City Building

City Building

Nine Planning Principles for the Twenty-First Century

John Lund Kriken, FAIA, AICP

With Philip Enquist, FAIA, and Richard Rapaport

Princeton Architectural Press, New York

Published by
Princeton Architectural Press
37 East Seventh Street
New York, New York 10003

For a free catalog of books, call 1.800.722.6657.
Visit our website at www.papress.com.

On the cover: San Francisco digital context model
© Skidmore, Owings & Merrill LLP
All images © Skidmore, Owings & Merrill LLP unless otherwise noted.
65B: Hedrich Blessing
106BL, 106BR, 221BL, 224CL, 224CR, 232CL: Tim Griffith
189TR: Timothy Hursley
209: Doug Fogelson
232CR, 232BL, 232BR: Tom Fox

Project Editor: Clare Jacobson
Designer: Jan Haux

Special thanks to: Nettie Aljian, Bree Anne Apperley, Sara Bader,
Nicola Bednarek, Janet Behning, Becca Casbon, Carina Cha,
Penny (Yuen Pik) Chu, Carolyn Deuschle, Russell Fernandez,
Pete Fitzpatrick, Wendy Fuller, Erin Kim, Aileen Kwun,
Nancy Eklund Later, Linda Lee, Laurie Manfra, John Myers,
Katharine Myers, Daniel Simon, Andrew Stepanian, Katie Stokien,
Jennifer Thompson, Paul Wagner, Joseph Weston, and Deb Wood
of Princeton Architectural Press —Kevin C. Lippert, publisher

Library of Congress Cataloging-in-Publication Data
Kriken, John Lund, 1938-
City building : nine planning principles for the twenty-first century /
John Lund Kriken with Philip Enquist and Richard Rapaport.
p.   cm.
Includes bibliographical references and index.
ISBN 978-1-56898-881-8 (alk. paper)
1. Skidmore, Owings & Merrill. 2. City planning—Philosophy—
History—21st century. I. Enquist, Philip (Philip Jerome), 1952- II.
Rapaport, Richard. III. Title. IV. Title: Nine planning principles for the
twenty-first century. V. Title: Skidmore, Owings & Merrill's nine critical
planning principles for the twenty-first century.
NA737.S53K75 2010
711'.4—dc22
                                        2009011140

Contents

<u>Part III:</u> The City of the Future/The Future of the City

Foreword

Philip Enquist, FAIA

John Kriken's *City Building: Nine Planning Principles for the Twenty-First Century* challenges those currently involved in the design of cities as well as those considering a career in the field, to think deeply about how cities are made and how they can positively change and evolve. I hope the audience for this book will also include civic and political leaders, preservationists, developers, environmentalists, as well as citizens who love their cities and recognize the benefits urban life well-realized can bring.

John's book addresses the fundamental questions of city growth and decline and the need for sustainability in virtually all aspects of urban life. He asks: How can humankind best occupy the land and do no harm? How, within the dramatic context of ongoing change in urban populations, can cities still be made increasingly livable? How in the face of the growing forces of globalization, can cities retain their unique culture, reflect their particular climate, and maintain special characteristics of geography, history, and landscape?

In the broadest sense, John's book illustrates how to apply best-practice principles to successfully manage the interrelated, complex, and often-confusing subject of twenty-first-century city building. I believe that in this work, John has successfully made the argument that citizens of our planet must collectively address these issues as if the future of humanity depends upon it. Because, quite simply, it does.

Preface

John Lund Kriken

It is my hope that the ideas contained in this book will provide new tools for people from a wide range of design disciplines and interests, to encourage them to think, talk about, and participate in the design of the world's existing and soon-to-exist cities. Good city building is not created by complex statistics, functional problem solving, or any particular decision-making process. Successful cities instead come from people advocating easily understood human values and principles that take into account the sensory, tactile, and sustainable qualities of environment and design in relation to what is the best of human endeavor.

These principles can be applied universally, recognizing, of course, the need to vary them by local climate, culture, geography, and history. I hope that the projects and work presented here to illustrate these principles will encourage those who are skeptical about the need for thoughtful city building to consider that cities can and indeed are being designed, built, and rebuilt in careful, caring, and cognizant ways. I find much hope in the growing public awareness that the earth's resources are finite and precious, and thus must be carefully preserved and fairly allotted. This understanding, I believe, will incite members of my profession and people concerned about urban life to do what we all should have been doing long ago: using land more responsibly and respectfully, and building city densities within the context of smart and appropriate infrastructure. At the same time, planners must also pay attention to the requirements of local climate and the need for renewable energy sources.

Please join us in the crucial work of twenty-first-century city building. It is an urgent undertaking in which all caring citizens can and should participate.

Part I:
An Introduction to City Building

The Millennial City

With language itself, the city remains man's greatest work of art.
—Lewis Mumford, *The Culture of Cities*

It is a simple yet utterly unsettling statement: for the first time in history, the majority of the world's people live in cities. The United Nations Department of Economic and Social Affairs, in noting this epochal moment, estimated that as of 2007, more people lived in cities than outside them.

This trend toward urbanization will continue. By 2015, the UN estimates, our planet will be home to twenty-two "mega-cities," each containing over 10 million inhabitants, with sixty-one other cities achieving populations over 5 million. Similar predictions tell us that by the 2030s city dwellers will make up nearly two-thirds of the world's population, a staggering 5 billion.

This grand relocation of humanity into the world's cities is as significant in its own ways as the transition ten millennia ago from hunting and gathering to fixed agricultural settlement. It demands that those of us who call ourselves "city builders" ask and answer critical questions. Are we prepared for what may well be known as the Age of Urbanity? Specifically, have those who plan and design cities, particularly architects, urban designers, and landscape architects, armed themselves with the tools, strategies, and principles to make the transformation to *Homo urbanus* as positive, people-centric, and ennobling as possible?

Today's answer is a troubling "no." Current political leaders, developers, architects, and planners are by and large unprepared to solve the crowding, pollution, lack of open space, grinding commutes, and mind-numbing visual sameness that are the consequences of unplanned urbanization. Equally important, it is simply unacceptable now to thoughtlessly use up dwindling natural resources and irreplaceable agricultural lands and open spaces. The clear and present danger of global climate change, the destruction of New Orleans, the shocking 2006 oil price rise, and the subsequent global economic decline together warn that design and development "business as usual" will mean a drastic decline in the quality of people's lives all over the planet.

This book, then, attempts to inventory today's most useful urban planning tools and show how they have been, and can be, combined with best practices and principles to produce the desirable future that coming generations deserve as their birthright.

The challenge is to design cities that possess, as a part of their design DNA, a transit-enabling density, a unique, exciting environment, a quality infrastructure, and a settlement pattern that enables sustainable growth. The aim is to create cities that become "mega-tools" enabling billions of people to live in harmony with their environment. The goal, then, is nothing less than to meet our profession's rendezvous with twenty-first-century urban destiny. We are aided by the fact that, if there is one constant throughout the history of cities, it is the inevitability with which urban centers have reinvigorated, rebuilt, and reinvented themselves. They have done so in what scientists may someday determine is a genetic imperative to meet the needs of growing and evolving populations. They may also do so in ways that enhance value for the visionary developers who have the courage and foresight to build with principles of urbanity in mind.

The urgency of this task seems self-evident even beyond the need to deal with the immediate issues of ongoing urbanization. Our profession also needs to account for such factors as the decline in livability that is—and will increasingly become—the fate of urban dwellers in the unhealthy, unplanned, ad hoc settlement patterns that are, in many places, today's mean.

On the far side of the residential equation, and equally unworkable, are the gated communities, shopping malls, and other single-minded—and frequently simple-minded—developments that sprawl out in the suburbs in seemingly random fashion. These turn a blind eye to such basic principles as walkability, sense of place, neighborhood scale, preservation of irreplaceable green spaces and agricultural land, and perhaps even survivability itself.

In this book, I make the case that both urban blight and suburban sprawl limit the options to create habitable space that can be called life affirming. Either kind of feckless, reckless development tends to cancel out rather than enhance creation of a rich central urban core that can be celebrated as "downtown."

As a practitioner of what I have strived to make a more comprehensive, rigorous, and humane brand of city building, I take exception to those who give in to shortsighted expediency or the apocalyptic devil-may-care approach. I even admit to a measured, if currently out-of-fashion, optimism in the face of what is indisputably one of humanity's most daunting challenges.

Let it be said here that I am neither an urban "nostalgiac" nor a devotee of neo-totalitarian central planning. Instead, I propose that millennial city building be based on a forward-facing set of guiding principles and best practices that can help city builders meet the critical needs of our rapidly urbanizing planet. Throughout this book, I demonstrate how applying these principles can enhance the quality of life, encourage sustainability, and reward those who believe and invest in the principles.

Let us also emphasize that the new city building has room for unique, individual expression by millennial architects and designers. Rich cityscapes can result from applying sensible and sensitive best practices, paying attention to the critical elements of what Nathaniel Owings, founder of Skidmore, Owings & Merrill, called "the spaces in between," not coincidentally the title of Owings's 1973 book. In the following chapters, I demonstrate how setting development at a human scale can be a potent antidote to urban sprawl, to blank street-walls, and to other manifestations of thoughtless urban development. Other values that I propose include density, accessibility, diversity, and, perhaps most important, sustainability. It is critical that all these values be considered in the context of the flexible planning required to accommodate the certain uncertainty of long-term growth.

It is equally important to recognize the need to create identity-rich, mixed-use neighborhoods that offer both affordable housing and easy access to educational facilities, transit, commerce, and the other amenities that give city life its appeal. The absence of these is a root cause of automobile-centric suburban sprawl, while their presence can increase the magnetic attraction of city living.

I also argue that, in the coming Age of Urbanity, thinking solely in terms of individual design projects will be inadequate. Rather, I show why, in the twenty-first century, an enthusiastic interest in architecture must partner with the design principles that are both common to all successful cities and foundational for the profession I call city building.

This book is organized into three parts.

Part I examines the past and defines the current practice of city building, addressing its shortcomings and proposing a comprehensive framework for rethinking the approach to cities in the future.

Part II translates this framework into nine best-practice principles that I feel are common to successful, livable urban environments. These principles are illustrated in a global portfolio of city-building projects that show how best practices have been applied successfully—and sometimes not so.

Part III makes the case that, far from being the problem, cities, properly organized, can be a mechanism for sensible, sustainable uses of increasingly scarce resources. I also argue that education and training in design and architecture must be reshaped to meet the requirements of twenty-first-century city building, and I conclude with a call for a truly national planning process and a comprehensive framework for settlement.

The Missing Elements of City Design

Every day across the world, tens of thousands of people are moving into cities, a trend that will almost certainly continue well into the twenty-first century. Equally certain, unless cities implement new approaches to urban planning, is that they will be unable to manage population growth or meet the resulting demands on resources. In other words, cities that continue to mismanage growth either will drown or will starve.

Unfortunately, if we extrapolate current trends into the future, governing entities at virtually all scales will be unable to meet basic civic infrastructural requirements or provide an acceptable environmental quality of urban life.

The work of twenty-first-century city builders thus becomes a race to find ways to identify and improve unproductive elements of urban decision making. To do this, we all need to look at the process itself. We find first of all a major and obvious flaw: that most "deciding" takes place at the wrong level of government. Instead of occurring at a regional, national, or even international scale, where an overview of the important planning elements can be examined most effectively, deciding happens primarily at the city and even district or neighborhood scale.

Transportation issues, resource allocations, and land-use decisions need to be made at the highest possible level, because cities within a region are generally in competition to maximize their tax bases. They thus have little incentive to coordinate planning across the region. On a smaller scale, neighborhoods also compete for scarce city services. The result is a similar lack of mutual understanding and cooperation.

Private sector developers and their designer-architects add to the decision-making challenge. First, their focus tends to be on project elements rather than on a comprehensive whole. This often leads to urban design projects lacking a larger sense of vision or context. Architects also have a natural inclination to create landmark buildings that stand apart from their surroundings. All cities need landmarks, but when too many buildings strive to be unique, they end up eroding a coherent city or even neighborhood identity. In other words, for a landmark to work, it needs a harmonious background against which it can contrast.

Unfortunately, the traditional method of coping with planning dysfunctions at virtually all geographic scales has been to attack them separately, giving little consideration to essential interrelationships. Generally in these cases, the solutions treat symptoms rather than underlying causes. This approach is worse than ineffectual. It tends to create new problems and impede real solutions.

To give one example, a city may choose to grow by taking high-quality agricultural land out of production and developing it. What happens next? The city eventually finds itself short of fertile land for local agriculture. The symptom-oriented response? To pay for new water resources and massive fertilization to enrich and irrigate less-productive land. The result? High costs, agricultural inefficiency, and environmental degradation. A cause-oriented approach, by contrast, favors preserving high-quality agricultural land and instead guides new development to nondisruptive, more ecologically sound land or infilling within urban "brownfield" sites, whenever possible.

A Framework for Settlement

To deal with the various manifestations of an inadequate city-building framework requires a comprehensive, wide-view approach to the way land is occupied in the first place. As a first step toward developing this kind of realistic "framework for settlement," government entities with mandates over multi-city areas need to declare overriding responsibility to manage their region's growth in all its various manifestations.

To enable government to make a shift of this magnitude toward more-functional development and conservation control, the public must understand and accept the benefits of a framework-for-settlement approach. For developers, positive reinforcement rather than punitive enforcement must be provided. Any framework for settlement must therefore be based on incentives and self-interest rather than on mandates or regulation.

I believe that regional thinking can be encouraged by inculcating three necessary planning elements into traditional city design thinking:

1. The need to guide the location of population growth.

2. The need to think of population growth in terms of the environmental "carrying capacity" of a particular location.

3. The need to relate conservation and development decisions to quality-of-life issues, including accessibility and necessary infrastructural improvements.

The various means to guide and accommodate population growth were recognized decades ago in studies like the 1970 United States Federal Service Systems for National Land Use, which is discussed later. This and other attempts at comprehensive national land-use planning are not in widespread use today because of lack of political will and a general failure to comprehend the long-term and large-scale benefits of guided growth on a regional scale.

The Need to Guide Population Growth

One of the fundamental truisms of urban design is that the city is in a constant state of transformation. Some cities are growing because of an expanding economic base, an increased birthrate, or an in-migration by people in search of jobs. Other cities are losing population because of a declining birthrate, a shrinking economy, or a loss of key industries. These various conditions require different planning approaches, but all involve the basic need to guide population growth at a regional, or even larger, scale.

Cities in decline are amenable to large-scale guidance in the form of incentives to attract new investments. These incentives help create the jobs capable of "holding" a population in place; they give a city options beyond simply watching its population pull up stakes to find more favorable economic conditions. City-to-city migration is enormously wasteful, as it abandons investments in buildings, streets, sewers, and other expensive urban infrastructure in the declining city that then need to be duplicated at a substantial cost in growing cities.

Cities experiencing population growth are faced with other choices that involve the need to guide that growth. To begin with, a city's population can be selectively intensified within the existing urban areas. This so-called infilling is one of the most economical and environmentally sound ways to grow. Similarly, the city's population growth can be redirected to nonurban areas that have sufficient environmental "carrying capacity" to mitigate the population's natural impact on land, air, and water. In all cases, the growing population must locate in proximity to supporting infrastructure, especially transit.

Matching Population Growth with Environmental Carrying Capacity

The environmental carrying capacity of a particular city or region is a broad and important measure of its sustainability. Establishing such a carrying capacity is done to appropriately relate use of air, water, and land to population growth and its limits. The ideal of carrying capacity is to achieve a balance between population size and environmental quality of life as they apply to the following elements:

1. Air Quality: People must reduce greenhouse gases in the atmosphere to reduce and ultimately reverse global climate change. Clean air is also a critical urban quality-of-life and public health issue. To maintain air quality, government must consider strict limits on the location, number, and use of polluting sources in relation to the population size and to the carrying capacity of the area's air basin.

2. Water Quality and Quantity: The carrying capacity of an area's water supply can be defined as an acceptable quality and quantity for home, agricultural, and industrial uses. Government must balance the location, number, and use of water-polluting sources against acceptable levels of water purity, clarity, and taste. Remedies include bio-filtration of water runoff, planting drought-tolerant landscape, protecting drinking water, and building smarter, more efficient, and more effective storm-water and sanitary treatment facilities.

3. Land Consumption: Typically today, cities indiscriminately consume the available land around them. To avoid continued loss of valuable, irreplaceable land, authorities need to define the suitability of land to support population. Land devoted to agriculture, watershed, forests, animal habitats, or scenic beauty and land prone to natural disaster should be identified as unsuitable for development or as suitable only under certain conditions. The remaining land, deemed suitable for development, should become the sole focus of urban growth and supporting infrastructure.

Balancing the environmental carrying capacity of each of these three elements against population growth can enable city builders to guide sustainable settlement improvements as they simultaneously reduce pollution. This strategy can also increase the carrying capacity on what might be considered a sliding scale: as polluting sources are reduced for an area (as there are fewer polluting cars and more nonpolluting transit resources, for example), the population may safely grow.

Of all the current techniques for guiding growth, balancing carrying capacity in relation to population and polluting sources is the best documented and most easily understood by the public. Media reports have exposed viewers and readers to various metrics of air quality, water quality, and water quantity, which are regularly measured, scored, and reported.

The Need to Relate Population Size to Quality-of-Life Goals

Over the last half-century, people have come to recognize the need to approach city design and planning problems by studying the connections between city form, human purposes, and the sensory qualities associated with renowned cities. From the 1950s through the 1980s, the noted urban theorist Kevin Lynch propounded what he believed were the qualities common to successful cities. These, Lynch believed, could be stated as "norms" for guiding the design of cities virtually anywhere. He called this approach the "Normative Theory of City Design."

Lynch's normative theory contrasts starkly with the emphasis that most city designers of the time placed on fragmented, noncomprehensive, "single-function" development techniques. Lynch found these "functional" approaches to development limiting and ill-equipped to deal with the purposes and qualities crucial to good city design. Based in part on Lynch's theory, I present a set of principles that have proved useful in guiding and communicating the conceptual process of city building. They convey easily understandable connections between livability and the activities necessary to achieve it.

Historically, the best, most renowned cities have a distinctive character, a memorable feel, as well as the ability to function in a civically coordinated way. This distinction is desirable not only for the sake of livability but also for economic success. Livability, as defined by best-practice principles, creates worth in a variety of ways, including quality-of-life improvements and higher real estate values. I believe that applying these principles can help make cities better even as they grow larger. Out of necessity and self-interest, both public and private sectors must see environmental quality to be in their interest and, indeed, vital for the health of the planet and its people.

I thus propose nine principles, intentionally general propositions, that have proved useful in both our national and our international planning practice. Their utility derives from an ability to help define, in comprehensive ways, the character of successful settlement. The principles are useful at geographic scales ranging from nations down to states, regions, cities, districts, and neighborhoods. They even apply at the level of streets, open spaces, and individual buildings. I believe that my nine principles for twenty-first-century city building characterize both best practices for good city design and the qualities essential in the growth of all highly livable cities.

Principle One: Sustainability
Committing to an Environmental Ethic

Principle Two: Accessibility
Facilitating Ease of Movement

Principle Three: Diversity
Maintaining Variety and Choice

Principle Four: Open Space
Regenerating Natural Systems to Make Cities Green

Principle Five: Compatibility
Maintaining Harmony and Balance

Principle Six: Incentives
Renewing Declining Cities/Rebuilding Brownfields

Principle Seven: Adaptability
Facilitating "Wholeness" and Positive Change

Principle Eight: Density
Designing Compact Cities with Appropriate Transit

Principle Nine: Identity
Creating/Preserving a Unique and Memorable Sense of Place

This roster of principles is always evolving, and I invite readers to consider their own additions.

A Brief (and Personal) History of Urban Design Theory and Practice

My colleagues on this book and I completed our professional education in the 1960s and '70s, when interest in revitalizing American cities was nascent. It tended to concentrate on what was unfortunately termed "urban renewal," along with suburban expansion, new town construction, and transportation improvements centered on the automobile. Urban planning was largely dominated by engineers producing studies claiming to prove that new, wider arterial streets and fast-moving highways were essential to the public good. Cities were being remade in the image of the automobile, and the architecture of the time exemplified that reality. Design tended toward anonymous minimalism, inspired, it seemed, by the vast amount of raw concrete being poured for the rapidly expanding interstate highway system. Sadly, the style termed "brutalism" was having its day.

In the United States, at least, those decades were times of nearly universal, if sometimes misdirected, optimism. It was epitomized by the belief that the future would, as a matter of course, bring technical solutions to all settlement woes. We were taught that every problem could be solved by thinking really big. If California needs water, why not just build an undersea pipeline to Alaska? Similarly, the early practice of our professional generation had little concern for protecting the environment or preserving the qualities of existing cities. What little thought given to the natural environment centered on the expectation that it could be harnessed or harvested for near-term human benefit.

The focus in those not-so-innocent times was on new suburban growth and "slum" clearance. Since then, we have "discovered" a number of planners, designers, and scholars who were clearly not in the urban studies mainstream but are now honored and studied for giving us a healthier, more positive analysis of the world's cities. What follows is a brief overview of some of those inspired and inspiring voices whose works have encouraged the best of contemporary urban design and who have become major and progressive influences on our thinking about cities.

Large-Scale Architectural Design

The fundamental need for city planning has existed as long as there have been cities. It is easy to imagine an assembly of Sumerian engineers and scribes pacing off the perimeter of their city-state's mud-and-brick enclosure on the Mesopotamian plain circa 3500 B.C. Over the next 550 decades, the Chinese, Egyptians, Indus people, Greeks, Macedonians, Persians, Romans, Incas, Mayans, Aztecs, Spanish, Khmer, British, French, Americans, and others all added their particular insights into the art and science of planning cities. In 1791 Pierre-Charles L'Enfant created radial boulevards for the new American Federal District that would become Washington, DC. He presented the plan to President George Washington, who was by trade a surveyor.

For American planners of my era and generation, the practical history of city building began toward the end of the nineteenth century, underscored by the celebrated quote from the architect and urban planner Daniel H. Burnham, "Make no little plans, they have no magic to stir men's blood and probably could not themselves be realized."

Beginning with Burnham's planning for the 1893 Chicago World's Columbian Exposition, the tendency, especially among architects, has been to view urban design in terms of large, multiple-building architectural projects. Burnham's work on the exposition site plan led to a series of unified neoclassical buildings surrounding a formal lake. It provided a powerful, memorable image. Free from the chaos of normal urban life, the grounds were called the "Great White City." Burnham, in turn, worked closely with the landscape architect Frederick Law Olmsted, whose projects included the Columbian Exposition's Midway Plaisance, Chicago's Jackson and Washington parks, New York's Central Park, and landscaping around the Capitol in Washington, DC.

The triumphs of Burnham and Olmsted had a profound impact on both the public and the American architectural establishment. Their influence carried forward into the early part of the twentieth century. From then on, cities would be built and renewed through projects involving hundreds if not thousands of acres and scores if not hundreds of buildings. Throughout the century that followed, a number of similarly colossal urban projects were proposed and designed. Some of them were relatively benign, and actually built, such as the new Brazilian capital, Brasília; others were malignant and mercifully stillborn, like Albert Speer's grotesque Germania, intended to transform Berlin into Adolf Hitler's world capital.

By the 1960s the trend was toward exciting, utopian approaches to city design, exemplified by such projects as the General Motors Futurama exhibition at the 1964 New York World's Fair. Also exemplifying this trend was the work of the Japanese architect Kenzo Tange. To increase the amount of habitable land around Tokyo, he proposed building islands in the middle of Tokyo Bay for thousands of units of terraced housing, with a network of highway bridges connecting the islands.

In Tange's conception, the distances between islands were too far to walk. This suggested to him a new scale of spatial perception, which he tellingly referred to as "the superhuman scale." As unpleasantly Nietzschean as this sounded, it was not a far-fetched vision for future cities. Today, many of the world's cities are primarily experienced at 60 miles per hour out the windows of trains, buses, and automobiles. Though never built, Tange's concept was visually exciting and representative of both the power and the limitations of urban design as architecture. Today, the tradition of large-scale urban design projects is embraced by many of the world's best-known architects. While there has been occasional "magic" in such projects, they have more often been destructive to human scale and to the qualities I believe are essential to creating livable cities.

Design of the Public Realm

In 1909 Burnham submitted his plans for managing the growth of Chicago. Like his 1893 Columbian Exposition program, Burnham's Plan of Chicago also dreamt big. The design elements of the two projects were very different, however. The Chicago Plan proposed a long, wide waterfront park on the shore of Lake Michigan, with boulevards radiating away from the waterfront's city center. With this plan, all Chicago citizens could benefit from the prescription of the City Beautiful movement: that all urban dwellers live within walking distance of an open space or park. Burnham's plan was the first comprehensive program for an American city, albeit one with ambitions to transform Chicago into "Paris on the Prairie," as the rubric of the day suggested.

Unlike the design of the Columbian Exposition, the Plan of Chicago was not based on building design. Rather, it keyed off the power of the public realm, its streets, parks, and public facilities. Significantly, the plan sought to establish a loose framework for the tens of thousands of privately constructed buildings rather than shoehorn those buildings into a framework established by official fiat.

Today, at the beginning of the twenty-first century, the Burnham plan that has guided Chicago's growth and development for a century continues to exemplify a planning process that emphasizes the public realm and exemplifies the City Beautiful movement. Largely pioneered by Olmsted, the City Beautiful movement was responsible for the development of many large urban parks throughout the United States. Beginning at the close of the nineteenth century and continuing into the early twentieth, what is today called "urban planning" was often referred to as "civic design," emphasizing the importance of the public place. Today, the civic realm remains the most important framework for thinking about cities in functional, aesthetic, and, perhaps most important to the current world, environmentally sustainable ways.

Human-Scale City Design

Focusing on the aesthetics of city design inevitably leads to the works of Gordon Cullen (1914–1994), the British planner, theorist, artist, and author who was the founder of the Townscape movement. Like Burnham and Olmsted, Cullen thought of cities in terms of the public realm, but he added a new conceptual tool to the planner's kit. What he called "townscapes" referred to the urban domain as experienced sequentially on foot. Cullen's lifework was to teach the importance of making human-scale development explicit by the size of open spaces, materials, landscape, lighting, and street furniture. The concept of townscapes is the planning equivalent of the ways architects use various materials to highlight and humanize individual building design.

Cullen viewed the city as a series of highly identifiable outdoor "rooms" and was interested in the quality and character of those rooms as well as their relationship to the sequence of a townscape. He recognized how space can be made to feel comfortable or awe-inspiring and how it can be made to propel a viewer dramatically from one memorable space to another.

Cullen believed that three-dimensional models and two-dimensional drawings of urban plans, while necessary, were not always the best tools for studying design in the public realm. He maintained, and I concur, that the perspective given by those tools was something like the view of a city from an airplane. Instead, Cullen's graphic approach was to consider, model, and draw the city as experienced *on foot from eye level*. Through this methodology, he defined what is still the most important way to see and design urban places, a technique that should be central to the work of all city builders.

Value-Based City Design

Kevin Lynch was a mid-twentieth-century American urban theorist, MIT professor, author, and practitioner of city design. His point of view was unique, in that, rather than focus on buildings or open spaces, Lynch was interested in how people experienced cities and what they remembered about a city's neighborhoods and distinctive spaces. Lynch was not satisfied with city planning based on process-oriented decision making, functional problem solving, or comparative statistical analysis. Rather, he proposed that the test of a good city was its "legibility"— how it was perceived and understood by dwellers and visitors. Lynch concluded that certain basic values are common to successful and livable cities and can be defined as principles to guide city design.

Lynch's professional lifetime journey was the search for a more comprehensive approach to city building based on the sensory qualities of the environment. His thoughts about cities and the natural world have significantly influenced the work of several generations of city planners and are an important starting point for modern planning.

Like Lynch, the Canadian author and urban activist Jane Jacobs believed that cities are best understood by observation and common sense. Jacobs fiercely fought the "urban renewal" of the 1950s that invariably cleared large areas of existing cities to rebuild them with wide streets, large blocks, repetitive buildings, and monolithic land uses. These projects mirrored the suburban world in which people lived in one place, shopped in another, and worked in still another. In the United States at the time, urban transit systems were being dismantled at the behest of Detroit automakers to advance the requirements and patterns of private automobile use. Sadly, at the turn of the twenty-first century, this same pattern is being repeated in many developing countries.

Jacobs, who became increasingly influential, persuasive, and successful at fighting thoughtless urbanization, died in 2006. Her death deprived the world of a powerful voice advocating the dense infill development mixed with fine-grained urban commerce that is proving more livable, more sustainable, and more economically resilient than the now largely discredited philosophy of "urban renewal" in the 1950s and '60s.

Designing with Nature

The process of understanding and communicating the qualities of the natural environment as they relate to city building was simplified by the 1969 publication of Ian McHarg's *Design with Nature*. Born in 1920 in Glasgow, Scotland, McHarg became professor in Landscape Architecture and Regional Planning at the University of Pennsylvania as well as being a renowned landscape architect, planner, writer, and lecturer. McHarg made a breakthrough in mapping complex natural systems and environmental features at regional scales. He taught that regional land planning was the way to determine which areas were appropriate for urban growth and would have the least disruptive impact on that region's ecology. Thanks to McHarg, planners now have a system that helps define sensitive areas within a region, including watersheds; steep, unbuildable slopes; irreplaceable land; and areas prone to floods, storms, earthquakes, forest fires, and other hazards.

Regional analysis encompassed wildlife habitats, migration corridors, areas of scenic importance, valued forests, and the like. McHarg's designations provided a way to identify environmentally sensitive land that required protection or was otherwise unsuited for development. Prior to McHarg's regional range of view, environmental concerns tended to be evaluated on a parcel-by-parcel or, at best, a city-by-city basis. Unfortunately, these were contexts in which threatened environmental systems could not be easily defined or understood. They were thus likely to be sacrificed to the immediate economic benefits of development. McHarg's insights into mapping enabled creation of a methodology that overcame the tendency to view development in a fragmented, small-scale way.

The careers of Frederick Law Olmsted, Daniel Burnham, Gordon Cullen, Kevin Lynch, Jane Jacobs, Ian McHarg, and other enduring urban thinkers of the twentieth century have commonalities beyond the desire to create humane and human-scale cities. Perhaps most important, each was able to take a larger view that combined design and planning so that they could deal with the same critical elements of city building that city builders face today: intelligent settlement, improved environmental quality, and planetary sustainability.

The Role of Design in Today's City Building

Today, what I might call "the present tense" of city building is broadly concerned with functional, visual, and tactile relationships between people and their environment, both natural and built. At its foundation, intelligent modern city building focuses on the ways those relationships can be maximized and improved. This simple mandate includes all the substantive areas of planning: housing, transportation, open space, institutional services, infrastructure, industry, and commerce.

The practice of designing cities is based on the assumption that the physical environment can be usefully shaped and that a desired physical form can be created through various design methods. Any coherent philosophy of city building must also assume that economic and political forces can be influenced by the design process to achieve desired results. Typically—but not always—city design is understood to function as part of the public realm, from which it can stimulate, guide, and influence actions in both public and private sectors.

The public-interest emphasis of a city design practice derives from the traditional responsibility of government for such key functions as stewardship of open space, transportation networks and streets, community services, and utilities. By helping determine the design and configuration of these basic services, city design can guide overall environmental quality and help coordinate subsequent private development.

Although the current practice of planning still emphasizes management of the public sector, for an increasing number of large privately financed developments, city design services are often directly engaged by developer clients or by a combination of public and private entities. Design studies in these cases begin with an investigation to determine the appropriate purpose and feasibility of the project. Plans present alternative ideas for the character, function, and creation of a quality environment. The goal is to guide both new private development and redevelopment, both of which accommodate public-interest requirements.

City building makes a major contribution to the even more encompassing field of environmental design by coordinating and connecting the contributions of building architects, landscape architects, engineers, and planners, with the ultimate goal of bridging the gap between design and planning. Collectively mobilized, this interdisciplinary team approach can balance the pressure for growth. Employing compatible building design, adequate access, and necessary services, a planning program can meet the requirements of modern development, environmental conservation, open-space preservation, and sustainable growth.

The Design Process

City design problems are highly complex by nature. Countless and diverse issues need to be addressed on multiple levels and across disciplinary lines. Because design is an intrinsically visual process, a "diagrammatic approach" is useful, representing various issues, principles, and choices as simply as possible through drawings and diagrams that break problems down into digestible components. These "pieces of the puzzle" can then be combined and interwoven in ways that are easily communicated to professionals and lay audiences alike. The following sections show the typical city-building design process in action.

Context

The first task of the city builder should be to examine the context of a project site, in other words, to "read the land" in ways cognizant of the natural systems that can affect a project's environmental qualities and design nuance. Understanding a project's context also includes mastering existing public policy and land-use regulations. In this early part of the process, it is crucial to look at a site's constraints as well as at opportunities to achieve the optimal type, mix, and density of possible uses. Defining context also involves identifying the correct level of potential development, given time and budget constraints. Context defines how issues of planning and design relate to the principles of sustainability, livability, and perhaps even survivability.

Project context also requires community participation—involvement by the people who will be most affected by the project. Popular input is a critical source of design intelligence as well as a way to gain overall consensus. In many if not most projects, this input has a crucial impact on the plan's achievability, quality, and success.

Alternatives

Developing alternatives is the next step in the city design process. Alternatives describe different ways to solve the same problem. They are the means to compare various ways to accomplish design goals. They can also help convey why the selected method works best. In defining alternatives, it often helps to break the project down into specific choices for such aspects as circulation, land use, mix, and density.

Breaking a project down enables decision makers to select choices that are not biased or confused by unnecessary complexity. A good solution for one subject may otherwise be rejected because it is combined with a bad solution for another. Ultimately, the desired alternatives, once recognized, can then be recombined into an overall plan.

Choice Selection

Choices among design alternatives need to be made on the basis of their relative social, environmental, and economic benefits and consequences. Design choice must also be based on the implementation techniques that best fit the capabilities and resources of the governing, managing, and financing entities.

In large-scale city-building projects, fundamental trade-offs are intrinsic to making important design choices. It is often not possible to optimize every part of every design alternative, ideal as that might be. Limitations are inherent in the city design process itself. Sometimes the limitations come from lack of resources; other times, from the clash of contending agendas. Often they arise because two or more ideas, often ideal in and of themselves, simply, inevitably, bump up against one another. When trade-offs are necessary, they need to be made explicit to project decision makers.

The optimal circulation system for a new neighborhood, for example, will almost certainly be affected by the land dedicated to parks, open space, and buildings. Choices balancing land for roads and land for other uses must be made, but they need to emerge from a process that enables the most intelligent and beneficial choices for the largest number of people over the longest period of time.

Images

Solutions that come out of this step-by-step city design process are most powerfully represented through images, drawings, diagrams, and models. At their best, these images communicate the sensory, physical qualities of thoughtful design policy. The use of imagery serves two purposes: comparing and testing alternative concepts during the design process, and communicating important design principles. When solutions have been determined, the design images, together with stated principles and technical descriptions, can serve to express agreed-on design policies that then guide those charged with implementation.

Guidelines

Guidelines for such factors as building usage, site coverage, location, height, and bulk are well-known tools of city design. In many urban contexts, guidelines can also define a desired architectural character. Such guidelines might describe preferred materials, color value, and ground level or rooftop treatment, as well as size and location for signage and way-finding. In all cases the rationales for creating these guidelines are

1. To relate density and use to the capacity of streets and utilities
2. To avoid major conflicts between the objectives of individual developers
3. To improve overall environmental quality as a product of master planning

For guidelines to be accepted, they must be based on sound values of public interest. No matter how well thought out the guidelines, the subsequent period of public comment will often be contentious. Despite, or perhaps because of, opposition, the process at its best can sharpen the overall project design and smooth stakeholders' acceptance of reasonable guidelines. To maximize architectural creativity, guidelines should not only be simple but also leave room for interpretation and reinterpretation over time. Guidelines tend to be most successful when they pair what is desired with what is to be avoided.

Design Scales

City design must contemplate geographic scales that range from the tiniest detail to the largest overview. The latter may be at the national or state scale but more typically is the regional or district scale. This descends to smaller planning scales, including streets, blocks, and individual buildings. Each scale presents different insights and challenges, but all can ultimately be related to the overall principles for livable cities. Later in this book, projects are compared that have huge geographic variations of scale and show how both the similarities and the differences can inform an overall solution.

Regional Scale

As a species, we are learning more each day about the effect that interlocking ecological systems can have across immense geographic distances and time spans. Today, however, environmental disruption is occurring widely in the world's metropolitan regions because of their development and growth. Typically, this disruption occurs because the planning mechanisms needed to avoid it do not exist at the appropriate scale of governance. Cities (where most real planning authority resides), for example, have no mandate to deal with critical problems at the regional scale. Throughout the world, there are few incentives and lawmakers have little political will to encourage cities within a region to collaborate on finding collective solutions to their respective, and often similar, problems.

The San Francisco Bay Area is an example of debilitating regional "Balkanization." Within the region's 7,000 square miles, nearly one hundred city governments and over one thousand special agencies and districts compete for authority, control, and tax revenue. Out of these, only two authorities, the San Francisco Bay Conservation and Development Commission (BCDC) and the Metropolitan Transportation Commission (MTC), actually have the power to guide planning at a regional scale—and only in specialized spheres.

In the 1960s and '70s, overall planning efforts by both the federal and the California government proved unsuccessful in ameliorating the self-centered planning that, even today, compels cities in a region to expand their tax bases through wasteful, inefficient, or inappropriate land uses. These uses tend to be commercial, because they require less tax support for infrastructure and services. Residential uses typically require more services such as schools, parks, and public safety than do commercial uses. Commercial development, with its typically higher tax rates, also enables cities to collect more money while keeping residential taxes relatively lower. With each city thinking first about its own tax base and last about collaborating on necessary regional issues such as residential development, wetland require-ments, and agricultural land preservation, the result is often an overabundance of "auto rows" and retail malls.

Lack of ability to plan on a regional scale is also responsible for the expansion of housing in lowland townships such as those around China's Yangtze River Basin, Northern California's Sacramento River Delta, and Louisiana's Mississippi River Delta. In each case, land is relatively inexpensive but has a high risk of flooding. Regional oversight guidelines can prevent devel-opment in ecologically sensitive or hazardous areas that in a disaster come under the aegis of federal and state government for hugely expensive recovery and cleanup efforts.

The solution to the lack of regional planning is not necessarily creation of a single civic entity out of hundreds of townships—although governmental simplification is often a good idea, it is usually politically difficult to achieve. The solution is to require local offi-cials to "think regionally" and begin to act collectively on issues of shared land, air, and water resources. They have to take a regional approach to environmental hazards as well as to regional services such as transit. Fragmented solutions to these problems have become, quite simply, unsustainable.

City Scale

It is at the city scale that streets, sidewalks, parks, transit systems, communication networks, and power, water, and sewer utilities are built and maintained. It is at the city scale as well that regulations are promulgated to preserve buildings and open space in the urban core, as well as to control the density, location, and character of new development. Services at the city scale ideally include education, police and fire protection, local transportation, emergency health care, cultural affairs, and recreation.

The opportunity to design a city "from the grid up" came along rarely for earlier genera-tions of urban planners. In recent years, opportunities have increased, with new cities being planned and built in support of industrial, port, and trade development throughout Asia and the Middle East. In the future, designing new cities will likely become increasingly common because of the growing pressure to urbanize in virtually all parts of the world.

One key benefit of building a city from scratch is, ironically, to better manage the grow-ing population of existing cities. Thinking of new cities can be useful in helping manage subur-ban sprawl. As urban areas grow outward, they create, among other problems, impossibly long commutes. A better approach to managing largely unplanned, sprawling growth can often be through developing dense, carefully planned new cities able to support nearby employment and sustainable growth.

Most frequently, thinking at the city scale involves the design of urban elements larger than neighborhoods and districts. This is also the scale used for the long-range planning of existing cities.

City-scale thinking should also consider future needs for urban preservation, new higher-density development, and all the attending infrastructure and service requirements. A city-scale overview can help connect or reconnect neighborhoods and unify disparate urban elements, including the redevelopment of waterfronts, the creation of new transportation corridors, city-wide transit systems, and large-scale street landscape and open-space improvements.

District Scale

The district includes downtowns, neighborhoods, civic places, universities, medical centers, and research and development campuses. The district is the level at which design can be most efficiently mobilized and directed toward the human scale.

At district scales, architecture, landscape design, and planning most closely and importantly intersect. Here the world is defined by concerns such as walkability, personal comfort, community safety, and collective purpose. At the neighborhood level, through careful application of twenty-first-century planning principles, the viability, livability, individuality, and "legibility" of a city can be assured.

As I have noted, the concept of the "legible" neighborhood was first proposed in the 1950s by the urban theorist Kevin Lynch. Lynch recognized that one of the important qualities of good city design was visual and emotional clarity, which, he suggested in his 1960 masterwork *The Image of the City,* was defined by "the ease with which [the city's] parts can be recognized and organized into a coherent pattern." In *The Image of the City*, Lynch juxtaposed a "legible" Boston and an "out-of-focus" Los Angeles where, he asserted, "the grid pattern itself is an undifferentiated matrix, within which elements cannot always be located with confidence."

One of the important lessons of Lynch's work is that it has provided planners with insights into why world cities are either memorable and distinct or illegible and unfocused. He suggested, for example, that "good" cities were different from "bad" ones because they had districts where care had been taken to nurture a distinctive sense of place relevant to the locale, history, geography, and climate.

Lynch's incisive civic overview has been validated time and again in cities old and new. He teaches us that, while a city can have a memorable neighborhood without being great, a city cannot be great without having a series of dense, interconnected, identifiable, walkable, livable, visually compelling, and transit-enabled neighborhoods.

Downtown Scale

Downtowns are primarily defined as places of work, although many successful downtowns, most prominently in Chicago, New York, Tokyo, London, and Hong Kong, are moving toward a 24-hour-a-day, mixed-use, office/commercial/residential model. Successful downtowns tend to be compact, which allows them to concentrate infrastructure and makes them walkable, to support easy face-to-face contact between people doing business. The densities of downtowns vary widely. Generally, at the highest density, downtown land is the most valuable, public transit has its largest ridership, and the business role of the downtown is significant regionally, nationally, or internationally.

Residential Neighborhood Scale

The residential neighborhood is where people spend much of their lives outside work. A city is made up of many residential neighborhoods. They are typically identified by their schools, public parks or recreation areas, and nearby centers for shopping or social life; some are further identified by natural or built features.

What is a livable residential neighborhood? At almost a primal level, in such a place, residents coming home from an evening of overindulgent socializing would have no difficulty recognizing their own street and building as a distinctive and welcoming presence. Further, if the building has multiple units, the exteriors of individual apartments might well be differentiated from others in the building. How is this achieved? Some of the qualities of identity can derive from the architecture and be communicated through planning guidelines and policies.

In San Francisco, for example, residential design guidelines encourage the use of bay windows. Whether gracing a modern or a historic building, these windows help break the building's façade into smaller, identifiable constituent parts and are a reminder of the ever-present San Francisco Bay views.

Retail District Scale

In today's global marketplace, modern retail districts are units of nearly endless duplication. The universal reach of retail marketing means repetitive malls with standardized exterior and interior designs for the "usual suspects," well-known chain stores. There is increasing recognition, however, that interesting retail can grow out of the commercial expression of a particular geography or culture. In the United States and elsewhere, the tide of suburban malls may be ebbing, with local "main street" shopping again gaining traction. With the global economic downturn of the late 2000s, the nature and status of urban retail remains very much in flux.

Nevertheless, aside from certain steroid-pumped mega-malls, the most extensive retail districts in North America are located in transit-rich downtowns such as Chicago's Michigan Avenue, New York's Fifth Avenue, San Francisco's Union Square, and even Beverly Hills's Rodeo Drive. Suburban malls are sparked by a very different motivation from that of urban shopping streets. They are almost always based on the ability of customers to drive there quickly and park easily and cheaply. Suburban malls will continue to flourish as long as energy remains relatively inexpensive (and perhaps even longer). It is not beyond imagining that suburban mass transit/light-rail, buses, or vans will not only help keep suburban malls viable when energy costs rise but perhaps also serve as a catalyst to their densification. Examples of this suburban-to-urban transition can be seen around a growing number of rapid-transit stations in Hong Kong, London, and the San Francisco Bay Area. The growth of mid-rise, mixed-use, transit-oriented developments has helped push what were primarily low-density residential areas toward a density that is urban and sustainable.

Civic Place Scale

Every city has its center of governmental and civic life. Generally, these are treated as special places, distinctive and symbolic of their public functions. Civic places are most often defined by their landmark buildings, special parks, and plazas that serve as formal or informal public gathering places.

Civic center open spaces are often the location of commemorative memorials. The center of China's national government, for example, on Beijing's Tiananmen Square, is marked by its Monument to the People's Heroes. The National Mall in Washington, DC, has the Washington, Jefferson, and Lincoln memorials, among others. A civic place is often the center for a community's cultural life, as well. Shanghai's City Hall, for example, located in People's Park, is surrounded by an opera house, art museum, and the Urban Planning Exhibition Hall. In many cities, such as London, these civic and cultural uses are not concentrated together but instead widely dispersed.

Historically, the "publicness" of civic districts has often been conveyed by large plazas and generous sidewalk-setback landscaping. These communicate a welcoming character, a gravitas, and a visual contrast with the street walls or concrete setbacks of most commercial districts.

Campus Scale

Campus development, whether dedicated to academic, research and development, or medical uses, is an endeavor at much the same scale and complexity as neighborhood and, in certain cases, even at city scales. At the campus scale, there is often a desire to unify the building and landscape character to create a memorable and distinctive place.

To be successful, campus planning must span an extremely long development life and allow for the fact that future growth needs cannot be precisely defined. Campus plans must therefore provide a simple, easy-to-understand framework that both guides and unifies current work and is highly adaptable to changing requirements.

Paying attention to potential growth and leaving room for inevitable change are particularly relevant in the design of medical campuses. Yet, because the dramatic growth of medical services in the last decades has rarely been anticipated in past designs, an ongoing struggle occurs to transform those campuses into legibly designed urban districts with a sufficient infrastructure and a plan that is open enough to allow for long-term growth.

Similar to a city, an academic campus must accommodate places for education, social life, recreation, residence, and entertainment. The resulting academic campus environment should also become an intrinsic part of the learning experience by providing places for quiet contemplation as well as an educational "polis" or "marketplace" for social gatherings and the free interchange of ideas.

The campus must be compact to maintain acceptable walk times between classes. Locating buildings close together requires careful planning and an administration that accepts the principle that every new building cannot be a stand-alone landmark—not an easy goal to achieve in an era that hungers after landmark architectural expression.

One of the key problems with industrial campuses is that, from their inception, they tend to be single-use sites with isolated buildings afloat in a sea of parking lots. High-technology R&D campuses often require large floor areas to promote maximum interaction among employees. This frequently leads to isolated structures, built along cul-de-sacs and on large blocks that both limit access to transit and block pedestrian movement.

An important initial step to creating open R&D campuses is to limit the initial size to that of a typical residential neighborhood and mix in a series of other uses. A key next step is to integrate or reintegrate the site into its surroundings by designing pedestrian corridors that connect to nearby housing, commercial, and recreational sites.

Production, Distribution, and Repair District Scale

Urban production, distribution, and repair districts are generally understood to be mixed-use areas that serve multiple small industrial, "back office," and other service functions. Particularly in fast-growing cities, these areas are especially fragile and often threatened by redevelopment into economically more profitable uses such as housing, entertainment, or retail. While functions like food preparation, auto repair, printing, industrial and technology incubators, and other small service-related businesses often lack the economic clout to protect themselves, they are critical to the overall functioning of the city and may need to be protected by zoning.

One possible solution to preserving endangered PDR districts is the Asian model, which builds up rather than out. While American PDR districts tend to be one and two stories, in Hong Kong the lack of space has led to creation of service neighborhoods of up to ten stories. These use such novel methods as giant elevators to move tractor-trailers from the street to higher-story loading docks.

Air, Sea, and River Port District Scale

Ports are often critical economic engines for their respective urban areas. Yet they also tend to be locked in an uneasy relationship with their cities, particularly as they grow. As centers of commerce, both airports and seaports attract industrial uses and are often catalysts for scores of trade-related satellite businesses. As a city grows outward, air, sea, and river facilities once at the outskirts are often transformed into uneasy inner-city neighbors.

In New York, Chicago, Hong Kong, and elsewhere, older airports have simply become surrounded by the expanding city, which is then forced to build a newer, larger airport even farther from the city center.

In rapidly growing Shanghai, the docks along the Huang Pu River, which historically defined the city's edge, grew overcrowded with commerce and forced the city to relocate its shipping northeast to the Yangtze. This, in turn, enabled planners to take a new look at the deserted dock lands and transform them into highly valuable downtown waterfront neighborhoods. London's Canary Wharf is an outstanding example of this kind of serendipitous transformation.

Public Realm Scale

The most detailed elements of scale in the urban planning and development palette involve the interaction of streets, blocks, buildings, and open spaces. It is through the interplay of these components that all cityscapes are created and the livability of a city largely determined. Each element is discussed next.

Street Scale

The best cities tend to have the greatest number of streets. Today, experience tells us that a city with many narrow streets will function more smoothly than a city with fewer, larger ones. Narrow streets tend to be pedestrian-friendly because they are safer and easier to cross and because vehicular traffic moves more slowly on them. More streets offer increased options for travel and are less vulnerable to traffic gridlock.

Block Scale

Blocks vary in size and shape. Those shapes may be derived from topography, natural features, view-corridors, or the formal geometry connecting landmark destinations as in Washington, DC, Berlin, and Paris. What is most important is that blocks provide an overall street network that, for the most part, enables pedestrian, transit, and vehicular traffic. Best-practice principles tell us that a block's size must be large enough to support its intended uses and small enough to make foot travel around it easy. Alarm is the proper response when a design proposes blocks longer than 100 meters.

Building Scale

At the building scale, designers first need to consider the architectural question of how to conserve and retrofit older structures of special use or historic interest. For new buildings, thinking begins with guidelines to ensure that structures fit together compatibly and support pedestrian comfort.

In terms of the overall city-building tool kit, planners need to think of individual structures as elements that can define a district or an entire city. In particular, they need to closely examine the design, size, and placement of buildings in terms of creating an appropriate sense of scale. Two important factors are the compatibility of buildings in a district and a particular building's unique "landmark" identity within the district.

Open-Space Scale

A defining element of the public realm of city building is the thoughtful use of the open space between buildings: parks, plazas, streets, and sidewalks. This common ground is shared by all citizens. Open spaces should express a city's unique identity, culture, and climate, as well as the character of its separate neighborhoods, streets, and blocks. Open space includes appropriate lighting fixtures, transit shelters, benches, play equipment, and all other kinds of street furniture.

Open space, urban landscaping, and native plantings do far more than improve the urban experience, which they also do. They begin to repair the degraded environment, contributing to a city's sustainability by several means: cooling the air, consuming carbon dioxide, minimizing ozone, providing habitat, especially for birds, and promoting storm-water bio-filtration. The "green roof" movement that is rapidly spreading is an example of how ecologically challenged cities can be transformed into centers of environmental sustainability.

Part II:
Nine Principles for Twenty-First-Century City Building

Introduction

Building successful twenty-first-century cities will require new modes of thought about growth, particularly as it relates to sustainability. This new thinking must be capable of encompassing and even transcending the kinds of technical problem solving explored in Part I. It will not be enough to simply throw around catchphrases like "green buildings," "sustainable growth," and "reduced carbon footprint." Instead, planners and architects need to think in terms of active principles that assist in the ongoing task of designing rich, rewarding, transit-enabled, high-density cities, taking into account issues of air, water, vegetation, habitat, soil, and other essentials of sustainability.

It is also important to think about innovative city building in relation to historical and geographic factors, even those considered "long ago and far away" but that are nonetheless important in a city's present and future life. During Hurricane Katrina, for example, the long-term destruction of barrier wetlands scores of miles downriver from New Orleans played a tragic role in the city's flooding. In the development of Shanghai's Chongming Island, for another example, planners recognized the need to preserve agriculture near a large city, even if farming might seem beyond the purview of the best-practice principles of urban design. Like it or not, the reach of the city and hence the requirements for city planning extend far into the regional, and even national, context.

What city builders thus need is a set of overarching principles that provoke thought about larger concerns fundamental to improving and ensuring the quality of urban life. Equally important, designers must preserve and enhance the natural environment that all cities inhabit. These principles are basic to the process of persuasively communicating the need for city stakeholders to think about urban growth in terms of creating livable, sustainable places.

Part II presents nine principles of modern city building and offers projects that exemplify those principles, or in some cases do not. The principles were applied in a wide variety of planning modalities. They provided insights that helped move projects to consensus and completion. The statement of each principle includes a verb, such as "committing," "renewing," "maintainting," or "facilitating," that suggests the actions that need to be taken. The use of active verbs in the principles is not accidental. Exceptional city building must be an active and ongoing process.

Maps and Plans

Much can be learned from comparing maps and plans for regions, cities, neighborhoods, and individual projects. I illustrate the use of the principles described in Part II in a wide range of case studies, each one introduced within its city or region. Wherever possible, I present the case studies at the same scale, so that the relative sizes of parks, blocks, streets, districts, and neighborhoods can be compared.

Principle One:
Sustainability

Committing to an Environmental Ethic

The Problem: Environmental exploitation and misuse, energy waste, degradation of land, and pollution of air and water.

Sustainability, the first principle of intelligent twenty-first-century city building, naturally underlies this book's eight other principles. Broadly speaking, sustainability refers to the conservation and protection of irreplaceable and nonrenewable natural resources. The subject of sustainability is one of the alpha topics of our time, extensively discussed and written about, if not always comprehensively acted on. The ubiquity of the discussion is enough to suggest that city building in the twenty-first century will be largely governed by the requirement for sustainability. Over the next decades, the city-building profession will need to reckon with a finite supply of energy and with issues of global climate change. These facts mandate a powerful and ongoing commitment to an environmental ethic in urban design and planning. Two themes need to be addressed in dealing with the development of such an ethic: the natural environment and smart city building.

The Natural Environment

In the new world of sustainable development, planners must begin by considering whether a project will consume irreplaceable lands: prime agricultural land, land that supports ecosystems affecting plant and animal life, and land with scenic qualities. Further, developers must carefully evaluate an area for its suitability, avoiding land subject to flooding, wildfires, storms, wind damage, and earthquakes. Water and air are fundamental to supporting population and, above virtually all other resources, need to be protected and conserved.

Protecting the water, air, and other elements of the natural environment is typically addressed through measuring environmental carrying capacity and land-use management.

Environmental Carrying Capacity

It has become a familiar practice for planners to study comparative data on air and water quality and quantity related to population growth and concomitant pollution. This relationship is useful in determining the development capacity within specific air basins and watersheds. It is a relationship that can change for the better over time. Through intelligent environmental stewardship, an area's capacity to sustain population can increase while protecting desired air and water quality and quantity.

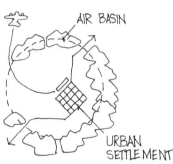

Land-Use Management

To avoid destructive natural hazards and to protect or regenerate irreplaceable lands, including wildlife habitats, animal migration corridors, riverfronts, watersheds, and high-quality agricultural lands, planners must consider new land zone designations. These will define where and under what conditions nondestructive urban development may take place and what lands must be protected.

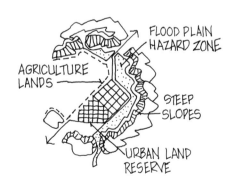

Building Smart Cities

In fulfilling the second, built, component of sustainability, energy consumption for lighting, cooling, and heating buildings is a major concern. Consumption is typically limited by requirements for appropriate, energy-efficient materials for walls, windows, and roofs as well as for highly energy-efficient mechanical and electrical equipment. While these requirements may add to initial construction costs, it is well understood that energy conservation has a high investment return over the life of a project.

Smart cities are also defined by a commitment to compact, dense development to minimize invasion of valuable irreplaceable and agricultural lands. In addition to protecting land for food production, smart development needs to address concerns for water supply, water quality, and air quality. Any program must also allow for efficient infrastructure, including utilities, transportation, and support services. Smart cities have alternative ways to get around and are comfortably walkable.

In regions throughout the world, freshwater is a limited, increasingly precious, and potentially conflict-engendering commodity. City builders must consider a number of strategies to conserve water. These include drought-resistant planting and climate-appropriate landscaping, recycling "gray water," capturing runoff, creating more permeable ground surfaces, and using water-efficient methods and equipment. "Green roofs" to control water runoff and naturally cool buildings are increasing in popularity, one indication that the lessons of sustainability are taking root.

Air needs to be accounted for, and not simply in terms of pollution. In cities like Stuttgart, Germany, the north sides of outlying hills are the collection point for summertime "pools" of cooling air that the afternoon breeze moves into the city. These pools, which act as a natural air conditioner, need to be protected and preserved. On Treasure Island in San Francisco Bay, afternoon breezes tend to be uncomfortably cold, and a novel approach was taken to shelter pedestrian environments from the wind by creative siting of buildings and reorientation of streets.

Building Infrastructure to Lead Development

Today, even though infrastructure investments are largely funded publicly, they almost always follow random, ad hoc development decisions. Unfortunately, "following the developmental money" tends to create disconnected, dysfunctional, and unsustainable settlement patterns. Instead, infrastructure that supports sustainable goals should become a priority, in order to guide new city growth to locations that meet those goals.

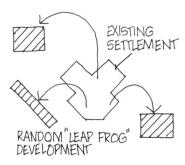

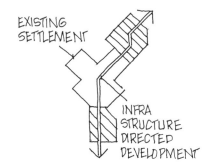

Managing Settlement

Sustainability ultimately demands that the nature and location of new development be managed so that cities can choose to infill, tucking new growth into existing urban infrastructural boundaries, rather than locating it on undeveloped land. To avoid random leapfrog development on the outskirts of cities, "urban growth boundaries" can be a useful strategy: these limit the land available for new development and direct such projects to positive locations, promoting compact development near existing infrastructure and encouraging infill. Urban growth boundaries have been used successfully in Greater Portland, Oregon. The boundaries can be periodically evaluated—twenty years seems to be the logical time span—and adjusted.

    Managing settlement can also be achieved by limiting the pressure for suburban land development from population growth. For example, population can be retained within economically declining cities by using incentives to attract new jobs and other reinvestments. Another approach is to raise the population density within existing cities, especially around locations that have good transit access.

1.1. Creating a Framework for Sustainable Settlement

The Federal Service Systems for National Land Use

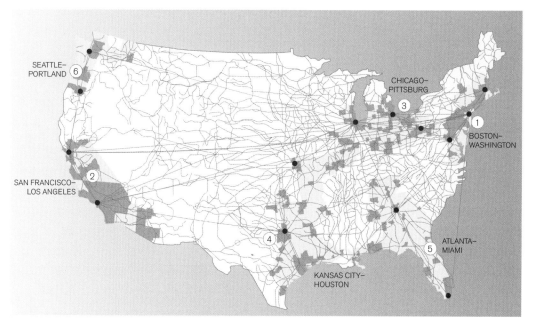

United States corridors of concentrated development

In 1970 SOM founder Nathaniel Owings made a proposal to the United States Bureau of Land Management to develop a national framework for settlement. Called the Federal Service Systems for National Land Use, the plan was designed to test whether strategic investments in infrastructure might promote more sustainable patterns of urban settlement. It was Owings's contention that this kind of approach could be presented in terms of incentives for positive action instead of the traditional punitive measures implemented through regulation and zoning controls. The framework proposed what would in effect be a national land-use plan, with three distinct approaches to managing a region's development. Each in its own way was necessary for sustainable city design.

1. Maintaining Population in Cities in Decline

The first approach was aimed at keeping population in cities suffering economic decline. Critical choices needed to be made to give those cities' residents options to stay where they were rather than force them to leave their homes for jobs elsewhere. The approach entailed supporting and redeveloping a community's economic base through carefully selected infrastructure investments that would attract talent and create jobs.

The settlement plan suggested that, in North America and elsewhere, programs could be brought to life through resources specifically designed to redevelop existing buildings and to dedicate underused urban land to new "infill" development. At its most basic, this first settlement approach was designed to take advantage of the existing and enormous investment in a city's civic, industrial, and residential infrastructure.

2. Guiding Population to Appropriate Locations

Owings's second proposed approach to national growth management was to guide population to appropriate locations within the region, using infrastructure as a "lure." This proposal ran counter to the land settlement situation in North America that largely exists to this day, in which public infrastructure passively follows private development. This "inducement to sprawl" occurs because communities are typically forced to hold their infrastructural fire until settlement patterns are established through land speculation. Then, typically, the first money can be raised to support those new services. The proposed land settlement alternative would be to use new infrastructure investments in transportation, water, power, and waste disposal to attract development to planned communities within land already designated for future population growth.

3. Intensifying Population in Existing Urban Areas

The national framework's third approach to settlement involved increasing population

The three approaches to manage settlement

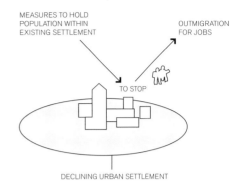

To hold

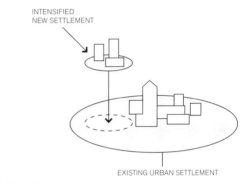

To intensify

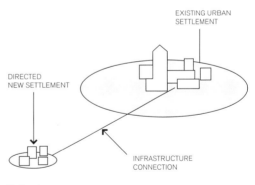

To direct

density in existing urban areas. Targeted to places experiencing new job creation, it would encourage the associated population growth on urban land capable of infill redevelopment at higher densities. To help achieve this residential intensification on a livable scale, public investment would be used to expand the carrying capacity of infrastructure systems in environmentally sensitive ways.

Virtually all city-building projects use one or more of the three settlement patterns proposed in the National Land Use plan. Woven together, they are able to provide a comprehensive prescription for a sustainable approach to regional and national development and population management.

Another important facet of the National Land Use plan was the development of land zone classifications. These identify a region's most valuable and threatened areas and attempt to check urban sprawl by guiding new settlement to other, nondisruptive, locations. The sustainable land zone concept was to be administered by a governmental body with jurisdiction over a region's metropolitan area land use. The plan created four land quality categories, with settlement locations supported and guided by coordinated, publicly funded infrastructure investment.

1. The agricultural land zone: The most productive farmlands would be included in this zone and classified as "non-buildable" or as "conditionally buildable" at densities low enough to enable ongoing productive agricultural uses.

2. The conservation land zone: This zone would include ecologically, scenically, or historically important land, recreational areas of exceptional quality, and habitats of unique or endangered animal or plant species. Fire, flood, erosion, and earthquake areas, open water, shorelines, and aquifer recharge land would also fall into this category. In the conservation zone, lands would be classified as either non-buildable or conditionally buildable under controls that protected the qualities that put the land in the zone in the first place.

3. The urban land zone: This zone would include lands not falling into the first two categories and either immediately suitable for urban development or already urbanized. Lands in this category would be administered by local governments according to regional standards.

4. Settlement reserves: Lands not falling into any of the first three categories would be zoned as settlement reserves. They could be used for future development, settlement, open space, or a variety of other public and private purposes.

Throughout this urban land zoning process, areas suitable for development or redevelopment were to be identified in terms of their environmental carrying capacity. The determination of an area's capacity was made by a "land census" of the amount of development and the number of people the land could support before air and water quality began to degrade, among other factors. Carrying capacity incorporated a sliding scale on which population limits could be adjusted upward as higher environmental quality was achieved through new technology or infrastructure investment.

Applying a framework for settlement to the Boston–Washington corridor

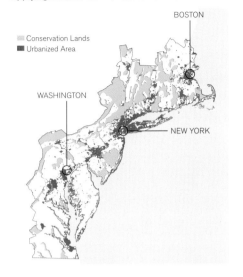

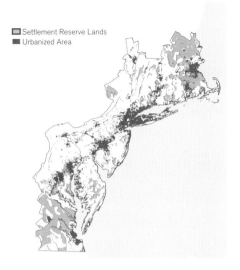

Conservation lands that are to be protected from settlement

Potential settlement reserve and existing urbanized lands

- Core, Community Renewal
- New Towns in Town
- High Access Corridor Industry
- Beltway Centers
- Linked Towns
- Corridor Communities
- Metro Communities

- Transit - Integration
- Automobile - Intercept
- Airport - Access
- Port Development

Government-assisted opportunities to guide new development
to settlement reserve land or to intensify existing urban land

The National Land Use plan also called for developing quality-of-life standards. This process assumed that cities needed to create and maintain a certain lifestyle to be livable and attract the talented proto-urban dwellers whose presence helps "electrify" a city's culture and who are generally able to live wherever they choose.

To create this cultural and commercial "gravitational force" required, first of all, amenities: a range of housing choices, adequate parks and recreational areas for the population size, and cultural, civic, and entertainment facilities. Other parts of the livability package were quality education, easily available health care, and easy transit and travel services—home-to-work, home-to-school, and home-to-recreation.

One key lesson learned during development of the plan was that public investments in urban infrastructure had to be highly coordinated and managed. This had historically been done at the more circumscribed city level. What was clearly necessary, however, was to recognize and meet environmental concerns before a city expanded in unplanned ways. This could be done only by coordinating infrastructure investments in transportation, water, and power at state and federal levels. In the development of most cities, this necessary level of coordination had been difficult—sometimes impossible—to achieve.

The National Land Use plan pioneered recognition of the clear connection between environmental quality and the creation of real-world value. While the absolute quality of a region's environment might vary because of its economy, geography, culture, and climate, the value added by thoughtful development was virtually a universal phenomenon.

Although the plan was not adopted at the time, the Federal Service Systems for National Land Use provided a vocabulary and syntax of sustainability that is one of the most important tools for intelligent use of precious land. Today it is clear that value-based city design and the use of infrastructure investment to guide settlement, when properly applied, do establish environmental benefits, increase property values, and ultimately improve the quality of life.

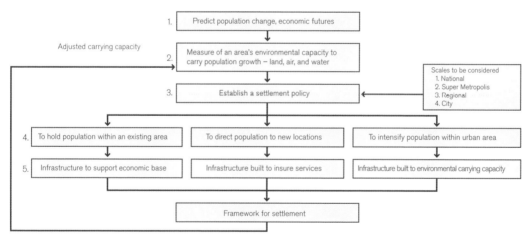

Standards and planning procedures to establish and maintain
a framework for settlement

1.2. Choosing the Right Future
The California Tomorrow Plan

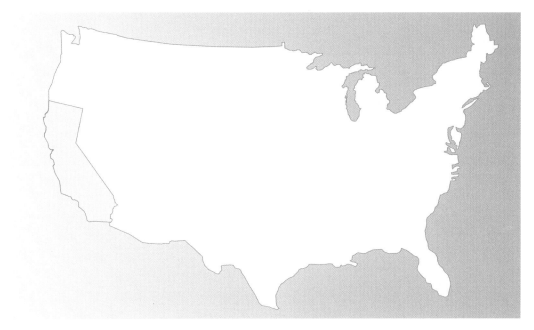

The state of California

In the early 1970s the concept of a framework for settlement proposed in the Federal Service Systems for National Land Use plan was given a chance to be reintroduced and refined. This time the target was smaller, but by no means inconsiderable: the state of California.

The plan was sponsored by and named for California Tomorrow, a nonprofit organization dedicated to creating greater public awareness of planning issues that were thwarting a more sustainable, livable, and productive state. The California Tomorrow Plan presented the future of the state as a series of discrete planning and development choices. It made the point that these choices could have tremendously positive or negative consequences.

To distinguish between the diverging outcomes, the plan presented two very different narratives of future California. The first conceptualized an unsustainable "California One," hobbled by the limitations of symptom-based problem solving or no problem solving at all. The other, the sustainable "California Two," presented a far more positive future based on recognizing and dealing with underlying dysfunctions and ensuring that connections were made among social, economic, and environmental policies.

California One: an unsustainable future corridor

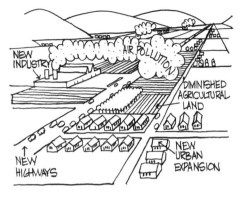

Agricultural lands are eroded by ad hoc urbanization.

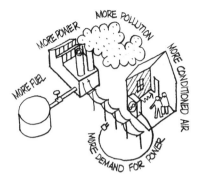

The reckless exploitation of energy increases.

California Two: a sustainable future

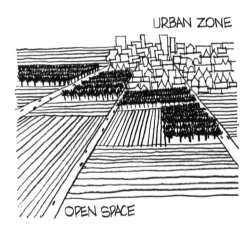

City growth stops at the edge of the urban zone.

New policies promote efficient waste disposal and encourage recycling.

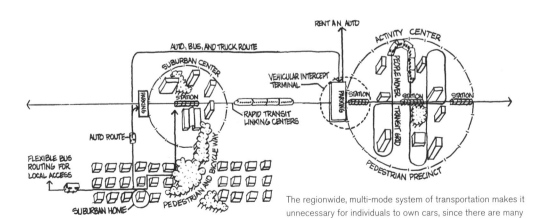

The regionwide, multi-mode system of transportation makes it unnecessary for individuals to own cars, since there are many attractive alternatives.

The "good" California Two plan was organized into three subject areas: land, structures, and people. It was driven by the need to achieve four distinct policies:

1. Establish a framework for settlement.
2. Develop new patterns of consumption.
3. Guarantee economic sufficiency.
4. Ensure political participation.

Together these policies were intended to form a common framework for developing and coordinating state planning.

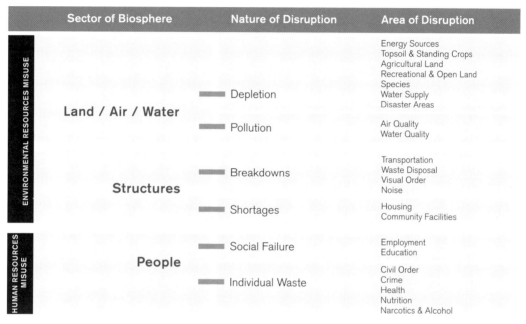

Major disruptions establish three categories for statewide policy coordination: land/air/water, structures, and people.

Establishing a Framework for Settlement

To begin with, the California Tomorrow Plan called for protecting land, air, and water under the aegis of a very different kind of state government. This government would be empowered to establish geographic zones that defined areas where development could and could not take place. The state would also be responsible for setting standards for air and water quality. The zones would be the basis for development and conservation based on environmental standards, population policy, and overall guidelines for regional development. State approval of regional plans for the location and design of new settlement and reconstruction of existing settlement were to be based on environmental health and safety standards and job opportunities.

All of California's 100 million acres are surveyed to identify lands for protection and lands for future settlement.

Conservation zone: agriculture

Conservation zone: desert

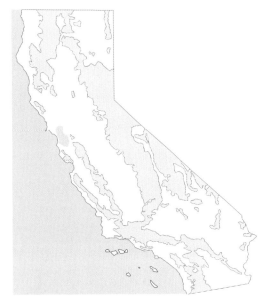

Conservation zone: steep slopes

Conservation zone: forest watersheds

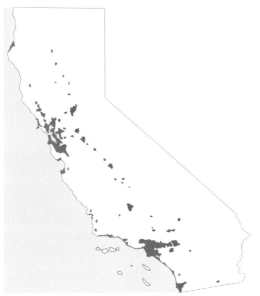

Urban zone

Remaining land reserved for possible settlement or other public or private purposes

Developing New Patterns of Consumption

The California Tomorrow Plan was intended to form a common framework for setting and coordinating development policies. In the California Tomorrow settlement framework, the state would assume responsibility to protect land, air, and water. Updated building codes would be designed to support rehabilitation more than new development of structures, upgrading and intensifying existing settlements with the intent to reduce suburban automobile travel. The human component of the new patterns of land consumption also emphasized education curricula on comprehensive resource management and its relationship to state resource conservation and development goals.

Guaranteeing Economic Sufficiency

The California Tomorrow Plan was designed to balance individual economic interest with the ability of society to actually pay for conservation and development goals. Development would be used to combine revenue-producing investments with non-revenue-producing investments in a balanced economic package that would be attractive to money markets. The plan would also provide education to furnish residents with the motivation and skills needed for available job opportunities.

Ensuring Political Participation

Responsibility for the plan was designed to lie with the governor, a newly empowered State Planning Policy Council, and the legislature. Regional plans were to be created and carried out by regional governments. Community councils and local governments were given responsibility for determining the specifics of the regional plans, including the location and design of public facilities such as schools and parks, of regional and state transportation networks, and of housing and other structures and their supporting services.

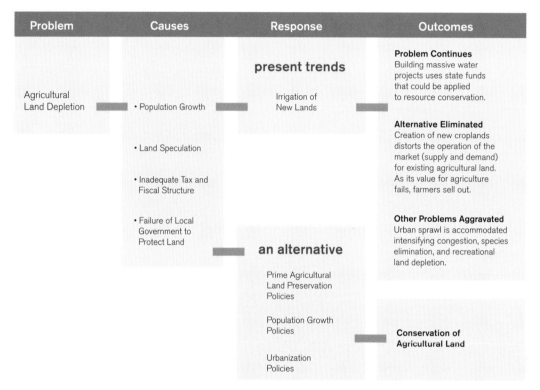

Typical problem solving tends to treat symptoms, but the problems always get worse unless causes are eliminated.

Far too ambitious for its time, the California Tomorrow Plan took on a number of sacred cows, including developers, agribusiness, and the auto industry—powerful interests that virtually guaranteed that the plan would not succeed. Requiring massive change and some public inconvenience, the plan was an early attempt to find a decent and livable path to environmental survival, and today seems very contemporary indeed.

The California Tomorrow Plan produced a series of statewide conferences, a newspaper, a book, and a paperback edition of the plan. Perhaps of greatest importance, the effort led a generation of California urban designers to recognize that choosing and implementing comprehensive planning solutions was as important as it was difficult.

Issues addressed by the California Tomorrow Plan were strikingly coincident with many of those explored in the federal context by the National Land Use plan. An important goal of the California Tomorrow Plan was to shift policy makers away from single-purpose problem solving toward dealing more comprehensively with the underlying causes of unsustainable, out-of-control statewide growth.

One of the study's conclusions was that California's damaging patterns of settlement resulted from the combination of a fast-growing population, insufficient public control over destructive development activities, jurisdictional power grabs, and intergovernmental disputes. The California Tomorrow Plan also recognized that damaging settlement patterns resulted from thoughtless development. Destructive consumption of land and resources was possible, in turn, because land was relatively cheap. The plan asserted that, to ensure a productive and healthy environment, new policies had to encourage both new settlement frameworks and more environmentally sound patterns of land, water, and air use.

With its publication, the California Tomorrow Plan won wide praise, at least among the state's editorial writers. It was heralded as an example of the potential benefits of making correct, comprehensive, and sustainable planning choices. Although not implemented, the plan was widely used as a teaching resource and a "prod" to largely unresponsive California legislators and other public officials, who recognized that the plan would impose a number of unpopular standards. The plan did, however, become a model for similar undertakings in other regions, states, and nations. Like the National Land Use plan, the California Tomorrow Plan was a milestone along what proved a very long road to heightened consciousness of the need for a sustainable framework for settlement at a regional scale.

San Francisco from the Marin County greenbelt

1.3. Expanding a City/Sustaining Green
The Chongming Island Master Plan, Shanghai, China

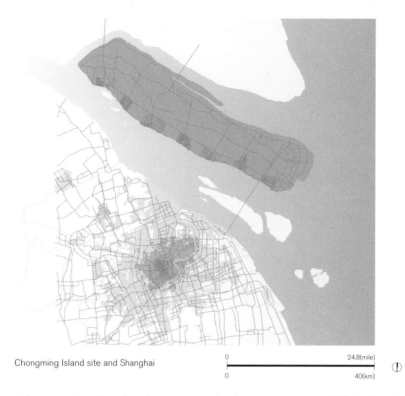

Chongming Island site and Shanghai

0   24.8(mile)

0   40(km)

After two decades of exuberant growth, the government of China has begun to refocus its millennial development philosophy in the direction of environmental sustainability. The decision in early 2004 to call off construction of the Hutiao Gorge Dam in Yunnan Province was an example of China's increased sensitivity to its natural environment. A similar focus on sustainability lay behind the decision by regional planners to choose the SOM entry in a 2004 master planning competition for the development of Shanghai's Chongming Island.

A 750-square-mile alluvial island at the mouth of the Yangtze River, Chongming is approximately 20 miles east of downtown Shanghai. With a new bridge/tunnel scheduled to connect Chongming directly to Shanghai, the island was directly in the path of seemingly unstoppable sprawl generated by China's great urban economic locomotive.

Since it was formed by the silting action of the Yangtze River, Chongming has developed into Shanghai's "rice bowl." It is today one of the world's largest alluvial islands and has some of China's richest agricultural land. Maintaining this agrarian orientation was the key to the plan to develop compact new communities on the island while preserving and advancing farming as the island's core function.

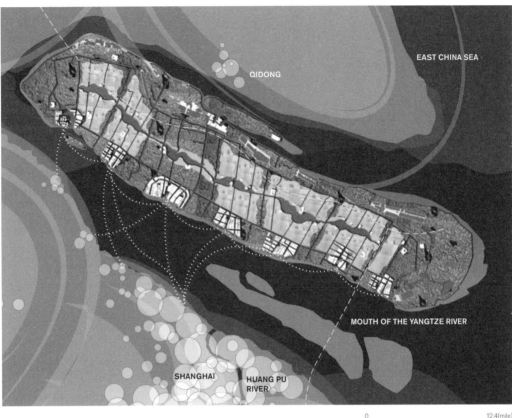

A fifty-year plan for Chongming Island

0	12.4(mile)
0	20(km)

In the SOM plan, Chongming was repositioned as a "green island" with its urban development confined to eight new, pedestrian-friendly cities. Each community would consist of walkable, transit-enhanced districts built at a density high enough to enable a population of 800,000 to live and work in only 15 percent of the island's land. The proposal included a "green" framework for energy and water treatment facilities, along with a transportation infrastructure bringing rapid transit connections to the center of each new town.

The plan set aside a percentage of Chongming's land for parks and open space, enough to make Chongming Shanghai's largest urban park. The Chongming Plan also protected wetlands that are one of Asia's primary avian flyways.

Sustainability was the key concept in the Chongming plan, which mandated that agriculture remain the island's primary function. Even more sustainable, the plan proposed to dedicate the island's agriculture to producing organically grown, high-quality, high-value fruits and vegetables.

Based on examples of intensive, high-value crops such as those in California's Napa and Sonoma valleys, Chongming's new high-end agricultural focus would enable local farmers to

The Principles to Guide Growth

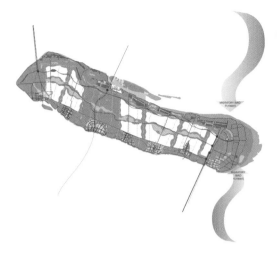

1. Protect wilderness areas and ecosystems.
Restore wetland wilderness areas. They form strong natural habitats for a broad community of wildlife.

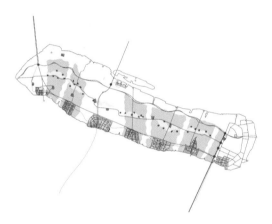

2. Introduce organic farming.
Maintain farming as the island's core business, shifting the focus to organic products and direct sales to Shanghai restaurants. Higher-quality produce will increase farmers' income.

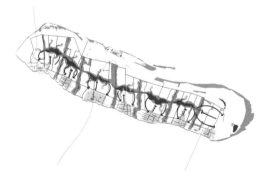

3. Develop green systems.
Tie all cities to bio-filtration. Introduce an island-wide lake system to maintain quality freshwater. Introduce renewable energy sources.

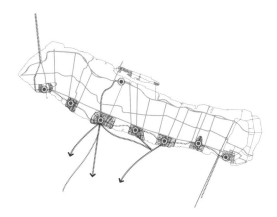

4. Ensure transit.
Preserve the historic farm grid of narrow streets throughout the island. Minimize overscaled highways. Connect all cities by rail to Shanghai. Introduce light-rail between cities. Expand the existing bikeway to all villages and cities.

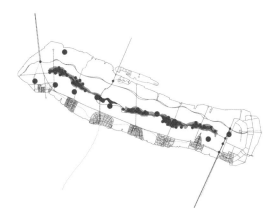

5. Protect the farming villages.
Define and protect forty farm villages organized around lakes in proximity to the farmlands so that farmers can live close to their work.

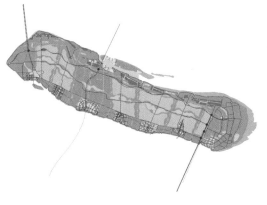

6. Create compact, walkable coastal cities.
Organize eight cities along the south coast, focused on rail transit corridors. Introduce a mix of uses within each city, to encourage more local trips than trips to Shanghai. Locate jobs, schools, and housing in each city.

Introduce organic farming.

Protect the farming villages.

Protect wilderness areas and ecosystems.

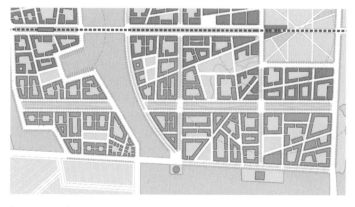

Create a city of distinct neighborhoods and small, walkable blocks.

Aerial view of Pearl Lake City

enjoy an unprecedented return on their labor. This increased profitability would be ensured by creating farmers' markets in central Shanghai. The markets would enable farmers to sell directly to the city's upscale shops and restaurants, providing the quality fruits and vegetables increasingly demanded by China's newly affluent middle class.

Included in the plan were a number of literally groundbreaking agricultural techniques capable of overcoming such problems as the infiltration of seawater into underground aquifers under stress from increasing development and more intense agriculture. The plan called for a chain of artificial lakes running down the island's spine, to provide additional potable water and create hydrostatic pressure that would push back against the permeation of brackish water. The lakes were also planned to be linked by canals to Chongming's periphery, to transport polluted water through wetlands, which would act as natural gray-water "bio-filters."

1.4. Guiding a Nation to a Post-Petroleum Future

The Bahrain National Plan

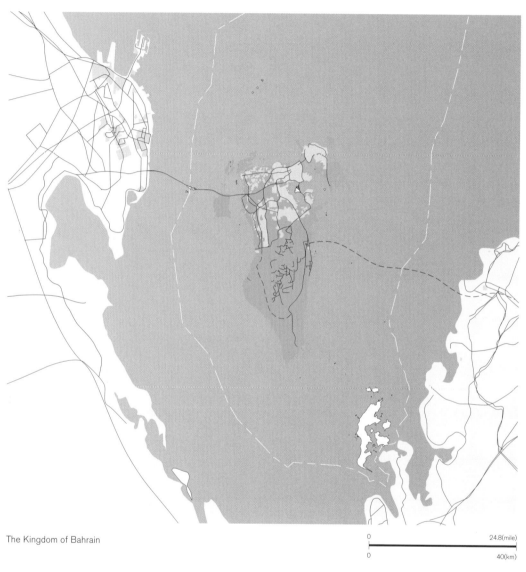

The Kingdom of Bahrain

| 0 | 24.8(mile) |
| 0 | 40(km) |

In 2007, following an extensive, intensive, 18-month process of research, analysis, consultation, and writing, SOM planners submitted the Bahrain National Planning Development Strategies (NPDS) to Crown Prince Shaikh Salman Bin Hamad Al-Khalifa. The Bahrain plan studied the kingdom's sustainability in a variety of aspects. These included preservation and restoration of Bahrain's rich natural heritage both terrestrial and aquatic, and a plan for infill and sensitive development that would take pressure off the ongoing filling-in of Bahrain's precious shoreline. Equally important, the plan presented an economic program that would enable Bahrain to become the world's first petroleum state to wean itself off oil and create a sustainable economic infrastructure.

The NPDS was the first effort of its kind in the Persian Gulf. It also placed Bahrain in the select company of Ireland, Singapore, and Denmark, the only nations to inventory their land and infrastructure and use that information to transform themselves economically, socially, and environmentally into prosperous, sustainable twenty-first-century states. Underlying the urgency for a national plan was recognition that Bahrain, with its limited supply of easily exploitable oil, would also be the first to run dry. This imperative lay behind the need for Bahrain to be the first Gulf nation to implement a comprehensive plan for a post-petroleum future.

The NPDS was unique in its scope: to inventory virtually every aspect of the nation's infrastructure and national life. The plan studied what Bahrain is and is not, charted its areas of excellence, and described aspects of life that required attention and improvement. The NPDS can also be seen as a step along the way to creating national land-use and developmental inventories that SOM had begun four decades earlier with the Federal Service Systems for National Land Use and the California Tomorrow plans. The NPDS exemplified a process designed to

Areas to conserve: where not to build

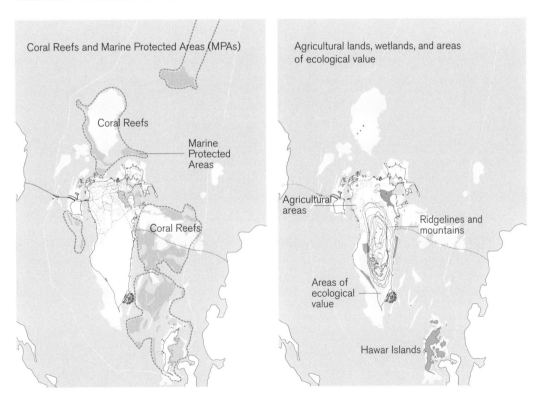

Coral Reefs and Marine Protected Areas (MPAs)

Coral Reefs

Marine Protected Areas

Coral Reefs

Agricultural lands, wetlands, and areas of ecological value

Agricultural areas

Ridgelines and mountains

Areas of ecological value

Hawar Islands

address the role that sustainable land-use development can play in ensuring stable, predictable, long-term, and, most important, sustainable growth.

The plan illuminates a vision of an economically sustainable Bahrain to which the world would come for business, trade, and leisure. It presents strategies designed to give Bahrain worldwide visibility as one of the Gulf's key financial, business, transportation, tourism, and electronic data hubs. This is a role for which Bahrain is uniquely suited: it is a regional center for today's jet- and Internet-enabled world economy, just as, during its millennial history, Bahrain was an important ancient trading crossroads.

The Bahrain plan addressed such critical challenges as depleted natural resources, inadequate housing, lack of zoning, weak transportation infrastructure, insufficient public open space, the need for educational improvements, and the need for comprehensive employment. By dealing with these issues today, Bahrain is attempting to move toward the stability and sustainability that are the outcomes of an orderly and creative planning process. Ultimately, by adopting the kind of unified, sustainable land-use decision-making process highlighted by the NPDS, Bahrain has the opportunity to overcome what is a very difficult world and regional economic downturn and continue to move ahead as the prototype of a successful twenty-first-century post-petroleum nation-state.

Areas to conserve: where not to build

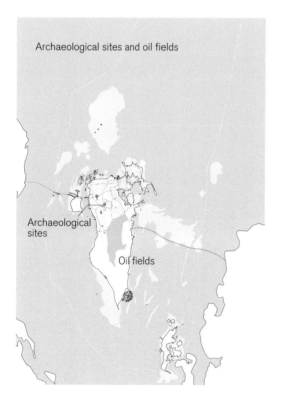

Archaeological sites and oil fields

Archaeological sites

Oil fields

Areas of future development: where to build

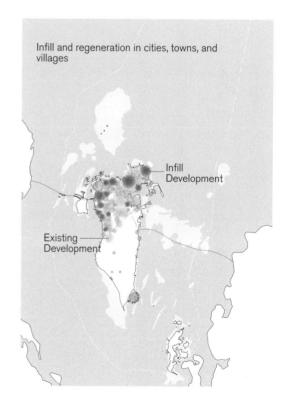

Infill and regeneration in cities, towns, and villages

Infill Development

Existing Development

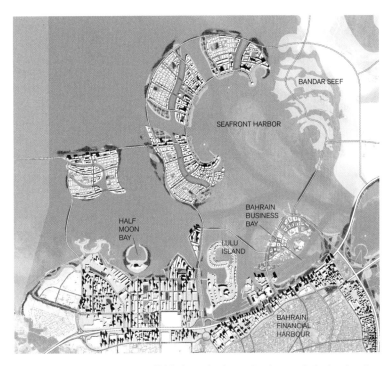

Old Harbor redevelopment and new waterfront park system

Areas of future development: where to build

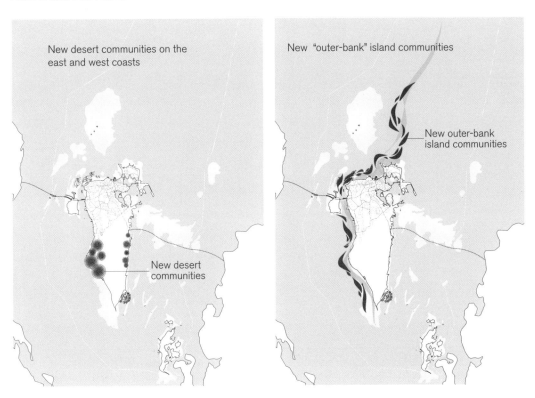

New desert communities on the east and west coasts

New desert communities

New "outer-bank" island communities

New outer-bank island communities

City high-density centers are located along the redeveloped waterfront and provide public access and parks along more than 40 kilometers of the shore.

Principle Two: Accessibility

Facilitating Ease of Movement

The Problem: Congestion, gridlock, time lost, gated and walled-off districts, lack of pedestrian safety and comfort, dependence on automobiles.

One of the foundational ideas of the city is to facilitate easy and economical exchanges among people, goods, services, and ideas. Historically, urban settlement patterns tended to expand around transportation and trade hubs, almost always where trails and waterways connected or crossed. In modern times, rail, highway, air, and even electronic links have facilitated and, in turn, been facilitated by city development. A nighttime photo of North America from outer space luminously illustrates how the continent's cities developed along these major transportation corridors like pearls on an economic necklace. This intensive settlement is most clearly visible along the northeast corridor between Boston and Washington, DC, in the urban industrial belt strung along the Great Lakes, in the Atlanta-to-Miami corridor, and along the Pacific Coast between Los Angeles and San Francisco and between Portland and Seattle/Tacoma. The necklace patterns are also visible along central China's Yangtze Basin, between Guangzhuo and Hong Kong in southeast China, along Germany's Rhine River, and between Tokyo and Osaka in Japan. Over time, these chains of cities tended to combine to make powerful regional economic units, which in turn grew and strengthened because of continuous reinvestment in infrastructure as the interlocking demands of population growth and commercial connections increased.

Moving Goods and People

Today, the most successful of these cities tend to be centered on highly compact downtowns, which are accessible by foot, with transit fundamental to achieving ease of getting around. Surprisingly, perhaps, typical American downtowns are 150 to 200 acres, which can be traversed on foot from the center to the outer edge in 15 to 20 minutes. In successful downtown districts these comparatively dense areas typically have the highest property values. Value, in this case, derives from the proximity and synergy of mixed commercial, office, and, increasingly, residential uses. City centers not coincidentally tend to have the richest transit access. The most desirable residential neighborhoods are similarly walkable, defined by a density above 15 dwellings per acre, and are characterized by convenient walks to schools, shopping, and transit connections.

Cities that have not facilitated ease of movement tend to depend primarily on the private automobile for transportation. Auto-centricity caused these cities to spread out and become pedestrian-unfriendly largely because the space required to park cars tends to equal the space taken by the buildings the parking serves. This necessitates spreading out commercial and office development so that each building can be set in its own captive parking lots. This, in turn, necessitates making everyday trips outside the building by car or, at best, by foot across expanses of asphalt.

These spread-out, auto-first downtowns have other drawbacks. Getting around in them requires people to spend unreasonable amounts of time and cities to devote large amounts of street space to autos. Streets become too wide to cross on foot, traffic lights must be set for longer cycles for car movement and shorter time for foot traffic, and in every respect the arterials become uncomfortable, unhealthy, and unpleasant for both pedestrians and drivers. Similarly, neighborhoods that are gated and separated from the city in cul-de-sacs or dead-end streets tend to block convenient pedestrian access and encourage automobile use instead of walking.

In many spread-out residential neighborhoods, the dominance of auto travel has also tended to concentrate commercial services in strip developments along fast-moving arterials. It is axiomatic that, on these wide streets where pedestrian use has not been considered, urban land value is lowest.

Land value, pedestrian and driver safety and comfort, and the concentration of urban amenities all argue for creating dense urban areas in which getting around is easy. Facilitating ease of movement is a critical principle of planning. Five distinct design methods help achieve it: compact development, concentrated destinations, small blocks and streets, system redundancy, and multiple modes.

1. Compact Development

Compact development minimizes the distance people need to travel and therefore the time and energy required to walk between home and work destinations. Compact cities also support convenient transit and commercial services.

SPRAWL CITY
2 HRS TO WORK

COMPACT CITY
30 MIN. TO WORK

2. Concentrated Destinations

Work destinations that are spread over large areas can never be served adequately by private vehicles or public transit. For automobiles, the streets can never be wide enough; for transit, the population within walking distance is never enough to support the service. To somewhat offset this lack of density, planners can design concentrated work destinations. These might include downtowns, mixed-use industrial/R&D campuses, and business parks, all supported by a transit infrastructure for short daily home-work commute trips. In each situation, however, walkability needs to be a bottom-line goal.

CONCENTRATED
WORK DESTINATIONS

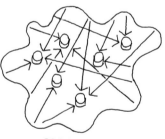

SCATTERED
WORK DESTINATIONS

3. Small Blocks and Streets

Large blocks with wide streets are pedestrian-unfriendly and vulnerable to breakdowns. Planning for small blocks and the narrowest feasible streets promotes comfort and safety for those on foot, which, in turn, encourages pedestrian use. With smaller blocks, there is less out-of-direction travel for pedestrians and vehicles. At the same time, pedestrians crossing the street have fewer vehicular lanes to cross. In Portland, Oregon, shorter blocks resulted in one of the most pedestrian-comfortable downtowns in the United States. In contrast, Beijing, China, is built around huge boulevards bordering giant blocks, making it one of the world's least pedestrian-friendly cities.

4. System Redundancy

A plan of multiple parallel streets can distribute traffic to other roads when capacity on one is reached or a traffic breakdown occurs, thus minimizing traffic congestion. Multiple streets are also adaptable to higher capacity by changing from two-way to one-way travel. The success of Portland's transit system is in part due to one-way streets dedicated to transit, so that light-rail speeds in and out of the downtown unimpeded by automobiles.

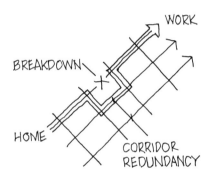

5. Multiple Modes

Providing adequate travel corridors for all modes of movement—pedestrian, bicycle, transit, and private vehicle use—creates the greatest flexibility for managing urban traffic.

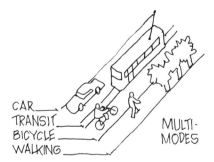

Circulation

Consuming between 20 and 30 percent of the land area they are designed to serve, transportation, circulation, and access corridors play a critical part in the planning process. Five major design methods facilitate maximum circulation and mobility using a minimum of land.

1. Land Reserves

To avoid higher future land costs and expensive disruptions from later acquisition and demolition, it is important to establish adequate land reserves for movement corridors that may be required in the future.

2. Corridor Location

To establish the walkability of an area and protect pedestrian comfort, major movement corridors need to be located at the edges of neighborhoods and districts. Conversely, those corridors must not be located in urban spaces where they wall off important views and amenities, such as waterfronts or other publicly valued natural features. San Francisco's Embarcadero Freeway, for example, stood for nearly three decades as a virtually impermeable barrier between the waterfront and the downtown. Its destruction in the Loma Prieta earthquake of 1989 was almost universally applauded by a population that regained its magnificent waterfront through what many thought was an act of a merciful God.

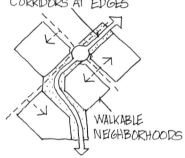

3. Geometry and Scale

For much of the twentieth century, traffic engineering focused on driver safety, which promoted wide streets to accommodate high-speed travel and wide turning radii. In recent times, emphasis has shifted to pedestrian comfort and safety, with new techniques to slow traffic. Wide traffic lanes tend to encourage

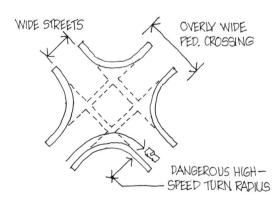

speed, while narrow lanes encourage traffic to slow down, aiding both pedestrian and driver safety. Similarly, a large curve at street corners increases both traffic speed and overall street-crossing width, which reduce pedestrian safety and comfort. It is a good exercise to imagine many of our existing wide streets narrowed by redesign with broader sidewalks, landscaped medians, or even "ribbon" wetlands that can filter water runoff and help reduce pollution.

4. Street Types

Types of streets vary widely. They may be defined by formal or informal geometry, established as grids, designed in capitol webs, or curved to accommodate existing topography. Street type is crucial in establishing block and parcel sizes, which delineate and define most aspects of a city, including neighborhoods, parks, and buildings.

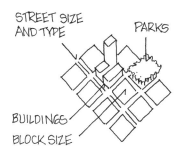

    Streets can be undivided or separated by a central median. The latter provides a safety zone for pedestrians crossing wide streets. In a divided boulevard with two medians in the center, stop-and-go local traffic is diverted to side lanes. Medians can also separate light-rail transit or bicycle paths from vehicular traffic.

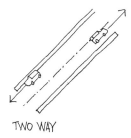

TWO WAY

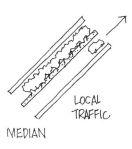

MEDIAN

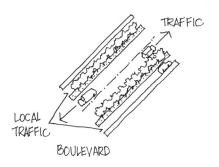

BOULEVARD

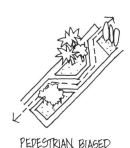

PEDESTRIAN BIASED

5. Street Design Treatments

Streets can have nearly infinite variations in the treatment of parking, sidewalks, landscape, lighting, amenities, and services. Sidewalk and street spaces, for example, can be totally dedicated to pedestrian traffic, to vehicular traffic, or to virtually any combination of the two.

In streets designed primarily for walking, landscape treatment forces vehicles to slow, because they have to zigzag through. In streets dedicated *solely* to pedestrian traffic, emergency vehicles have limited access. Streets that do not carry heavy or through traffic may become pedestrian- and bicycle-friendly. Cars can enter, but they must pass with great care. Enlarging sidewalks at street corners creates more space for pedestrians waiting to cross the street as well as narrowing the street width to make crossing more comfortable.

Many European cities offer useful examples of mixed-use streets. That lesson is being learned in the United States, where street spaces once unquestioningly devoted to auto parking are increasingly set aside for transit stops, sidewalk café seating, pedestrian promenades, rest areas, and landscaping.

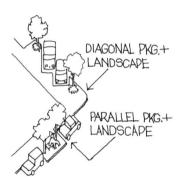

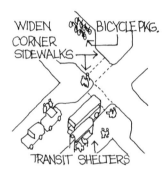

2.1. Locating Corridors to Preserve a Downtown

The Baltimore Expressway Plan, Maryland

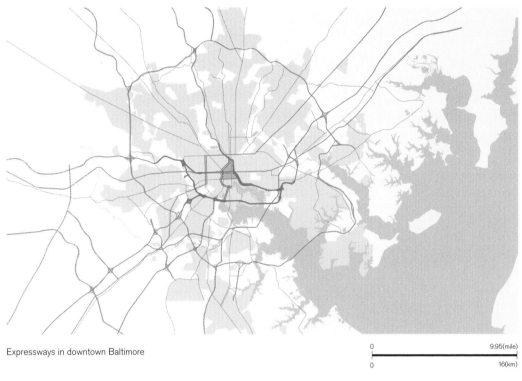

Expressways in downtown Baltimore

0　　　　　　　　　　9.95(mile)

0　　　　　　　　　　16(km)

One of the underlying doctrines that characterize best-practice city building relates to the medical injunction "First do no harm." A project that truly crystallized this understanding was a 1963 SOM study for a freeway plan to serve the Baltimore, Maryland, downtown and Inner Harbor District.

At that time, planners had little say about the design and placement of highways. Road engineers were considered the final and ultimate arbiters. However, as the SOM Baltimore study progressed, it became clear that "urban renewal" projects like this almost always ended up in areas that were environmentally sensitive, economically depressed, or racially segregated. In Baltimore, success meant undoing the entire plan of a harbor freeway. The consequences of not building the waterfront freeway were immensely positive, if not instantly apparent: the original plans would have precluded or made monumentally more expensive the development of the Inner Harbor into what is today the social and civic heart of a renewed Baltimore. If, in San Francisco, it took an earthquake to reconnect the downtown to its waterfront, in Baltimore, a thoughtful second look served the same function in a less hair-raising process.

The original plan for the downtown-serving expressway destroys Baltimore's Inner Harbor.

The revised alignment to the south retains the open harbor and shoreline amenity.

The shoreline amenity destroyed

The shoreline amenity retained

The Inner Harbor and central business district have become Baltimore's cultural and civic heart.

2.2. Creating Essential Access to Major Development

Canary Wharf, London

Canary Wharf site in London

| 0 | 9.95(mile) |
| 0 | 16(km) |

Over the last decades, getting around in London has been increasingly based on transit. Nowhere is this trend more powerfully exemplified than at London's Canary Wharf, the 70-acre mixed-use development in East London's once-decrepit Docklands. At Canary Wharf, transit access, dense development, and pedestrian ease of movement have been central to the project's success. Since the completion of its first phase in the late 1980s, additional transit improvements have helped make Canary Wharf an increasingly successful neighborhood, which has, in turn, led to more and better transit. Some experts even suggest that transit saved Canary Wharf and that Canary Wharf reciprocated by saving London. Hyperbole or not, the transit improvements at Canary Wharf truly were key to opening up the fabulously rich-with-potential 1,000-square-kilometer Thames Estuary to the east.

To facilitate transit and walkability, the 1997–98 Phase III SOM Master Plan for Canary Wharf called for creating new transit corridors, including stops for London's Jubilee Line and the Docklands Light-Rail (DLR) System. The plan recognized that without rich transit Canary Wharf simply could not succeed.

Unfortunately, while the early phases of Canary Wharf were being planned, there was a concomitant lack of political will to fund an extensive transit connection between Canary Wharf and central London. This setback played a part in the disastrous early 1990s bankruptcy

Canary Wharf Heron Quays construction progress, July 2002

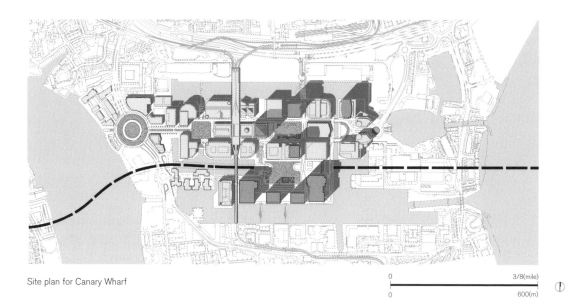

Site plan for Canary Wharf

0 .... 3/8(mile)

0 .... 600(m)

of the project. Ultimately, however, completion of the Jubilee Line extension to Canary Wharf in 2000 and inauguration of the DLR System have done much to enable the thriving 24-hour-a-day, 7-day-a-week mixed-use neighborhood that has become London's second downtown and Britain's de facto financial heart. Today, the Jubilee Line is functioning at full capacity, and 75 percent of Canary Wharf's visitors and workers arrive there via the Underground. The trip to and from central London is a mere 15-minute rail ride, and Canary Wharf's transit is within a 5-minute walk of more than 20,000 residential units.

Commercially, Canary Wharf's large floor plates and easy access have enabled financial institutions to maintain their headquarters and trading presence in London. The site has seen creation of some of London's most outstanding high-rise building design. Canary Wharf's commercial infrastructure has, in turn, helped facilitate Britain's continued central role in trading in the European Union and beyond.

Canary Wharf's successful, transit-oriented development was complemented by the project's attention to historical design precedent. To a large degree, that design care led sometimes

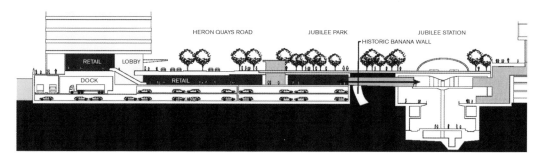

The retail level provides a weather-protected environment from transit to the street-level uses.

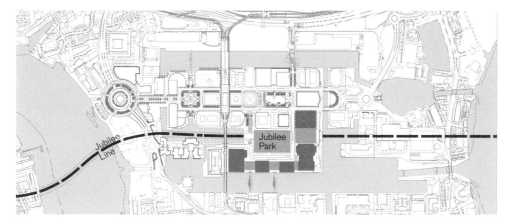

Heron Quays establish Jubilee Park as the civic front door to Canary Wharf, accepting the 44,000 who arrive daily by transit to work in the building shown in red.

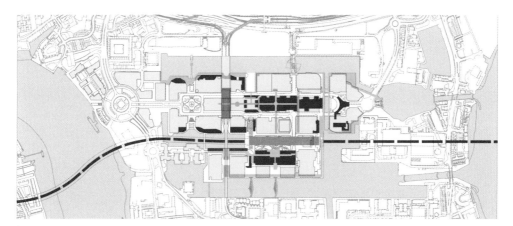

Retail connects transit to office buildings

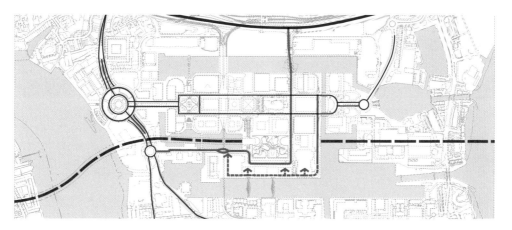

New roadways are illustrated in red. These links provide north-south and east-west connections to the district and Canary Wharf. A below-grade service route (dashed) provides access to the loading docks and parking, without negatively affecting the waterfront promenade above.

solipsistic Londoners to take quickly to their new neighborhood. Formal parks, landscaped streets, crafted street furniture, familiar palettes of building materials, and the project's River Thames orientation reinforced the bond between people and place. From its inception, the Canary Wharf Master Plan lived at the scale of a new urban neighborhood, with each element supporting and elevating the primacy of "district" over "building." Combining important architecture with overall district planning minimized discordant notes, and people who live in, work at, and visit Canary Wharf experience a unified, complete, transit-accessible neighborhood. Today, Canary Wharf is in Phase IV, its final buildout, which includes mixed uses and housing projects that will add over 20 million square feet of residential, commercial, and office units at nearby sites that were once out of the way, such as the Isle of Dogs and Leamouth.

Canary Wharf's success has also helped jump-start proposals for the new £10 billion Crossrail underground rail link that will further tie West and East London together and open up London's Thames Gateway region to the east. In connection with Canary Wharf, Crossrail will effectively "move the map" of London, as commercial and housing developments extend east along the Thames toward City Airport and the North Sea coast.

A new 14-million-square-foot downtown consisting of twenty-six buildings

2.3. Planning for Ferry Transit
The Treasure Island Master Plan, San Francisco, California

The Treasure Island site in San Francisco Bay

In 2005 developers and city officials approached SOM to help advance a plan for Treasure Island, the historic, possibilities-rich, 400-acre former Navy base lying 2 miles across the bay from downtown San Francisco. Because of limited vehicular access off and on the San Francisco–Oakland Bay Bridge, the planning team felt from the start that Treasure Island could be a demonstration project for a new kind of neighborhood development based on ferry and other transit, applying the most advanced principles of sustainability. The key was to create a community not only liberated from the notion that each housing unit must include parking space but also embracing walking and bicycling as the primary modes of getting around.

The Treasure Island illustrated site plan

| 0 | 0.55(mile) |
| 0 | 880(m) |

Treasure Island has a storied history. Beginning in the mid-1930s, the island was dredged from San Francisco Bay. Originally planned as a new airport, the island first became the site of the 1939 Golden Gate International Exposition. The 2-year-long world's fair celebrated completion of the Golden Gate and Bay Bridges, as well as 30 years of post-earthquake growth, which had transformed the Bay Area into a leading international industrial, educational, and intellectual center. After the fair closed, Treasure Island became the terminus for the famous Pan American China Clipper seaplane service to Asia. From World War II until the mid-1990s, the island was a United States naval facility and site for navy housing.

In 2005, with a large percentage of the island's housing already in civilian use, planners faced the imperative to stage development so that current residents in navy housing could segue seamlessly into the island's new neighborhoods. Another pressing issue was toxic contamination from six decades as a navy base.

The revised plan began by addressing critical negatives: the island's toxicity, the often-harsh west winds and persistent fog, and the dangerous ramps on and off the Bay Bridge, which hampered island auto traffic. Planning team efforts focused on finding ways to transform these shortcomings into sustainable advantages. The overarching theme was to remake Treasure Island into nothing less than a fine-grained, walkable, downtown San Francisco neighborhood and a model for sustainable urban life, design, and ease of getting around.

The 2006 plan for Treasure Island envisioned four residential neighborhoods and one commercial district enabling between ten and twenty thousand San Franciscans to live in the style and density of some of the city's other famed districts, like North Beach and the Marina. Island housing was designed at a density as high as 100 units per acre. This would be dense enough to support ferry service and to dedicate the majority of the island's acreage to a variety of open spaces, including wetlands capable of filtering island-produced "gray water," bike and walking paths, and a large detoxified demonstration site for organic gardening.

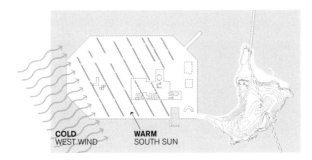

Street geometry

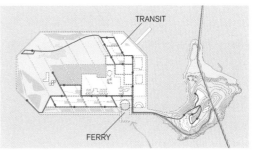

Intermodal exchange

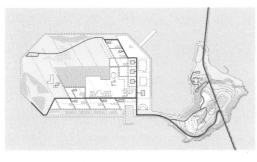

Automobiles and parking

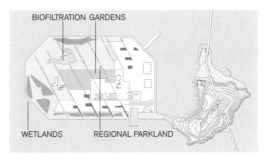

Neighborhood open space

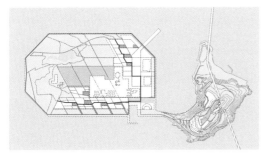

Pedestrian and bicycle access

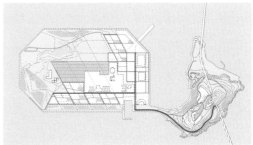

Street types

The plan's transportation component focused on pedestrian and bicycle uses connecting to frequent, fast ferry service to San Francisco. Siting ferry slips and a central terminal 500 feet inside the island's western perimeter would encourage residents to rely on the ferry, because those in the four predominantly mid- and low-rise residential neighborhoods would be only an 8-minute walk away at most, and the ferry a 13-minute ride to downtown. Locating the ferry terminal on the island's western flank both practically and symbolically represented the new community's direct connection with San Francisco.

Like city districts, the island's neighborhoods would mix a variety of housing densities and types, from two-story walk-ups to forty-story apartment towers. Housing options and price points ranged from apartment rentals to condominiums and single-family homes. Parking would be limited to areas outside the various districts, designed to be "out of sight" and thus to further encourage walking and transit use.

The planning team recognized that it was crucial to address the issue of constant winds and frequent bone-chilling island fog. A simple, novel scheme was developed to largely mitigate the island's difficult weather: the plan turned the development grid to the north and west, and proposed locating stands of new trees, berms, and buildings to effectively block bay winds from penetrating neighborhood peripheries. Shifting the grid also enabled maximum southern solar exposure throughout the neighborhoods, for enhanced personal comfort. Power for the new community would be assisted by sustainable photovoltaic arrays in concert with advanced wind turbines.

View from Treasure Island toward San Francisco (right) and Yerba Buena Island (left)

View from the San Francisco Ferry Building

View of the neighborhood core and the Golden Gate Bridge

2.4. Learning from Mistakes: Mixed-Access Streets versus Transit Malls
State Street, Chicago, Illinois

The State Street site in Chicago

0   9.95(mile)

0   16(km)

State Street in Chicago is a prime example of the snares of a popular urban planning scheme through the 1970s and '80s: creating auto-free pedestrian and transit zones. The project began in the late 1970s with the development of a 9-block "transit mall" along State Street, once Chicago's premier downtown shopping boulevard, famously dubbed "the Great Street." The initiative took advantage of federal funding and was seen as a way to boost State Street against competition from both suburban shopping centers and the upscale shops prospering along north Michigan Avenue. The design called for a curving two-lane bus-only transit mall, with widened sidewalks and new bus and subway shelters illuminated by huge modern lighting fixtures.

Although the plan was implemented, State Street continued to decline, with anchor stores (including Sears and Montgomery Ward) pulling out just months after the transit mall opened. Chicago was in the midst of a building boom, but State Street was not benefiting, and complaints about the transit mall were many and varied. Some criticized its curvilinear design (which ruled out most parades), the 50-foot-tall streetlights, the modern bus shelters, kiosks, and subway enclosures, and the 50-foot-wide sidewalks, which dwarfed pedestrians and made the street seem empty at the busiest of times. People also complained about the gray asphalt pavement, which deteriorated badly in the harsh Chicago weather. Most of all, Chicagoans wanted their autos allowed back on State Street.

In the 1980s a new task force studying State Street found that the site's physical condition had become a major impediment to attracting pedestrians, that the dark sidewalks were unsafe and uninviting, and that the absence of auto traffic made State Street isolated and limited access to its businesses.

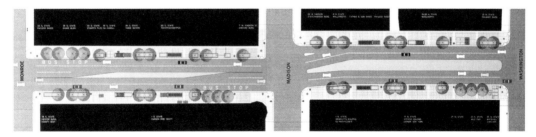

Street and sidewalk plan

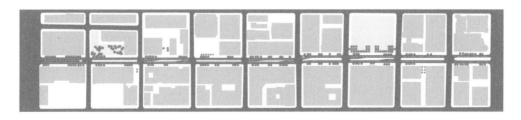

State Street site plan

| 0 | | 1/4(mile) |
| 0 | | 400(m) |

In 1991, assisted by funding from the new federal Intermodal Surface Transportation Efficiency Act, Chicago tried again. The new plan completely reenvisioned State Street, removing the bus transit mall and welcoming back cars. Once the city decided to bring back private autos and taxis, other design elements fell into place. Planners narrowed the sidewalks to their historic width of 22 to 26 feet. This concentrated people near store windows and created a greater sense of commerce, movement, and energy. Sidewalks were landscaped with sizable trees and seasonal plantings in low granite planters rimmed with iron railings. The gray asphalt pavement was replaced with rose- and limestone-colored concrete.

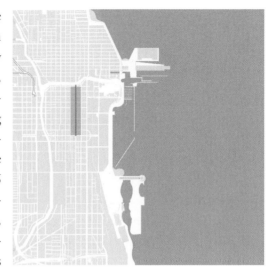

State Street location in the city center

The plan's centerpiece was a design concept for reconstructing State Street using historical precedent as a guide. The mall was removed, a four-lane street created, sidewalks narrowed, trees planted, and subway enclosures replaced. The historic 30-foot-high cast-iron light fixtures designed in 1926 were reintroduced. Besides enlivening the street, the fixtures supported street signs, banners, and seasonal decorations. Ultimately, the design team decided to underplay various street elements so that shop windows would be center stage.

Light standards and transit entrances establish the street's identity.

As the State Street redesign evolved through the 1990s, it was given credit for a renaissance along the street. New hotels opened, and a theater district began taking shape, anchored by the restored Chicago Theater. A number of other historic buildings were renovated, including several by the famed Chicago architect Louis Sullivan. Buildings converted into live-work space and apartments helped add a 24-hour vitality that is a hallmark of Chicago's now—finally—successfully re-renovated State Street.

Landscaping defines comfortable sidewalks.

2.5. Unblocking Movement
Far East Side, Detroit, Michigan

Far East Side site, Detroit, Michigan

0   9.95(mile)

0   16(km)

Detroit's Far East Side is a neighborhood that abuts the famous high-end bedroom community of Grosse Pointe, Michigan, and the contrast between the two could not be starker. The Far East Side was less a ghetto than an overgrown ruin. In 2004 a private development group led by Henry Cisneros, former U.S. Housing and Urban Development secretary, developed a master plan for redeveloping 1,200 acres, which constituted most of Detroit's Far East Side. The first 140-acre phase of the project began in 2005 and was a model and an advertisement for the rest of the phases.

In no other part of urban America is it possible to see such a contrast between adjacent developed and undeveloped neighborhoods. Even Newark and Chicago in their worst days of public housing could not match the stark transformation of suburb to wasteland across the width of a single street. A driver headed south from Grosse Pointe transited directly from a thriving neighborhood into a place where the houses were boarded up or burned down, with yards and alleys turned into dumping grounds for trash and abandoned cars.

A tour through Far East Detroit offered clues to the cause of the decay as well as possible solutions. Historically, early settlers had laid out this part of Detroit in what were called "ribbon blocks"—elongated strips—that had been useful for farming. But when the blocks were adapted into an urban form they became a disaster for vehicles and pedestrians alike: uninterrupted strips nearly a half-mile long.

Although they led down to the Detroit River, these extended blocks were unfriendly and wasted time and effort. For example, residents had to drive a car from the front of their house all the way around the block and then back again down the alley behind the house to garage it. Upkeep of the alleys, which ran parallel to the major streets in the neighborhood, had been largely abandoned by the city, so they became overgrown and almost impassable.

The first challenge was to break the oversized blocks down into a more human scale, closer to the block sizes in other major cities; Chicago, for example, has a grid of 300-foot-long blocks, between one-quarter and one-third of those in Detroit's Far East Side.

Far East Side proposed neighborhood master plan

| 0 | 3/8(mile) |
| 0 | 600(m) |

Planning began by introducing a new grid of east-west streets. These were designed not just to break up the north-south ribbon blocks but also to do so in ways that created an urban rhythm sensitive to important and indigenous factors. These included preventing the streets from becoming auto speedways from the suburbs into downtown Detroit. The proposal therefore limited east-west straightaways to no more than three blocks. Then, traffic would have to stop and turn a corner to get to the next east-west thoroughfare.

Another guiding principle for the plan was preserving existing structures, at almost any cost. Each neighborhood home that could be preserved meant one fewer that needed to be built. New street grids were thus planned to go through already vacant lots and around existing housing. By paying careful attention to the housing checkerboard, the plan destroyed only four structures in the first phase, three of which were in poor condition to begin with.

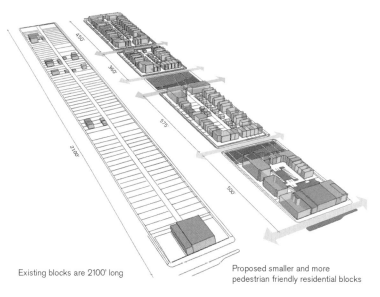

Existing blocks are 2100' long

Proposed smaller and more pedestrian friendly residential blocks

Create smaller residential blocks by introducing new streets to the 2,100-foot-long blocks.

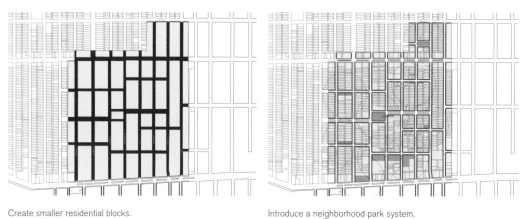

Create smaller residential blocks.

Introduce a neighborhood park system.

Locate new east-west streets on vacant land.

Strengthen retail and cultural corridors.

2.6. Restoring Access, Reversing Vacancy and Decline

ProCentro, São Paulo, Brazil

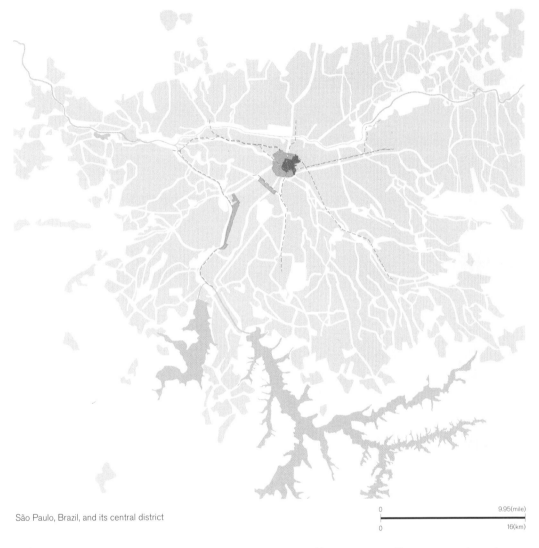

São Paulo, Brazil, and its central district

0	9.95(mile)
0	16(km)

In 1998 I was invited to São Paulo to deliver a series of lectures as well as to consult with city officials about renewing the central business district of South America's largest city.

Then, as now, Brazil was trying to narrow the extraordinary disparity between wealth and poverty. In São Paulo, in the 1990s, the automobile was considered an obvious distinction between rich and poor. In the name of social parity, therefore, the city government experimented by closing a number of streets in the historic downtown to car traffic and turning them over to pedestrians.

São Paulo's skyline is made up of thousands of concrete towers.

The street closings, unfortunately, produced a series of unintended and largely negative consequences. Pedestrian-only streets limited access to the city's high-density core and thus tended to create economic "dead zones." Over a few years, as the "broken window syndrome" took hold, building after building in the area went vacant. Safety and security became increasingly important topics among São Paulo planners and politicians.

Among the most visible effects of the decline were rust stains spreading across the windowless concrete "party walls" designed to be shared by adjoining high-rises. Here were depressing visual reminders of the economic depression in downtown São Paulo.

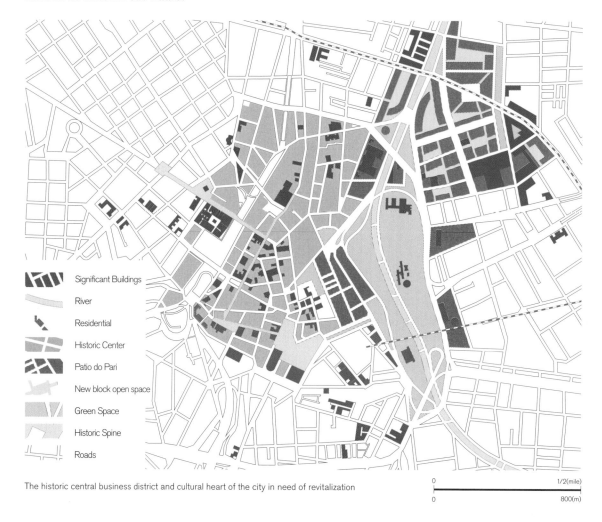

Significant Buildings

River

Residential

Historic Center

Patio do Pari

New block open space

Green Space

Historic Spine

Roads

The historic central business district and cultural heart of the city in need of revitalization

| 0 | 1/2(mile) |
| 0 | 800(m) |

Brazil is not a rich country and does not have a great deal to spend on urban design fixes. But São Paulans are extremely creative. Their creativity and cultural strength translated into an ability to move quickly when planning or design proposals made sense.

To begin the process of bringing the downtown back to life, certain streets reopened to auto traffic. This provided the taxi and drop-off access that could help repopulate empty blocks. To improve the downtown cityscape visually, plans were made to paint murals on the numerous dirt-streaked concrete blank faces of degraded high-rises.

This didn't seem to me to be a good idea; several hundred large-scale murals would blur into a chaotic, undistinguished mass of graffiti. The art would make the cityscape less comprehensible than it already was and might even project the negative character of the graffiti in many North American cities.

I had happened to bring with me a set of watercolors for amusement, and I made a few paintings of downtown São Paulo, highlighting various buildings in different tropical pastel colors. When I showed the paintings to city planners, they found the pastel shades agreeable and thought they could have a positive impact. The response was immediate, and an

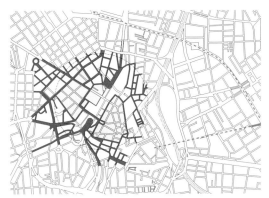

Existing vehicular streets (red) and pedestrian streets (yellow). Most vacant buildings were located on pedestrian streets.

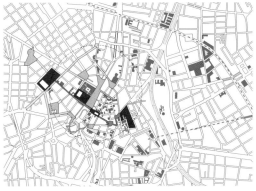

Historic east-west linkages and plazas (red) to initiate central district renewal

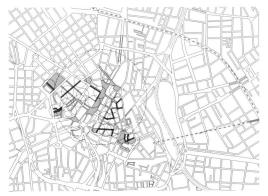

Proposed pedestrian zones (yellow) and new vehicular access (red) to restore declining districts

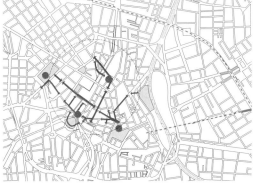

Transit station (blue) and pedestrian movements (red) establish the corridors of highest pedestrian density

Before: vacant buildings with dirt-stained concrete walls

organization called Paint São Paulo was founded. About 6 months later, when I returned to Brazil, I was astonished to see that over four hundred downtown buildings had been painted in those pastel shades. Best of all, the colorful display was one factor helping bring a sense of life back to central São Paulo.

I learned two lessons from São Paulo. First, for cities with few financial resources, simple ideas can be tested inexpensively and, if they seem to work, quickly implemented. Second, a positive visual appearance, though a smaller piece of the puzzle than redevelopment, was an incentive that helped reestablish lost civic value.

Watercolor study to show the impact of pastel colors on a gray cityscape as an alternative to previous plans to paint multiple murals

Yellow core tower

Pink tower of the central district

Principle Three: Diversity

Maintaining Variety and Choice

The Problem: Deprivation of services, lack of visual interest, unsatisfying environments, lack of affordability, and single-minded design thinking.

Science, history, and experience teach that diversity plays an elemental role in natural systems. Variety and choice are equally important for developing successful human-scale cities. Intrinsic in the livable city is choice of accommodations, job opportunities, services, cultural and religious activities, visual interest, elements of leisure and recreation, and close, convenient access to health care and education. Together these choices provide city residents the widest range of opportunities to live satisfying, well-rounded lives. For city builders the principle of variety and choice has two important aspects: visual variety and maximizing mixed use. If visual variety lightens the human spirit, a mix of residential, commercial, and service uses provides the motivating power to keep cities moving ahead and alive 24 hours a day.

Visual Variety

Good city environments possess a variety of buildings, old and new, large and small, daring and unassuming. Simple though it may sound, variety is essential to creating a visual interest that engages the imagination and captures the eye. A good city expresses and benefits from the richest possible variety of cultures, ages, languages, ethnicities, economic strengths, and lifestyles.

Since the middle of the twentieth century, and increasingly today, the scale and pace of development are making these elements of diversity disappear or at least become more difficult to bring together. In parts of Asia, whole neighborhoods are being built in a single phase with a single residential building type repeated. This "repetition compulsion" may meet programmatic goals, but it almost always lacks fine-grained, human-scale variety. It also fails to offer the choices of how to live, work, and play that add so much to a city's attraction. Diversity is inversely proportional to a culture's tolerance for (or at least acquiescence in) repetition. Experience shows that the best city developments create variety, choice, and economic diversity regardless of project size or rapidity of development. Three design methods can promote a visually interesting environment.

1. Conservation

Conserving notable landscapes, historic street patterns, and historically interesting buildings helps retain the cultural memory of a cityscape. Preserving the past also educates the population through comparisons between older and more contemporary building and landscape practices. Preservation is enormously important as an aspect of maintaining visual interest and defining the character of a

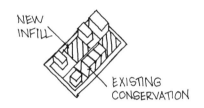

city. Today, we are building huge cities with tall buildings and a consequent lack of historic variety. Under these circumstances, visual diversity is even more important and must be established by other means.

2. Design Variations

Guidelines that call for design variations between buildings are important in all large-scale development projects. Guidelines may address varying façade treatments, entry characteristics, building heights, setbacks, landscape characteristics, and the like. The rationale for the variations can involve access to views and sunlight as well as the desire to enhance building identity and visual complexity.

3. Small Parcels

A useful strategy for creating maximum architectural variety is to enable many separate designers and builders to participate in a single development. Subdividing a project into the smallest feasible development parcels can create maximum architectural variety and avoid the repetitiveness and sameness of large buildings in large projects on large parcels.

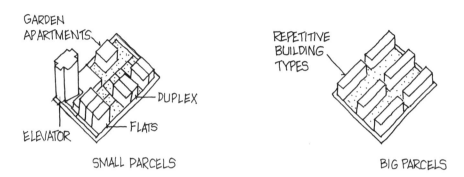

A multiple development approach has worked successfully in places like Freiberg, Germany, and Chicago, Illinois. In Freiberg the construction of a new village containing 4,200 residential units for between ten and twelve thousand inhabitants was parceled out to between five and ten investors per block, rather than the typical one per block. In Chicago the renewal of ten city blocks among the city's most degraded public housing areas was parceled out to a half-dozen different architects and developers to create a low-rise, mixed-use new neighborhood with an emphasis on diversity of style, building type, and, ultimately, occupant.

Mixed Use

Diversity is a welcome condition that is difficult both to achieve and to maintain. In a market economy, competition for a limited supply of living and working space will raise costs and often drive away the very kinds of residents and small businesses that are diversity's standard-bearers. When diversity is decreased, the loss to city livability is substantial. Municipal workers, for example, who tend to earn less than their private sector counterparts, are forced to live elsewhere and commute longer distances. Higher living costs can lead to a similar out-migration of artists and craftspeople, a fundamental loss to a city's cultural diversity.

Losing affordable work space can also create harm by decreasing new urban economic enterprise. Even necessary "back office" services that support everyday business life may be forced out of the city through high rents.

In the United States, over the last half-century, the typical approach to development has been the reverse of mixed use: creating huge single-use districts. With one area dedicated to suburban housing, another to detached, inward-looking industrial parks and high-tech campuses, and still others to the commercial malls that rest so uneasily on the American landscape, the outcome is an unplanned, low-density sprawl that has become a social, environmental, functional, and human blight.

Only in recent decades have planners put any energy behind reversing the single-use mentality. For example, business campuses are reorganized into higher density, walkable, mixed-use neighborhoods that place work, shopping, recreation, and residence in close proximity. As a rule, single-use campuses should not exceed 200 acres unless other uses are mixed in.

In the name of livability, therefore, it is critical for cities to find ways to keep space affordable so as to maintain human diversity. One way to protect the existing supply of affordable buildings is through legislation. In North America there is a trend among cities to require new market-rate residential buildings to dedicate a portion of a project to affordable housing or pay to build that housing elsewhere in that urban zone.

Such a requirement is different from past programs that created publicly subsidized housing set apart and ultimately stigmatized as "projects." Today, a premium is placed on developing affordable housing mixed within existing neighborhoods and districts and not readily recognized as "low income."

Affordability cannot be defined absolutely (and varies in fact from city to city). Nevertheless, it can be assigned a more universal meaning. Beginning with the truism that upper- and upper-middle-income families always have habitat choices, it is logical to then define affordability as the ability of middle- and lower-income families to have a similar adequate choice of urban habitats for both living and working.

The phrase *mixed use* has become a talisman in recent decades, representing convenience, round-the-clock safety, and maximized choices for living, working, shopping, entertainment, culture, leisure, and recreation. In Asia, housing, office, and retail uses are mixed in virtually every project, regardless of size. Some of these projects include leisure entertainment uses as well. Mixed use is a logical outcome for development in high-density cities. Four design methods help maximize mixed use.

1. Affordability

Cities and districts must conserve land or provide financial support to maintain affordable uses and encourage social and economic diversity. In fast-growing cities, housing offered at an affordable price typically becomes unaffordable when resold for profit. The best means for maintaining affordable houses thus is to make them rentals.

Throughout the first decade of the twenty-first century, housing was the most valuable

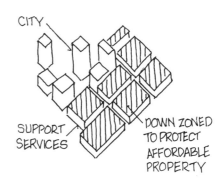

development use, and no other use could compete. Prior to that, office development was the alpha use. This led to an obvious imbalance that argued against mixed use. With the economic collapse of 2008, the necessity to think in terms of planned, balanced, and, hence, mixed-use development has become even more imperative.

2. Proximity

Mixed-use development should generally be located according to the frequency of visits to various uses. Destinations of everyday trips, such as supermarkets, should be planned closer to housing than those visited less, such as auto repair shops.

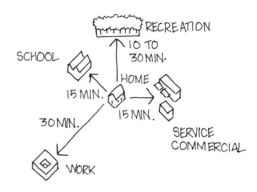

3. Critical Mass

The site size and array of uses within a mixed-use development must reflect functional, social, and economic requirements. The housing component, for example, has to be of a size and density to support walking to transit, services, and often-visited commercial uses. Similarly, the retail component should be adequate to support the population catchments of its service area. Conversely, population density has to be sufficient to support transit and retail services.

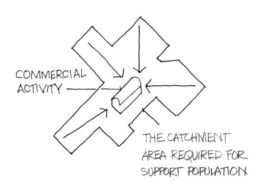

4. Type of Mix

Mixed uses can be configured vertically, such as housing over ground-level retail, or horizontally, as in separate adjacent sites. The horizontal plan might place different building uses side by side or build a new, dense residential neighborhood

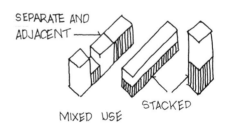

next to a commercial district. Retail shops are an exception to the practice of interspersing different uses. In retail shopping districts, it is best not to separate ground-level shops with non-retail uses.

Many tall buildings, particularly those built since the late 1990s, include combinations of uses, such as office, hotel, housing, retail, and services. High-rise mixed-use buildings offer a variety of functions without overwhelming a local market's ability to absorb a single use and, if flexibly designed, allow current and future market needs to be met.

3.1. Bringing Diversity to the Capitol

The Pennsylvania Avenue Renewal, Washington, DC

Pennsylvania Avenue site in Washington, DC

0   9.95(mile)

0   16(km)

Among the most widely noted city-building design work undertaken by SOM was the renewal of Pennsylvania Avenue in Washington, DC, from the 1960s through the 1980s. The project was successful in large measure because it applied principles of diversity in an innovative mixed-use development.

The Pennsylvania Avenue renewal program legendarily began in January 1961, the day of John F. Kennedy's inauguration. The new president was riding back to the White House and remarked about Pennsylvania Avenue's seedy appearance. What did the impoverishment of one of America's most important civic boulevards connote, Kennedy mused, and could anything be done about it? The process of rehabilitation began that year with the appointment of SOM founder Nathaniel Owings as chair of the Pennsylvania Avenue Commission. The commission's charge was to upgrade the blocks of Pennsylvania Avenue between the Capitol and the White House.

From its inception, the Pennsylvania Avenue renewal project was branded with Owings's emerging mixed-use imprimatur. This was particularly evident in the mix of uses proposed to bring 24-hour life to the area. At the time, planning as a profession was largely guided by what

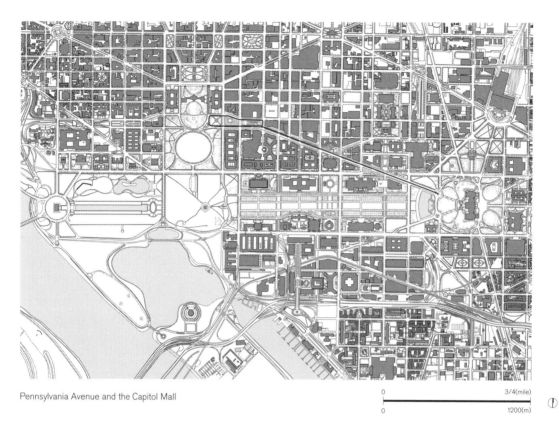

Pennsylvania Avenue and the Capitol Mall

| 0 | 3/4(mile) |
| 0 | 1200(m) |

has been called "the Magic Marker mentality," which favored segregation of land-use functions "by color," red perhaps designating a commercial district, blue an office district, and so on.

Owings's novel notion was to design layers of uses. At the time, mixed use was a hard sell to people (and to developers in particular). They didn't recognize the importance of including a housing component in large projects and designing office buildings to have retail at ground level. Owings persisted, however, and played a key role in making the Pennsylvania Avenue renewal the first major example of successful mixed-use downtown redevelopment. By helping developers understand that mixed use could be the "cement" holding a neighborhood together, Pennsylvania Avenue also became a model for using millions of government seed dollars to attract billions from the private sector.

Model of Pennsylvania Avenue from the Capitol to the White House

Looking toward the Capitol

New street life

Mixed use at ground level

Open space and landscape amenities

3.2. Designing Diversity into City Expansion

Saigon South, Ho Chi Minh City, Vietnam

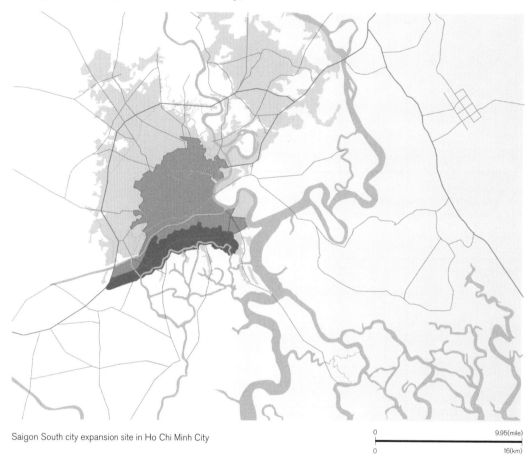

Saigon South city expansion site in Ho Chi Minh City

0	9.95(mile)
0	16(km)

Beginning in the early 1990s, Ho Chi Minh City's Saigon South development exemplified how a city could guide the nature and intensity of its own growth. In fact, growth could be directed to create a foundation of variety and choice even to those living beyond the project boundaries.

Saigon South began as a plan to expand Ho Chi Minh City (formerly Saigon), a dense older city, so that new development maximized wide-ranging infrastructure improvements and met difficult population-growth needs.

In 1993 SOM won an international competition to create a master plan for the entire east-west length of the southern edge of Ho Chi Minh City. The Saigon South project encompassed an area approximately 18 by 2 kilometers, connecting National Highway 1 to the city's Saigon River waterfront. Ho Chi Minh City's population was estimated to double from approximately

5 million when the project was conceived to 10 million by the 2020s. The project site was planned to accommodate at least 1 million of this projected growth.

The sheer size of the Saigon South Plan made it a catalyst for other major citywide improvements. On the project's long east-west axis, for example, the plan envisioned a transportation corridor that would upgrade over time from road to highway and from bus to fixed-rail transit. This new transportation corridor included multiple connections north to the existing city, providing improved access for residents of the whole city.

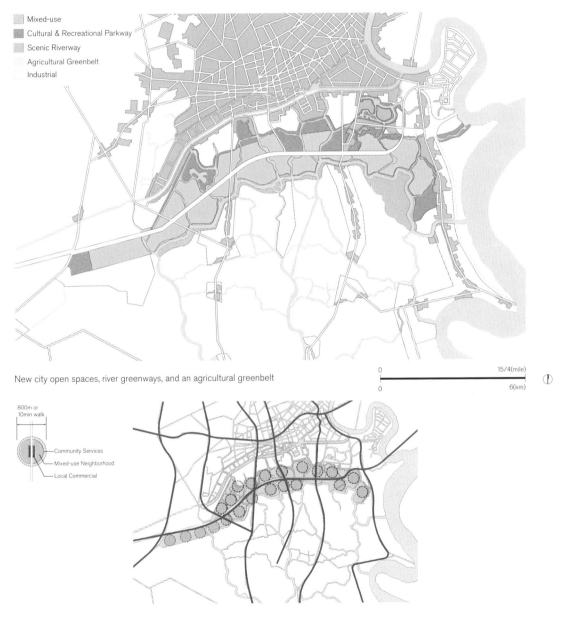

New city open spaces, river greenways, and an agricultural greenbelt

A city of islands, each island a walkable neighborhood

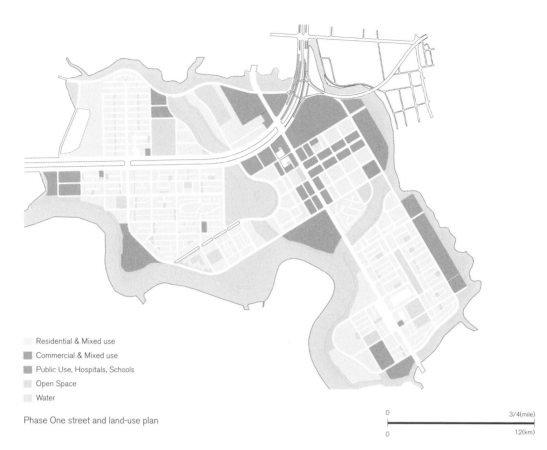

Residential & Mixed use
Commercial & Mixed use
Public Use, Hospitals, Schools
Open Space
Water

Phase One street and land-use plan

0   3/4(mile)
0   1.2(km)

The project also included a power-generating facility to provide dependable energy, which, in turn, could—and in fact did—attract major economic development. The Saigon South Plan created citywide facilities and amenities such as an international school, a hospital, a university, parks, and recreation sites. Taken together, these infrastructure improvements were planned to support high-density development that would otherwise have been set in Ho Chi Minh City's historic central district and been responsible for eroding the architectural quality of the downtown and its landscape.

A city of islands at the urban center

Fronting an expanded water channel and park, the crescent will become the social heart of Saigon South.

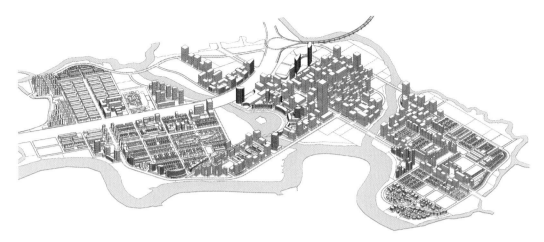

Phase One neighborhoods as built and as currently planned

The Saigon South Plan called for existing waterways to be retained for transportation, commerce, and recreation. The waterways, with minor modifications, also defined the edges of walkable land areas and formed the boundaries of the project's new neighborhoods.

Thematically, Saigon South was approached as a "city of islands," with each island constituting its own unique neighborhood. The Saigon South Plan also included approaches to encourage environmental sustainability. Retaining and celebrating the city's existing waterways, for example, and using them to define individual neighborhoods had the effect of catalyzing citywide programs to improve the water-quality and flood-control infrastructure. The plan's focus on the city's watercourses also led residents to become more aware of shoreline bird and animal habitats throughout the city and the need to maintain them.

The Saigon South Plan focused on walkable neighborhoods and included guidelines to increase diversity by preventing the repetitive "cookie-cutter" buildings that today typify most large-scale Asian residential development. Saigon South's neighborhoods were planned to express diversity in building design, density, street geometry, landscaping, and parks. In this

Diversity of building types

Diversity is achieved by a mix of building types and architects.

way, neighborhoods could express the variety and identity found in older, more "naturally" developed Ho Chi Minh City neighborhoods renowned for their livability. A key to diversity was the participation of many architectural firms creating unique designs under the aegis of the master plan guidelines. Perhaps most important, the overall plan was kept on course through periodic workshop sessions with the client, building architects, and government planners, reviewing the project's progress and planning upcoming phases.

The first phase of development

Riverfront building

Active street life

Landscaped street median

Night view of the city of islands

Park and pedestrian walks

3.3. Creating Variety within Uniform Residential Regulations
Tianjin Economic Development Area Residential Neighborhood, China

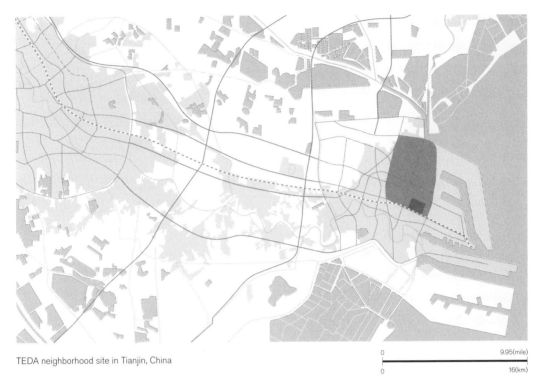

TEDA neighborhood site in Tianjin, China

0   9.95(mile)

0   16(km)

Housing and residential site-planning are highly regulated in China. Rules require, for example, that every dwelling receive a minimum of one continuous hour of sunlight each day. This has led to orienting most residential developments along repetitive east-west rows, spaced according to the building height so as to receive the required solar exposure.

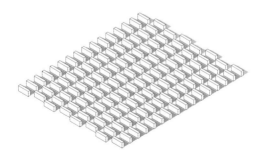

Uniform building treatment to meet the requirement for south sunlight

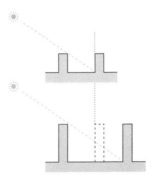

Low buildings, smaller separation; tall buildings, wider separation

Because taller buildings naturally cast shadows on lower ones, these sunlight regulations have made it difficult to vary building heights. Similarly, because each dwelling must have a south-facing room, residential buildings tend to be only one unit deep. While the reasons for these rules are admirable and humane, they lead to the design of monotonous, evenly spaced, east-west-oriented residential blocks.

With these constraints in mind, in 2004 SOM entered an international competition to design a community of residential towers for the Tianjin Economic Development Agency (TEDA), a master-planned development in the northeast coastal port city of Tianjin. The rationale was to design a project that could meet sunlight regulations while maintaining best-practice principles for sense of place, variety, and diversity.

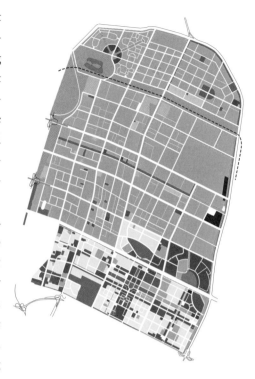

Location of a new neighborhood in the TEDA community

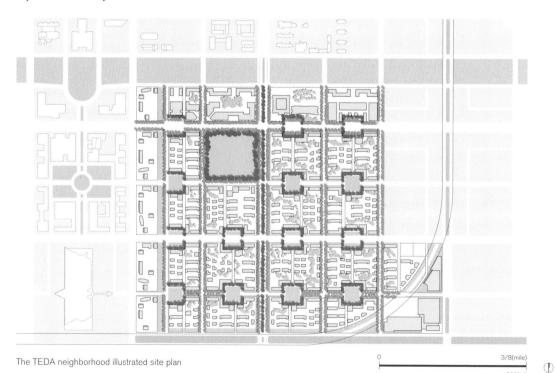

The TEDA neighborhood illustrated site plan

0   3/8(mile)

0   600(m)

In planning the TEDA Residential Towers, designers began with a street pattern fixed by a grid. A park system was superimposed on the grid and used to increase the separation between residential buildings progressively from north to south. This meant that a taller building could be built on the south side without the risk of shading lower buildings to its north.

Smaller parks and pedestrian pathways pass through the blocks to create unique landscaped enclaves for neighborhood shopping and services. The larger parks on the local traffic streets were also designed as "traffic calmers," islands of green around which traffic would be slowed. Larger parks were laid out in a regular pattern and uniquely landscaped to identify and distinguish neighborhoods.

The various building types and scales are visible along streets.

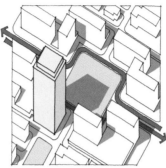

Tall buildings are located on the south side of a park so as not to shade buildings north of them.

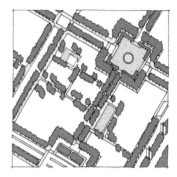

Open spaces vary in scale and are connected by landscaped pedestrian paths that pass through blocks.

The TEDA project retained the east-west orientation for sunlight, but diversity was achieved by using five or more dwelling types. Within each of the project's blocks, as well as along the outside street edges, guidelines encouraged a mix of three dwelling types to create a widely varied look and feel for every street. The edges of each neighborhood were defined by streets designed to carry the heavier traffic and take pressure off the internal streets.

Major parks

Pedestrian paths along internal streets

3.4. Identifying the Special Qualities of a Place

Knowledge and Innovation City, Shanghai, China

Shanghai's Knowledge and Innovation City site

0	9.95(mile)
0	16(km)

In 2000 SOM planners were approached to help refine plans for a city center for Shanghai's Yangpu District, an area noted as the home of seventeen institutions of higher learning, including Fudon and Tongji universities. The initial program had called for a series of high-rise buildings atop a five-story shopping mall podium that faced a ten-lane arterial with transit underneath. In this respect, the plans were similar to those of other district centers planned for Shanghai. Each was designed to serve as a shopping, commercial, and transit hub for districts with populations ranging from 1 million to 5 million.

A closer look at the initial plans suggested that such a high-density, antipedestrian approach to the development was wrong, and particularly wrong for a district centered on higher education. The major problem was that this kind of mixed-use complex simply did not support the social life and services that distinguish university life at its best.

The SOM team instead presented a new proposal that related more closely to the educational spirit of the district in terms of commerce, recreation, and lifestyle. The fresh approach softened the wide arterial street that fronted the site by adding a perpendicular University Avenue. This was a purposely narrow lane with wide sidewalks fronting small-scale commercial uses, with live/work spaces above. This was to become the social heart of the university district.

The west end of the avenue connected to Fudon University, one of China's most prestigious schools; the east end opened onto a "technology hub," a site planned to serve the entrepreneurial and research needs of faculty and graduate students. Beyond the hub, University Avenue terminated at a well-known 1930s sports arena, redesigned to incorporate recreation and health activities. The hub plus the historic arena not only served the needs of the district but also was a landmark giving Knowledge and Innovation City its unique identity.

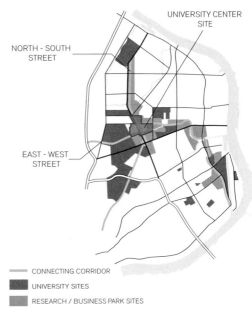

CONNECTING CORRIDOR
UNIVERSITY SITES
RESEARCH / BUSINESS PARK SITES

The district core and university locations with connecting streets

Buildings designed by five separate architectural firms help increase interest and variety, while an overall neighborhood feel is established through a series of district design guidelines. Along University Avenue, pass-throughs opening onto human-scaled courtyards are designed for small retail and open-space uses appropriate to an energetic academic setting. Importantly, the south sunlight regulation is more flexible for live/work spaces: if a unit does not receive two hours of sun a day, it is designated as work only.

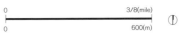

Site plan of university district hub

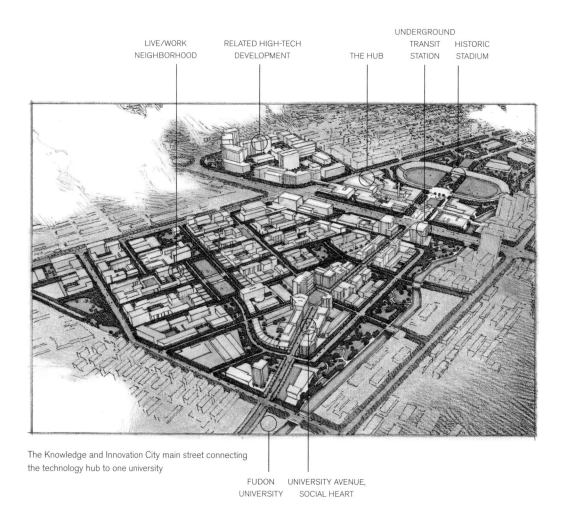

LIVE/WORK
NEIGHBORHOOD

RELATED HIGH-TECH
DEVELOPMENT

UNDERGROUND
TRANSIT
STATION

THE HUB

HISTORIC
STADIUM

The Knowledge and Innovation City main street connecting
the technology hub to one university

FUDON
UNIVERSITY

UNIVERSITY AVENUE,
SOCIAL HEART

The technology hub's plaza, leading to transit and the main street
social heart of the district

Another view of the hub plaza, leading to the restored historic
stadium

The initial vision of the main street as the social heart of the university district

The social heart as built: retail ground floor, live/work spaces above

Design diversity encouraged by guidelines and use of multiple architects

A typical live/work courtyard

Mixed-use walkable neighborhood

3.5. Building-in Diversity
Park Boulevard, Chicago, Illinois

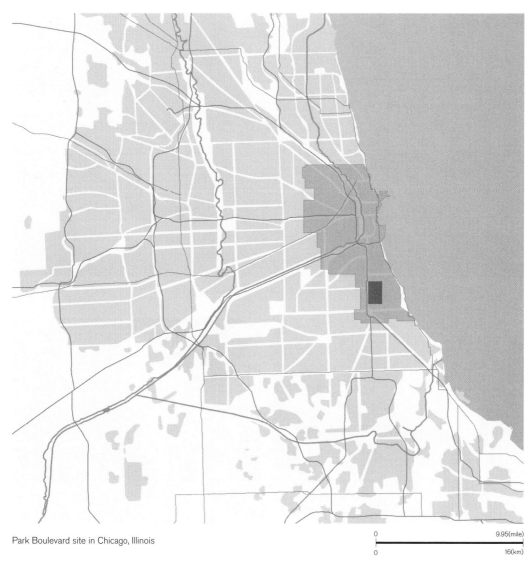

Park Boulevard site in Chicago, Illinois

0   9.95(mile)

0   16(km)

In 2004 SOM completed a master plan for Park Boulevard, the 40-acre former Stateway Gardens project. Park Boulevard was part of a comprehensive program by the Chicago Housing Authority to transform one of the city's most blighted late-1950s low-income, high-rise housing projects. In its conception, the Park Boulevard Master Plan attempted to exemplify how public and private sectors could collaborate to provide the planning, zoning, taxation, and financing needed to create a new, desirable urban neighborhood. From the start, diversity was a fundamental principle of Park Boulevard.

Located within an easy walk of a number of Chicago rail and bus transit systems, the new Park Boulevard was planned not as minority public housing but as a desirable new neighborhood that included a range of housing sizes, prices, and building types among its 1,300-plus units. These include single-family homes, townhouses, duplexes, three- and six-flat buildings, and mid-rise towers with units for sale and for rent.

Recognizing that lack of diversity has been one of the major shortcomings of large-scale, low-income housing projects, the SOM team ensured that Park Boulevard would have a variety of housing types by involving different developers who, in turn, hired different architectural firms.

Best-practice planning called for Park Boulevard to be built in discrete phases and designed so that each stage would provide the feel, sense of place, commercial and public spaces, and recreational amenities of the finished whole. A critical aspect of the plan was to reintegrate the site's roads back into Chicago's city street grid. This, in turn, increased the chances of creating a truly desirable, mixed-use, uniquely designed neighborhood on a site that had previously been a walled-off, architecturally monotonous no-man's-land of dangerous and dysfunctional housing projects.

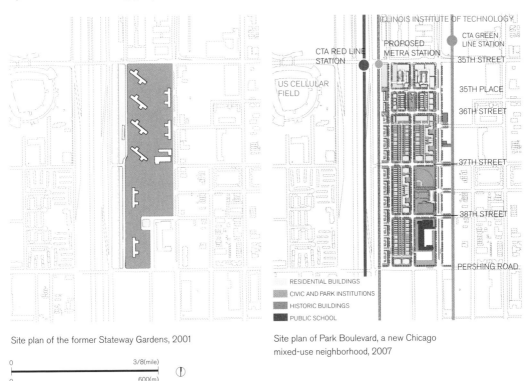

Site plan of the former Stateway Gardens, 2001

Site plan of Park Boulevard, a new Chicago mixed-use neighborhood, 2007

RESIDENTIAL BUILDINGS
CIVIC AND PARK INSTITUTIONS
HISTORIC BUILDINGS
PUBLIC SCHOOL

The Park Boulevard master plan

Architect collaboration at Park Boulevard: nine Chicago design
firms were involved in redesigning the master plan.

JOHNSON & LEE LTD

FITZGERALD ARCHITECTURE

BROOK ARCHITECTURE

BROOK ARCHITECTURE WITH FITZGERALD
ARCHITECTURE

WORN-JEREBEK ARCHITECTS

URBAN WORKS, LTD

LANDON BONE BAKER

KATHRYNE QUNN ARCHITECTS

MIMI MCKAY LANDSCAPE ARCHITECTS

Using multiple design teams per block for diverse architecture

Reintroduce the street grid

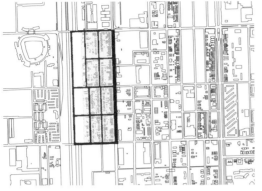

Small block mixed-use pattern

1949

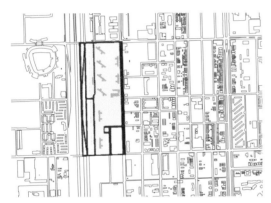

2001

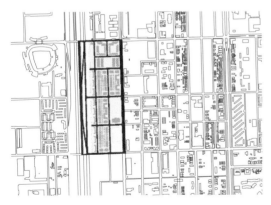

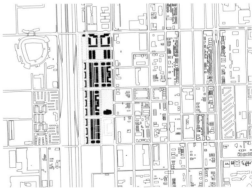

2005–2010

Principle Four: Open Space

Regenerating Natural Systems to Make Cities Green

The Problem: Loss of natural habitat, inadequate recreational space, an overbearing presence of buildings and hard surfaces.

Open space in an urban setting may be the single most defining design element in city building and far more important to livability than is generally understood. The type and character of open space vary by climate and culture, but good city building demands that some natural quality always soften the urban harshness and relieve the confinement of the built environment. In the 1900s the City Beautiful movement declared that the greening of American cities was essential to the mental health and physical well-being of urban dwellers. It still is, and today cities around the world are defined by and celebrated for their great civic open spaces: Washington, DC, has the National Mall; Mexico City, Chapultepec Park; San Francisco, Golden Gate Park; Chicago, the Lakeshore; Paris, the Champs Elysées; New York, Central Park; and so on. What all have in common is an open space that is the natural center of the city's civic life.

The principle of creating and regenerating urban open space is divided into three major areas: habitat and natural systems, recreation, and the presence of nature.

Habitat and Natural Systems

Large regional open spaces are found at the edges of cities or within natural systems that run through cities. These areas typically play environmental roles, providing habitat and migration corridors for wildlife. They may also be drainage corridors, lakes, rivers, and agricultural lands. Beyond offering visual relief, large habitat spaces are best suited for passive recreation and educational uses. Three design elements promote the environmental role of these spaces.

1. Migration Corridors

The locations and sizes of habitat open spaces should reflect species' migratory patterns, food supplies, and protection needs to avoid becoming endangered. Migration corridors exist at many scales, and human jurisdictional boundaries have to be ignored in planning them. In most parts of the world, corridors must be managed at a regional or national scale.

2. Watersheds

Rivers, floodplains, and drainage corridors need to be respected and maintained. Where they have already been altered by undergrounding or channelization, watercourses need to be restored and dedicated to open space and, if possible, to natural riparian drainage corridors. Urban run-off needs to be treated before returning to the natural watershed system. Water can be treated by the bio-filtration of vegetation along drainage corridors and within retention ponds.

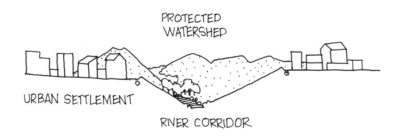

3. Isolation Requirements

Natural habitat locations often need to be removed from human contacts other than those for education and research. Wildlife, particularly birds, and off-leash dogs are incompatible. Birds, exhausted from migratory travel and needing rest and food, are forced to keep moving to avoid the dogs' natural enthusiasm. Less-sensitive open space may be used for walking pets, hiking, horseback riding, and bicycling.

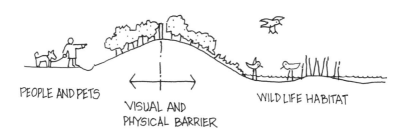

PEOPLE AND PETS

VISUAL AND PHYSICAL BARRIER

WILDLIFE HABITAT

Recreation and Urban Landscape

Good city design requires plans for open-space resources close to the city that are sizable enough to support the leisure requirements of a metropolitan population. Landscaped streets play an important role in connecting a city's open spaces. Good city building suggests that at least 1.5 acres per thousand population be set aside for larger "green" uses, if possible, located no more than 40 minutes from people's homes by transit or automobile. For a city the size of San Francisco, this would amount to approximately ten times the size of Golden Gate Park.

Parks within city boundaries are another important open space. They are typically human-made spaces planned for close-to-home recreation. City design principles suggest that approximately 2.5 acres per thousand people be set aside and located no more than 15 minutes from home by foot. Local neighborhood parks should be at most a 3- to 5-minute walk from home.

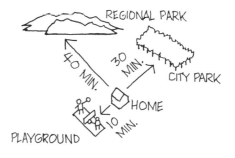

REGIONAL PARK

CITY PARK

40 MIN.

30 MIN.

HOME

10 MIN.

PLAYGROUND

Virtually all city landscape has been created by human intervention. Most forests have been cut down and regrown. Indeed, all of our best-known parks were planned and built on empty or already occupied land. City landscapes are for the most part human-made even when they appear to be natural and pristine.

Three design elements are considered in city landscaping: human activities, environmental purposes, and size requirements.

1. Human Activities

Part of a recreation space is typically set aside for specific sports and physical exercise. It is also possible and desirable to provide flexible play space that can accommodate a variety of

activities, in our increasingly multicultural societies. Space must be reserved for less-active pursuits as well, including walking, contemplation, picnics, and environmental education.

2. Environmental Purposes

City landscapes perform a number of beneficial environmental functions. Dense urban forests cool the air, minimize ozone, and consume carbon dioxide. Other landscape elements provide habitat and can filter polluted water runoff. Regenerated urban landscape can also be used to mediate toxic sites and brownfields.

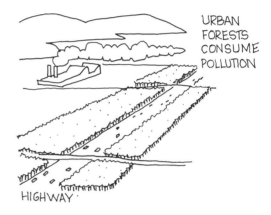

3. Size Requirements

Recreation spaces vary in size depending on use, population served, climate, and geography. I know of no scientifically established standards suitable for all cities. The values I stated earlier are based on observations of open space in successful and livable cities. But sizes and purposes of open space vary greatly according to a city's environment and culture. For example, at the heart of the ancient Iranian desert city of Isfahan is a 1,500-by-450-foot central plaza, or "Maydan." This space is defined by 30- to 40-foot-high walls. Its size and proportions can be understood only by knowing its purpose: as a cool, comfortable place to walk and meet in the evenings, far enough away from the walls that reradiate the intense heat from the daytime sun.

The Presence of Nature

Nature can be established as a presence in an urban setting in a number of ways. In Hong Kong, Shanghai, San Francisco, Chicago, and New York, views from the dense city across a body of water have an effect equivalent to views of open space. In the early 1990s a group of high-level Vietnamese planners and architects visited North America to study high-density downtowns. When comparing a street with a continuous frontage of tall buildings to streets that mix tall and low buildings, they recognized that even the "passive" natural presence of blue sky between widely spaced towers could provide a sense of nature and would be useful to incorporate into their indigenous designs for Ho Chi Minh City and Hanoi. Three design methods, conservation, views, and connection to views, are used to maintain the presence of nature.

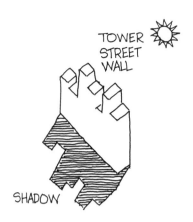

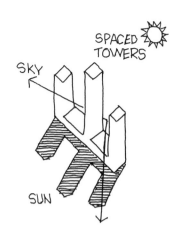

1. Conservation

Natural and human-made landscape features should be protected and preserved to provide both relief from city density and a unique identity and physical character for the city. These features include hills, water, native vegetation, parks, sunlight, and sky. A purposeful and correct reading of the landscape guided the 1989 master plan for the University of California, San Diego. The plan redirected growth away from the large, central eucalyptus grove that was generally regarded, before the plan was made, as little more than a land bank for future campus construction. The grove, however, was an important source of environmental benefit as well as a unifying identity for the campus. The master plan defined it as a central park to be conserved and maintained as the campus's most important open space.

2. Views

Views to and from natural features must be conserved to showcase a city's uniqueness. To maintain views, planners generally have to define guidelines for building height, spacing, and setbacks. It is possible that San Francisco, Hong Kong, and other hillside cities have relied on their spectacular views to "get away with" providing less neighborhood open space than high-density flatland cities. Hong Kong, framed between its harbor and its steep mountains, has shown little interest in or apparent need for public parks, even as its population continues to burgeon.

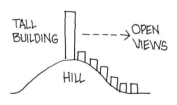

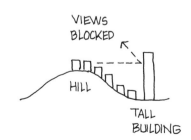

In the service of urban open space, it is imperative that city government take the lead. If not, decision making about the city's open space generally devolves to private interests, which, history indicates, will choose growth and building, often purposely misreading the landscape to serve developmental interests. This was certainly true in the case of the Los Angeles River, which, over the last century, has been "concretized" to minimize seasonal flooding and create more acreage for development. Today, the river stands as a monument to missed urban opportunities, lack of foresight, and thwarted creativity. Only time will tell if Southern California will recognize the opportunity to create a great civic landmark and to reclaim the billions of gallons of water yearly flushed through the Los Angeles River to the sea in a water-starved region. Plans suggest that winter floods could be captured in retention ponds and lakes to replenish the water table and irrigate the landscape.

3. Connections to Views

As we have shown, most of the world's major cities have been built on the edges of oceans, lakes, and rivers. To continue to grow, cities frequently filled marshes and other natural waterfront habitats. These practices are being discouraged in today's climate of environmental awareness. Still, filled wetlands frequently become a city's most valuable real estate because of water views and related shore amenities and thus contribute to a city's identity and livability.

The unintended irony of waterfront development is that reclaimed lands are the very ones that are most vulnerable to the kind of flooding predicted to result from global warming and concomitant mega-storm surges. To deal with the results of twenty-first-century climate change, it is imperative to develop environmentally sound approaches to waterfront redevelopment. Plans have to anticipate and provide a way to survive environmental change without walling off shoreline views and limiting water access by building new levees and dikes.

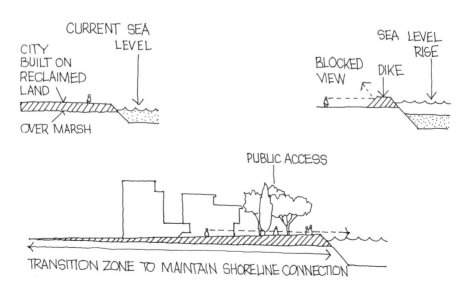

4.1. Greening the World's Densest City
Hong Kong Central Waterfront, China

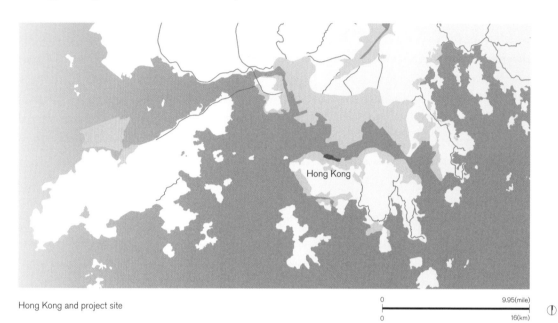

Hong Kong and project site

0   9.95(mile)

0   16(km)

In 1993 the government of Hong Kong proposed expanding the city's business center in conjunction with the rail link being completed to the city's then-under-construction Chek Lap Kok International Airport. The project was planned for a 60-acre landfill to be reclaimed where Hong Kong's Central District abuts the harbor.

There was considerable opposition to the proposal. Environmentalists worried that reclamation of the city's most recognizable landmark, the body of water for which the city is named (in Cantonese, Hong Kong means "fragrant harbor"), would be seriously diminished by a 1,000-foot landfill and new construction. Business interests were equally concerned that proposed high-rises in the project would destroy views and reduce real estate values in the Central District.

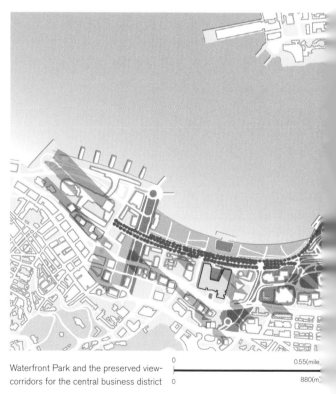

Waterfront Park and the preserved view-corridors for the central business district

0   0.55(mile)

0   880(m)

The original city plan with extended bay fill and new towers

The SOM proposal with the waterfront preserved and public open space

The project charge was to develop a counterplan designed to stop the government's massive harbor landfill that had been proposed to accommodate the original development program. In place of the landfill, the counterplan called for creating a waterfront park with a new, transit-based government complex on the park's city edge. Both park and government centers were designed to enhance Hong Kong's civic identity, which had been, until then, an afterthought in the world's most commerce-minded city.

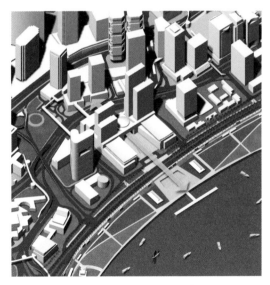

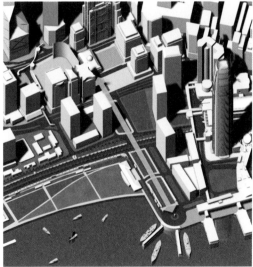

Part of a new city hall complex illustrates how view and movement corridors link all of the central district to the waterfront.

The historic corridor connecting Hong Kong's central district to the Star Ferry

The new plan also included view-corridors that reached back into the existing business district and maintained its visual contact with the water. The corridors themselves became sites for new low-rise cultural buildings, neglected elements in Hong Kong's development history. The new plan met the original goals for urban density by redistributing the massive housing and office component along the major transportation stops already being created by the new transit line to the airport.

The counterplan ultimately won out over the original conception, creating a new, powerful civic identity and a Civic Center capable of becoming Hong Kong's landmark social and cultural heart.

Open space and paths lined with cultural buildings on the corridor to the Star Ferry

The new open space provides a gathering place as well as welcome relief from Hong Kong's extreme density.

4.2. Unpaving a River
Los Angeles River Program, California

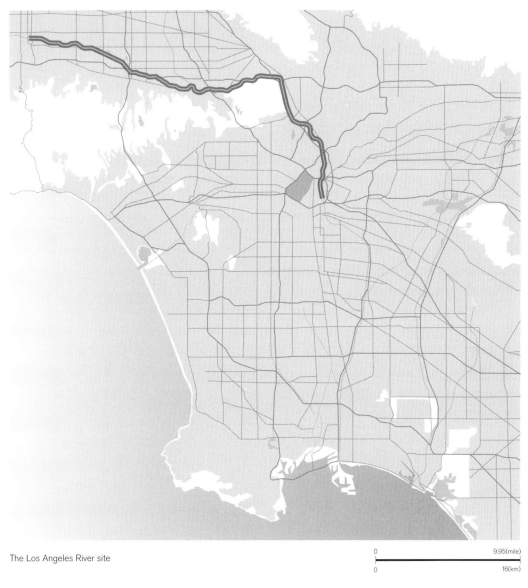

The Los Angeles River site

0	9.95(mile)
0	16(km)

Consider those "once-in-a-century" urban waterside projects that have defined the character and fabric of so many of the world's great cities. Daniel Burnham's 1909 Plan of Chicago has, over the last century, transformed Chicago's Lakeshore into one of America's most architecturally beloved, recreationally varied, and artistically rich downtowns.

More recently, Tempe's Town Lake Development, Chattanooga's Riverfront District, San Antonio's Riverwalk, Hartford's Adrien's Landing, Shanghai's Huang Pu River Redevelopment,

Ho Chi Minh City's Saigon South development, and similar plans have transformed decaying waterfronts into a multitude of lively and civically healing uses. These include reconnecting fractured street grids and isolated neighborhoods.

For the sheer possibilities of renewing dead-ended neighborhoods, opening fenced-off Mars-scapes, and providing environmental, cultural, and recreational benefits, virtually no project in the world matches the potential of an ecology-minded and people-centric revitalization of the Los Angeles River. These possibilities were explored in a 2005 request for proposals to transform 31 miles of the river into what would be a multipurpose linear greenway running virtually the entire length of the city. The project, with its combination of advanced engineering and imaginative planning, had the potential to be a grand civic unifier and create immense civic worth.

There was unfinished irony in the fact that the 1896 gift of 3,000 acres of land to Los Angeles by G. J. Griffith included not only what is today's Griffith Park but also 5 miles of riverside acreage intended for a grand riverfront park. Most of what should have been that promenade is today's Pasadena/Golden State Freeway Exchange.

Much of the Los Angeles River and its tributaries now are nature-taming concrete storm drains—sites that over the years have become iconic symbols of a human-made wasteland. Some stretches are truly little more than repositories for discarded auto tires or backdrops for TV cop-show car chases.

Because of groups such as Friends of the L.A. River, the California Native Plant Society, the Arroyo Seco Bikeway Project, and UnpaveLA, environmentally sound plans for the Los Angeles River are beginning to flow. Together, the creative proposals of these groups, educational programs, and pilot cleanup and replanting efforts have begun to work toward a comprehensive, long-term program for Los Angeles on the scale and scope of Burnham's Chicago Plan.

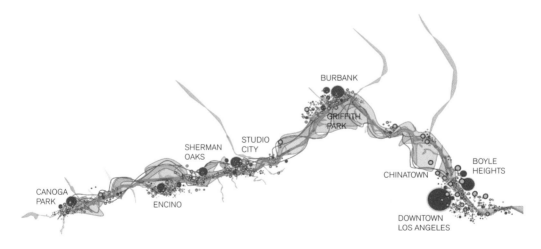

Site plan for Los Angeles River from Canoga Park to Downtown Los Angeles

The overall Los Angeles River Program is clearly a complex undertaking. Like the Chicago Plan, it would take most of a century to complete. Eventually it would include "re-greening" dozens of miles of riverbank with native trees, grasses, and shrubs, as well as building new kinds of user-friendly riverbanks. The thousands of restored acres of green would not only benefit citizens but also assist the city in slowing down global climate change.

Alongside the river, or perhaps, as some plans have suggested, elevated above it, jogging, biking, and roller skating paths would connect the entire length of the project. This could enable bicyclists to travel between Pasadena and downtown Los Angeles at speeds comparable to today's auto commute. Interspersed along this green thoroughfare would be mixed-use developments, schools, museums, art installations, and cultural centers—critical elements to strengthen the connection between the river and the communities that now coexist so uneasily alongside it. The river would be spanned at a number of locations, reuniting neighborhoods that were separated when the water was channelized, by providing easy pedestrian and bike access.

Some places on the Los Angeles River could serve as early "proving grounds" for how a sensitive treatment might be achieved. In Burbank, for example, Disney has built its Imagineering headquarters virtually up to the riverside fencing. Imagine if Disney were encouraged to integrate a campus into the newly planted and landscaped banks of a restored section of the river. Even in the river's most industrial stretches, beautiful structures, such as the Beaux Arts 4th Street and Macy Street bridges, could become beckoning gateways to revitalized riverfront communities.

Conceptual Approach

   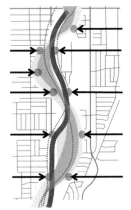

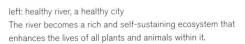

left: healthy river, a healthy city
The river becomes a rich and self-sustaining ecosystem that enhances the lives of all plants and animals within it.

right: A green/blue corridor
The river becomes a continuous mix of activities both urban and pastoral

left: A 32-mile Central Park
Braided ribbons of green and blue create a landmark urban public park that interweaves with the river.

right: A balanced landscape
A new kind of urban river carefully balances greenscape and hardscape in the river park.

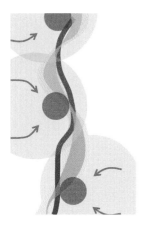 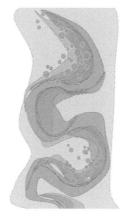 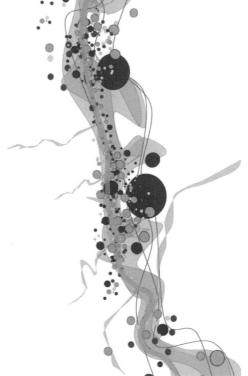

left: Bridges
Bridges are built to connect neighborhoods. Formerly an unknown resource, the river becomes the civic heart of the city.

center: Culture and history
Nature and culture are brought together along the river's corridor with curated cultural spaces. The river becomes a place to learn about the city's social, natural, and cultural histories.

right: A living legacy
The concept of 1,000 neighborhood centers over 1,000 years is a challenge to develop. It aims to communicate the long view, a plan for the future with principles to guide design over time.

A green/blue/gray freeway on which water and people can flow: Before and after

A balanced landscape, using greenery and hardscape to create a new kind of urban river: Before and after

4.3. Topping Off the Burnham Plan with a Green Roof

The Millennium Park Master Plan, Chicago, Illinois

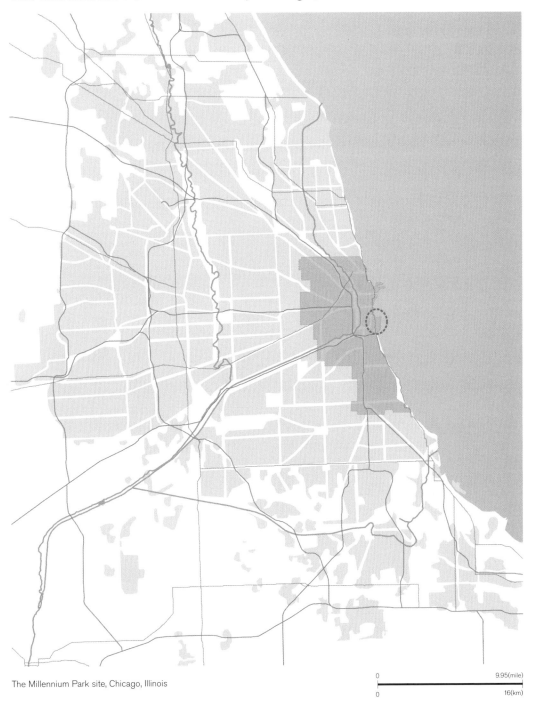

The Millennium Park site, Chicago, Illinois

0   9.95(mile)

0   16(km)

During the mid-1990s a shortage of parking at the Soldier Field football stadium led SOM planners to contemplate an abandoned railroad yard and parking lot along Michigan Avenue, north of the Chicago Art Institute. For decades the site had been an ugly gash separating Michigan Avenue from Grant Park and Lake Michigan.

Conversations about that space led to discussions about a project for the upcoming millennium celebration to transform this site into the final piece of Daniel Burnham's 1909 plan for Grant Park. At the time SOM was pioneering a number of projects exploiting air rights to create "found space," most prominently in London's massive Broadgate development. In Chicago, found space was the key to designing an elegant park to complete Grant Park's north edge.

Designers and structural engineers drew up plans for the site to create what would be the world's largest "green roof," overarching an underground parking garage and transit corridor with a stepped 16.5-acre park that would be a natural bridge between Michigan Avenue and Grant Park. Included in the plan was a plaza for a band shell and outdoor music performance

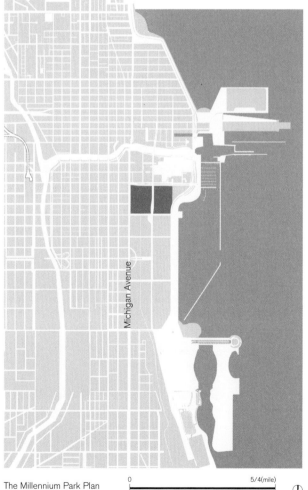

The Millennium Park Plan

Millennium Park, organized into separate donor projects

spaces, indoor performing arts facilities, and an ice-skating rink that could double as an outdoor dining area in warm weather.

From the start, the City of Chicago and the design team recognized that art would be a major component of Millennium Park. The City and arts community reached an agreement that the various sculptural elements should be designed to add to the artistic impact of Millennium Park in the way the famous Picasso sculpture has enlivened the City's Daley Plaza.

The sculptural imperative of the Millennium Park site was fulfilled by commissions for Anish Kapoor's "Cloud Gate," Jaume Plensa's "Crown Fountain," and, most prominently, Frank Gehry's band shell and pedestrian bridge connecting the park with the lake front. In its execution, the band shell is both structure and sculpture, its boldness mediated by the park's west-to-east, "past-to-future" landscaping. The result is an open space that quickly became one of the world's celebrated nature and arts settings and a crown jewel of the Chicago Lakeshore.

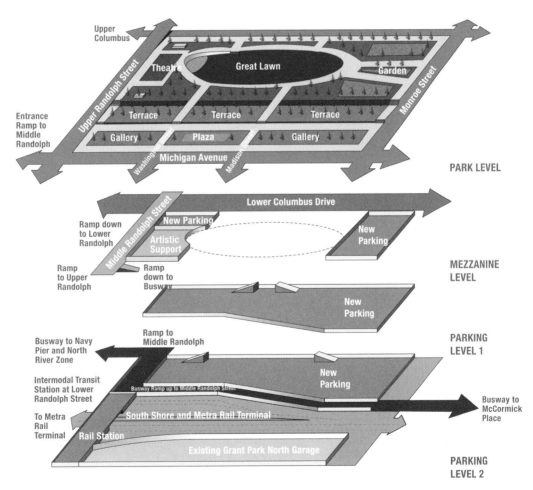

Cross section showing underground uses

The site with parking and rail lines before project

Completed Millennium Park

Great Lawn

Great Lawn and Pritzker Pavilion

Cloud Gate (sculpture)

The site overlaid with the Millennium Park Plan

The Crown Fountain

The Lurie Garden

McCormick Tribune Plaza and the Ice Rink

Wrigley Square

4.4. Developing a Public Greenbelt and Shoreline

Greenbelt Alliance/Bay Conservation and Development Commission Programs, San Francisco Bay Area, California

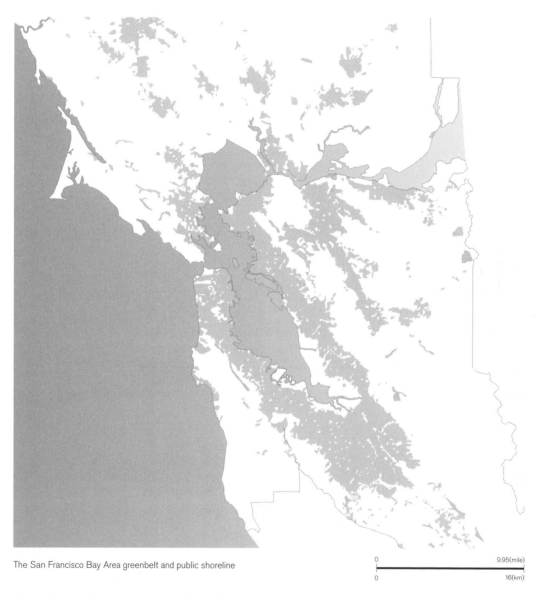

The San Francisco Bay Area greenbelt and public shoreline

| 0 | 9.95(mile) |
| 0 | 16(km) |

Beginning in the 1960s, principles and practices of sustainability articulated by the California Tomorrow Plan and the Federal Service Systems for National Land Use gradually were implemented through a number of major efforts to preserve open space. Two organizations crucial to carrying out this work were the state-mandated Bay Conservation and Development Commission (BCDC), founded in 1965, which focused on preserving San Francisco Bay, and the Greenbelt Alliance, founded in 1987, a California-based citizens' organization, dedicated to furthering the open space of the San Francisco Bay region.

Over the last two decades, the BCDC has been responsible for increasing public access to the bay from only 4 miles of shoreline to nearly 200 of the total 400 miles today. BCDC continues to base its work on the incremental review of shoreline building permits, guaranteeing that public access is maintained and the least possible amount of bay fill is used. Ultimately, BCDC has proved an effective advocate for the bay without using excessive regulation or eminent domain.

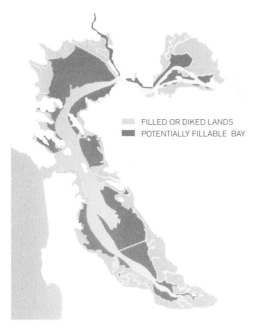

FILLED OR DIKED LANDS
POTENTIALLY FILLABLE BAY

Unprotected San Francisco Bay shoreline and potential fill areas, circa 1960

2008 San Francisco Bay and protected public shoreline access

Shoreline wetlands preserved

Public shoreline access with views to San Francisco Bay and the Oakland skyline

COMMUTE STRUCTURE OF
SUSTAINABLE METROPOLIS

EMPLOYMENT
CENTERS

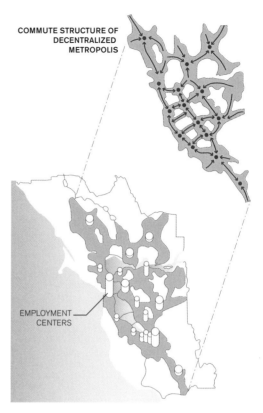

COMMUTE STRUCTURE OF
DECENTRALIZED
METROPOLIS

EMPLOYMENT
CENTERS

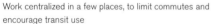

Work centralized in a few places, to limit commutes and
encourage transit use

Work located in multiple decentralized centers, which encourages
sprawl

Similarly, the Greenbelt Alliance has successfully implemented some twenty urban
growth boundaries around cities in five Bay Area counties. Urban growth boundaries are
designed to focus public and private investment priorities and ensure that pressures to spread
outward from an urban core are strongly redirected to existing "brownfields" or to compact
settlements along urban fringes. The encouraged patterns of growth are generally defined in
terms of transit-friendliness and a minimum net density of between 8 and 12 units per acre.
Boundaries need to be matched with a strategy for ensuring efficient, timely, and environmentally sound development. Under the greenbelt concept, incompatible uses, such as sprawling
residential and commercial strip developments, are largely prohibited.

The first modern greenbelt was created around London during World War II to protect
agricultural lands that became critical because of the German submarine blockade of Britain.
In the United States the first urban growth boundaries were officially adopted in 1973 by
Oregon. The state focused on an officially mapped line dividing developable land around
Portland from "greenbelt" areas to be protected for open-space and agriculture.

Fundamentally, growth boundaries are long-term regulatory tools, designed to stay in place for 20 years or more. To provide greater certainty for both developers and conservationists, the boundaries are rarely subject to revision and can be made permanent. In the Portland region, for example, they are responsible for protecting thousands of acres of pristine land from development while enabling the construction of over 300,000 new homes within the "green line." Boundaries have now also been implemented in Washington State, other regions of Oregon, Florida, Kentucky, Colorado, and Minnesota, as well as in Denmark and Canada.

In the United States, greenbelts can be created and maintained in a number of different ways. For example, open land outside cities can be donated or sold by landowners for conservation. Owners may similarly make a binding agreement that limits new uses or prevents development even though the land remains in private hands. Called "conservation easements," these agreements aim to protect values such as water quality and quantity, wildlife habitat, migration corridors, and prime agricultural land. In conservation easements, a landowner gives up development rights (often in exchange for a tax break), and a public or private conservation entity agrees to enforce the promise not to develop the land in perpetuity—that is, the agreement is binding on the owner who made it and on all subsequent owners of the land.

Today, the San Francisco Bay region greenbelt is one of the largest and most productive open-space systems in all the metropolitan regions of the United States. Over 1 million acres of greenbelt lands are permanently protected from development, a substantial increase since 2000. The acquisitions have been made by a combination of land trusts, state parks, and conservation easements.

Greenbelt land (green) at risk from new development (red), existing development (gray), low-risk areas (yellow)

Principle Five: Compatibility

Maintaining Harmony and Balance

The Problem: City neighborhoods and built elements that are out of place, discordant, and confusing.

City design is practiced on a variety of related scales with different purposes in mind. The largest scale, as seen in the Federal Service Systems for National Land Use, Bahrain, and other projects, can encompass an entire nation. Smaller scales descend to the region, city, neighborhood, and district. At the finest scale, design addresses the street, the block, and individual buildings as well as the critical "spaces in between," which is the title of the 1973 book by SOM founder Nathaniel Owings.

When considering a project at the smaller scales, an important design policy question becomes whether the context—that is, the sense of the whole—dominates the specific project or whether the project should stand out from the context as a landmark. If the decision is made to create a landmark, the next step must be to determine how that landmark should reference its context or background.

In the SOM planning practice, design compatibility has never meant replication. Rather, the quest for compatible design seeks to establish a range of visual tolerances that do not disrupt the character of a particular place. In deciding whether buildings are to stand out or fit in, the principle suggests that elements of similarity are just as important in establishing a recognizable, identifiable sense of place as elements of singularity. Thus the principle of compatibility is divided into three elements: relationship to context, building scale, and building character.

Relationship to Context

It is fairly simple to recognize when plans for district or city development are inappropriate: they are out of place, discordant, confusing, too big, too small, or simply "wrong" for the character of that place. Truly livable places tend to be appropriate in relation to the size and shape of the surrounding environment. Defining the character of a project is a critical factor in finding the appropriate in city design. To succeed requires, first, understanding the underlying nature of a project and then establishing the requisite physical qualities for its context. Two focal points are essential: design process and contextual character.

1. Design Process

At every scale of development, urban design must be studied and reviewed to determine the proper fit within its context. This process elucidates the issues of compatibility and provides insights into possible solutions. Many times city builders find that a community cannot focus on a solution for a civic land-use problem. When a downtown is in decline, for example, each political campaign season will bring with it new project ideas to counter that decline: a ballpark, a new city hall, beautification of a main street, and so on. In these cases, a change of context may be a way out of deadlock. Planners might, for example, restate the problem at a larger citywide scale, such as restoring a public shoreline, where benefits can be perceived by all public stakeholders.

In a public review process, illustrating the relationship of the part planners are considering to the larger whole often elevates the importance of that part and can provide new insights into how to approach the larger context. The ability to understand and communicate the broader context can be a critical missing element in the process of city design.

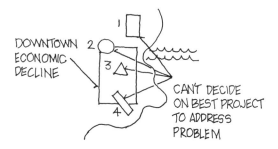

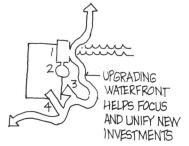

2. Contextual Character

Context is defined by a site's character, both present and historic; its current land use, infrastructure, natural systems, geology, and topography; and the buildings and landscape that surround it. Context should also take into account ongoing plans and public policies that will affect future building on the site.

To maintain livability, cities must manage development in ways that avoid overstressing existing infrastructure and community services. Similarly, city or neighborhood development must be managed to avoid the loss of precious assets such as views, historically important buildings and neighborhoods, accessibility, and unique landscapes, all of which can define context and civic identity.

While it is important to respect the context of a project, it is equally critical to keep an open mind about what the future can or should be. Cities need to be able to reinvent themselves. They thus need the ability to define alternative futures, even radically different futures, without necessarily being disrespectful of the past. A strict adherence to context might have meant, for example, that the John Hancock Tower in downtown Chicago, which at the time of its conception dwarfed all its neighbors, was out of scale and should simply not have been built.

To today's design mind, that is inconceivable: the Hancock Tower has become an irreplaceable symbol of Chicago. In recent years, many other cities have reinvented themselves through a design break with the past. Bilbao, Spain, with the Guggenheim Museum, and London with Canary Wharf and its new city skyline are examples.

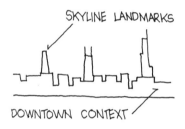

Building Scale

To define a project's character requires designers to identify both the type and the location of possible uses. Understanding the character and context of a project helps planners and architects decide if it is more important for buildings to blend compatibly together or stand out from one another in landmark fashion. In modern cities, a building's scale is the most important component of compatibility. Three design elements are helpful in deciding: parcel size, building size, and building bulk.

1. Parcel Size

Planning parcels of similar size create a common footprint for individual buildings and contribute greatly to establishing an overall building scale.

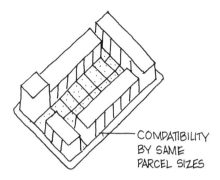

COMPATIBILITY BY SAME PARCEL SIZES

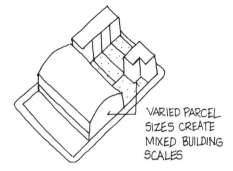

VARIED PARCEL SIZES CREATE MIXED BUILDING SCALES

2. Building Size

Regulating the building height, setback, and floor area for multiple buildings creates a strong sense of compatibility. However, minor height and setback variations are often desirable to make individual buildings more identifiable and a skyline more varied and interesting. In some circumstances, such as Chicago's Hancock Tower, exceeding the prevailing height by a large amount may be possible, even desirable, and still will not spoil the harmony of the overall neighborhood scale. Building elevation is a highly subjective decision, but, as a rule, it may exceed prevailing heights by one-half to two times, depending on the specific site. Beyond this ratio, a tall building can become freakish and out of place unless it is grouped with other tall buildings. London's Canary Wharf shows how a city can reinvent its skyline while respecting traditional view-corridors.

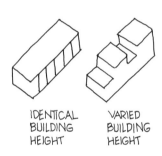

IDENTICAL BUILDING HEIGHT

VARIED BUILDING HEIGHT

3. Building Bulk

A new building that is too bulky can overpower and destroy the scale of the buildings around it. Bulk guidelines are especially necessary when the scale of existing buildings is fine grained. One way to measure a building's bulk is by drawing a diagonal line across the plan to compare it to the bulk of others and make sure that it is in scale with its neighbors.

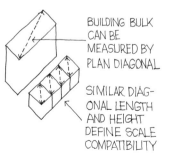

BUILDING BULK CAN BE MEASURED BY PLAN DIAGONAL

SIMILAR DIAGONAL LENGTH AND HEIGHT DEFINE SCALE COMPATIBILITY

Building Character

Beyond a concern for context and scale, the great architectural conundrum is the temporal style of a design. Should it be traditional and reflect the design around it? Should it break new ground? My view is that the character of a building should be both respectful of its surroundings and "of its time." In this way, history is made a visible part of the city's built environment. A building's "persona" is a subject defined by four design elements: architectural character, building color, building materials, and historic preservation.

1. Architectural Character

The character of buildings can be unified by guidelines for architectural features, including roof, window, and entry treatments. Of course, the most uncompromising distinguisher of character is the specific design style: Spanish Colonial, French Provincial, English Tudor, American Federal, and the like. Taken to an extreme, a specific style may create a false, stage-set effect. The desire to copy historic building styles continues to dominate much of suburban development in North America and has even invaded developments in China and Japan.

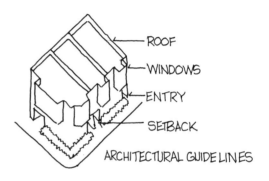

ROOF
WINDOWS
ENTRY
SETBACK
ARCHITECTURAL GUIDELINES

2. Building Color

Guidelines for the color of buildings generally refer to "color value." Light-colored buildings reflect shadow and sunlight; their surface character will change throughout the day. Dark buildings appear flat in sunlight and present powerful silhouettes against the sky. In heavily forested areas, dark buildings are more hidden and less intrusive. Either a light or a dark choice can make multiple buildings feel compatible.

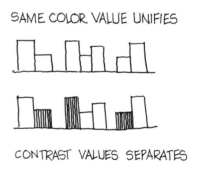

SAME COLOR VALUE UNIFIES

CONTRAST VALUES SEPARATES

San Francisco, for example, is known as a painted city because earthquake-resistant wood construction predominates in residential buildings. Each building is painted different colors, but they are made compatible by their common pastel range. The subtle color variations, together with the play of shadow on light-colored surfaces, contribute greatly to the city's unique identity and glowing presence.

3. Building Materials

Guidelines for specific building materials are often used for corporate or academic campus settings to create a more defined identity. Examples include Harvard University's use of red brick, UCLA's yellow brick, and Stanford University's red tile roofs.

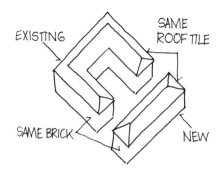

At the University of California, Merced, a new campus planned for the hot climate of the San Joaquin Valley, the first three academic buildings were designed by different architectural firms but were unified by the use of arcades and horizontal glass louvers to shade the building surfaces and walkways. The louvers provided a collective architectural "language" for the different buildings and supported the climate and sustainability goals of the campus plan as a whole.

4. Historic Preservation

To maintain the overall sense of a district's historic character, guidelines must require new construction to comply with regulations for historic district preservation and harmonize with important cultural assets. Harmony does not demand replication of historic style. A new building should both reflect its own time and be respectful of its older neighbor.

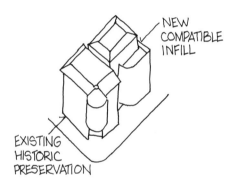

5.1. Protecting Heritage While Creating Identity

Taipinggiao, Shanghai, China

Taipinggiao site in Shanghai, China

0			9.95(mile)
0			16(km)

It is understatement to say that Shanghai experienced unprecedented growth between 1990 and 2005. The city's official population expanded from 14 million to nearly 20 million. This growth is manifested in more than two thousand new buildings over thirty stories high, extensive underground transit, highway systems, bridges, airports, museums, and other urban infrastructure improvements. Today, there are more high-rises in Shanghai than along the entire Pacific Coast of North America.

Most of Shanghai's high-rise development has taken place on sites a single building deep along a small number of famous streets supported by underground transit. The problem is that these strip development corridors stretch for many kilometers and discourage pedestrian use, the key objective of transit-served, high-density urban districts.

The city's development pattern is attracted by the identity of famous streets.

A new source of identity is needed for walkable, transit-served neighborhoods. This was the challenge for Taipinggiao.

In 1995 SOM was given the opportunity to redevelop a 160-hectare site in Shanghai's historic French Concession, one of the largest proposed developments within the city's central district. The challenge was to counter the urban sprawl by designing a mixed-use neighborhood that would have a recognizable character and identity comparable to Shanghai's linear, street-fronting developments. The team had to find a way to create a harmonious sense of place capable of attracting investor interest—an exciting, richly detailed, walkable, and commercially viable neighborhood.

The entire Taipinggiao site was covered by early-twentieth-century French Concession housing. These two- and three-story brick buildings fronted narrow, sycamore-lined streets crisscrossed by narrow interior pedestrian alleyways of architectural interest. By the mid-1990s people were living in Taipinggiao at very high densities, without sewage and individual water utilities. Within the site were two buildings that had played roles in the history of China's Communist Party. Aside from these, however, little interest was shown in retaining neighborhood buildings. At the time, in fact, rehabilitation of historically significant buildings in China was considered financially unfeasible. The value of redeveloped property was defined only by the highest total floor area of new buildings.

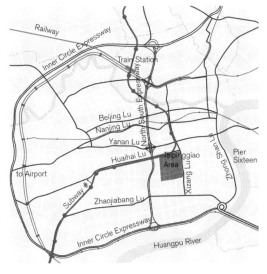

Taipinggiao is Shanghai's French Concession area.

Plan for Taipinggiao as new walkable neighborhood

The SOM development concept for Taipinggiao moved contrary to conventional wisdom by proposing to retain two blocks of the Concession buildings. The idea was to create a compatible context for the historic buildings by developing small plazas and narrow pathways for shopping, restaurants, entertainment, and living.

The Taipinggiao model, a valley of historic preservation, a lake, and a park surrounded by tall buildings

Concept drawing of the adaptable reuse of historic residential buildings

Concept drawing of the centrally located lake and park

A high-image central destination was enhanced by creating a landscaped park and lake. These two elements formed a kind of "central valley" of water features, parks, and historic buildings to be framed by future high-rises for office, hotel, housing, and entertainment uses. The Taipinggiao approach worked beyond expectation: by 2003 the historic shopping village called Xintiandi had become one of Shanghai's most famous destinations.

The restorational approach to the site illustrated two lessons. First, historic preservation is feasible when buildings are repurposed to more highly valued retail and entertainment uses. Second, when combined with a lake, park, and other natural features, this approach increases value for the high-density hotel, office, and residential sites surrounding them.

Ultimately, the sensation caused by Xintiandi spurred new interest in historic preservation in Shanghai—and throughout China, for that matter. Even the lake at Xintiandi, initially resisted by Shanghai government planners, became so iconic that more than a half-dozen similar water features have since been planned for the city. Taipinggiao has had a positive impact on Chinese development practices, because it successfully illustrated a direct connection between property value and the identity established by a compatibly scaled central core.

Night view of sidewalk cafés

The lake and park as built

Narrow walks that open to a courtyard

Historic buildings preserved with open space, to help create a unique neighborhood identity that adds value to the surrounding high-density redevelopment projects

5.2. Protecting Heritage While Managing Density

Foshan, China

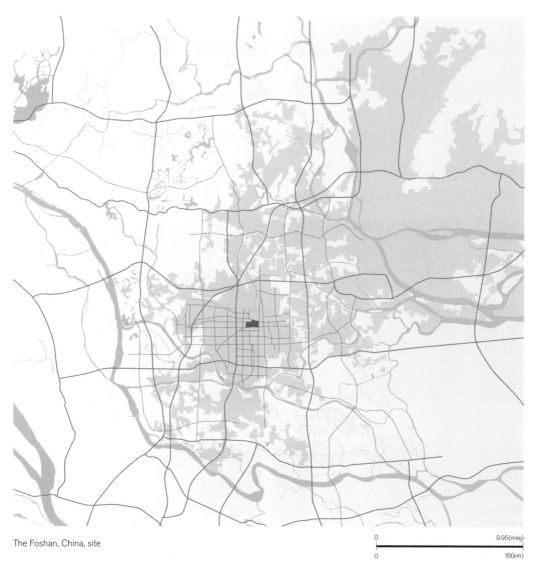

The Foshan, China, site

| 0 | | 9.95(mile) |
| 0 | | 16(km) |

Foshan is a city of 3 million people southwest of Guangzhou. The oldest part of the city centers on a 900-year-old ancestral temple and historic old town. Foshan is one of central China's renowned religious and cultural centers. In 2007 SOM was invited to plan the preservation and enhancement of the celebrated central district while enabling the city to develop a modern, transit-rich downtown.

With the success of Shanghai's Xintiandi District, Chinese planners began to focus on the value of their built heritage and to look for ways to integrate old and new. For Foshan, SOM was asked to preserve and upgrade the old town into a Xintiandi-style residential, retail, and entertainment district, as well as design a transition zone of live-work and residential spaces surrounding the old town, which would form a "central valley." From there, structures would gradually rise in height to an outer ring of higher-density tall buildings—the "hills" surrounding the inner "valley."

The new "hill" developments would be dense enough to support services and transit as well as provide funds to preserve and restore the old town blocks. The valley-to-hillside plan that SOM created offers sunlight and views for the tall, high-density developments as well as for old town Foshan. Height limits were included to preserve the historic temple's roof profile silhouetted against the sky.

The Foshan area plan

| 0 | 3/8(mile) |
| 0 | 600(m) |

The pattern of walks and historic buildings is preserved.

Building heights step up from the low existing buildings to the tall new buildings.

The Foshan valley-to-hill renewal may suggest a healthier approach to the high-rise building sprawl now encountered in many Chinese cities. "Valleys" of lower-height buildings can allow a new kind of diversity for high-density cities and define unique neighborhood identities of compatibly scaled districts that accommodate both tall and low buildings.

The view of the temple roof profile against the sky is protected by height limits for tall buildings behind them.

Low buildings make a valley that retains the historic fabric and promotes views and sunshine for tall buildings located along transportation corridors.

5.3. Retaining a Rural Landscape
Opérations d'Intérêt National, Paris

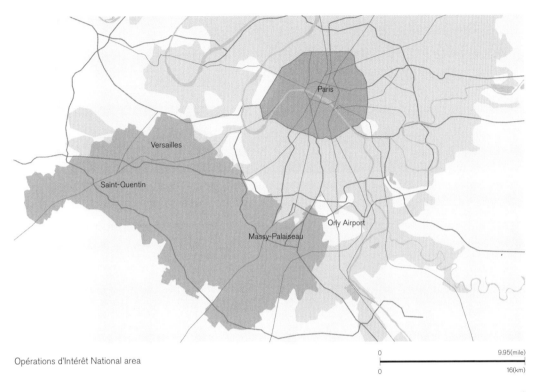

Opérations d'Intérêt National area

0		9.95(mile)
0		16(km)

In 2006 the French government invited SOM to participate in a competition to create a regional plan for the southwest corner of the Île-de-France region, the districts surrounding Paris. The "grande idée" of Opérations d'Intérêt National (OIN) was to stitch the region together into a renowned, public-private research hub in the mode of Sophia Antipolis, a successful development outside Nice. The Île-de-France was already the home of the National Institute of Nuclear Energy, Renault, and other public and private technology and R&D institutions and corporations. The competition was to find ways to capitalize on the proximity to the Palais de Versailles, with its world-renowned landscaped lakes and watercourses, and the area's strikingly rich agricultural valleys and plateaus.

OIN's goal was to create, by 2030, a high-technology district with sixty thousand new dwellings and the infrastructure, commercial, and service base required to support the development. The key was to develop a plan for the region to fulfill its technology future without violating its rich natural and historic character.

At the first take, the most obvious program for OIN would have been to design a series of new, themed towns located at the crowns of the region's defining plateaus, with a superhighway running through the district's agricultural heart. Instead, in the service of physical and visual compatibility, the SOM plan called for densification of existing townships in the region to allow them to absorb new homes while maintaining distinct boundary edges between urban and rural zones.

Rather than create a single Science City, the plan also called for distributing the technology infrastructure to the area's existing townships. This would have the effect of raising the density and improving the design quality of the villages while both preserving the regional character and allowing the valleys and plateaus to remain agricultural and undeveloped.

Instead of running a new highway through the region, the plan relied on greater population density to support a new central transit corridor. In total, the plan called for developing an area that was highly livable, with a new infrastructure that was appropriate and sustainable in relation to the size, shape, and original purpose of its surroundings.

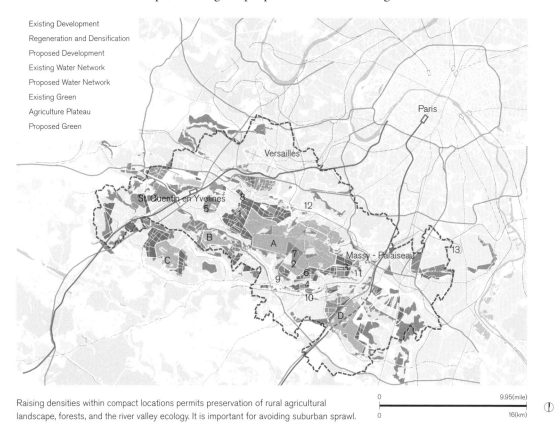

Raising densities within compact locations permits preservation of rural agricultural landscape, forests, and the river valley ecology. It is important for avoiding suburban sprawl.

Agricultural Plateaus	Significant Regional Institutions	7. CEA (Atomic Energy Commission)
A. Plateau de Saclay	1. Renault Techipole	8. ENSIA (National Institute of Food and Agroindustries)
B. Plateau de Magny	2. Centre d'Etudes Nucleaires	9. CNRS (National Center for Scientific Research)
C. Plateau de Cheveuse	3. Ecole Polytechnique	10. IHES (Institute of Advanced Scientific Studies)
D. Plateau de Limours	4. Université Paris Sud	11. ONERA (French Aeronautics and Space Research Agency)
	5. Université Versailles-Saint-Quentin-en-Yvelines	12. INRA (Institute for Agricultural and Food Research)
	6. INSTN (National Institute for Nuclear Science and Technology)	13. Aéroport de Paris Orly

5.4. Reviving Block Patterns and Building Types
Elephant & Castle District, London

Central London

The Elephant & Castle site in London

0   9.95(mile)
0   16(km)

Heavily bombed during World War II, indifferently developed into a shopping center and housing estates in the 1950s, and dominated by a traffic hub of bridges, roads, and transit lines in the 1960s, London's Elephant & Castle area had declined considerably from its celebrated status as "the Piccadilly of South London." In 2004, with the winds of gentrification blowing through the area, the Southwark Borough Council invited SOM to develop a master plan for a £1.5-billion regeneration of the area around the Elephant & Castle Underground station.

The initial program called for a new, mixed-use development consisting of high-rises, a pedestrian-friendly commercial center, housing for seven thousand, and transit stations and interchanges below ground. Original plans also envisioned a large, central park coupled with low-density housing. SOM planners, however, felt that playing off the district's historic character made better sense. They thus created a plan with a more urban feel derived from denser central high-rises, commercial areas, and civic spaces that stepped down to courtyard housing, so that the new residences could enjoy increased sunlight.

Instead of the formal central park, SOM planners chose an irregular street geometry that relied on a looser, more free-flowing urban grain to achieve a harmonious balance with the character of the surrounding district. This played off Elephant & Castle's location at the terminus of the Bakerloo Underground line and its status as the hub of bridges, roads, the Underground, and bus lines spanning the Thames, which met in the district center.

The SOM program took these converging routes as the natural outline for a series of ribbon parks that followed the flow of movement in the neighborhood. The plan ultimately produced a series of sequential streetscapes designed to pull people into and through a revitalized Elephant & Castle neighborhood.

New block geometry is skewed to match its context.

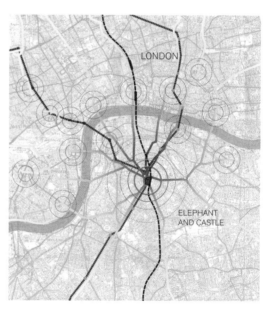

Transit-oriented new development in an older neighborhood

Street geometry studies

The Soho district street pattern

The City (financial district) street pattern

The Elephant & Castle street pattern

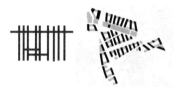

A dense rigid grid

An open irregular grid

A distorted grid, the concept adopted in the master plan

Courtyard buildings make a transition between the new higher density and the existing scale.

Principle Six: Incentives

Renewing Declining Cities/Rebuilding Brownfields

The Problem: Cities in economic decline, with infrastructure and buildings underused.

It is in the nature of cities to be in constant flux. Sometimes that fluidity is based on growth and development. In other periods, such as the late 2000s, that flux results from economic decline. In such a downturn, a wide range of creative incentives are available to help reverse, or at least mitigate, the trend.

A city or region in decline typically has underused land, infrastructure, and buildings. When recognized, these often become targets for governmental or private redevelopment seeking to attract new interest and investment. The goal is to identify more economically viable or socially desirable uses. A general rule is to think first about preserving existing buildings and adapting them to new uses. This enables designers to use them as historical templates for sensitive and relevant development. In many redevelopment projects, refurbished structures can be the intellectual bridge crossing the gulf between the architectural past and a rational design future.

In most cases public incentives are used to stimulate new development investment that can help achieve the goals of renewal. Of the many incentives, the most common are

1. tax reductions
2. subsidies for land costs
3. site assembly and preparation
4. new infrastructure for transportation and utilities
5. health care, education, and public safety services
6. open space and landscape beautification
7. additional density allowances

Incentives such as these are useful in attracting redevelopment inside cities. They can also be used to attract new development outside cities in environmentally appropriate locations. Such projects help combat sprawl by providing alternatives that are both competitive and sustainable.

In cities experiencing economic decline and population loss, incentives supporting new employment growth are a useful and important option. For example, Waukegan, Illinois, developed a comprehensive program to revitalize its downtown, which had lost over 40,000 jobs in recent decades. While it might at first seem overambitious and expensive to rebuild a city's economic base, doing so can avoid the even greater financial investment required to build a new urban infrastructure in a region on the rise elsewhere. Incentives can also be a major source of environmental enhancement in city renewal. Remember that livable cities are in themselves an attraction for talented people. These are the men and women who create exactly the kind of upward spiral of hope and expectation that can transform a good city into a great one.

If the legal status of a property seems to be an obstacle, this should not be taken for granted but be explored to seek a solution. It may turn out that properties can be bundled or an outmoded ownership situation changed. In the redevelopment of the former Montgomery Ward department store headquarters on Chicago's North Side in the late 1990s, for example, the city actually sent a team of real estate experts to the Netherlands to untangle an ancient trust and enable a long-vacant property to become a key part of the redevelopment.

To facilitate this kind and degree of change, master planning and infrastructure improvements are the primary elements that, together, define our approach to incentives.

Master Planning

A master plan provides a coordinated approach for attracting positive new investments to a city. In a situation of limited resources, a community needs to focus its capital and human energy on ideas that provide the highest possible return on investment. Master plans that are created as incentives for new development must have the unified support of a community's leadership, particularly when public money is involved. If there is no agreed-on focus, attention will drift to other promotional ideas and make moving forward difficult, if not impossible. Three design elements are crucial to giving a master plan an effective focus: development quality, beautification, and value enhancement.

1. Development Quality

An approved master plan with design guide-lines for circulation, open space, and phased building construction gives assurance to potential investors. With a master plan, the quality of development can be managed and maintained even when multiple developers participate. There is also less chance that an individual project within the master plan area will undercut overall value by incompatible uses such as blocking daylight or obscuring views with buildings and landscaping.

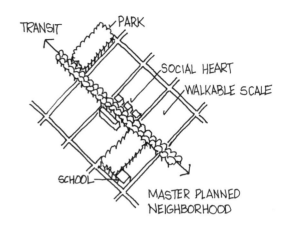

2. Beautification

Landscape beautification of the public realm, including streets, parks, and waterfronts, is a primary method for attracting development investments. Beautification elements include landscape, lighting, street furniture, commercial signage, and way-finding devices. If intelligently programmed, a relatively small proportion of overall construction costs put into beautification can have an outsized effect in enhancing the identity, value, and desirability of a project.

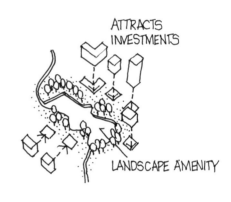

3. Value Enhancement

Assembling land into larger parcels and enabling additional density can add value to a property. This increased value is an attraction to investment in new development. Value enhancement does not threaten historic buildings if unused development rights can be traded for other development opportunities. The owner of the historic building gets paid for not using the right to develop it, and that right can then be applied to another property, usually in the same area.

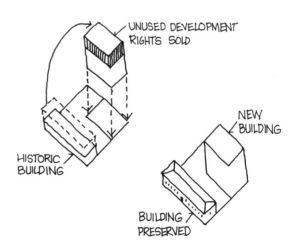

Infrastructure Improvements

Two types of infrastructure development can provide an incentive to additional private investment: access improvements and public facility development. Both add value and can be part of a community's economic development incentive package. Both are especially useful in helping reverse a city's decline.

1. Access Improvements

Transit and street redesign, new bicycle paths, pedestrian walkways, parking, and other access improvements can add value to a project property as well as to the larger community. Chicago's State Street, as described earlier in this book, was the focus of a 1992 redevelopment and enhancement program investing in new street furniture and lighting, as well as the conversion of a transit-only street back to general traffic use. The result, particularly the refinement of transportation uses, led to a dramatic upward spiral of State Street's value and a renaissance of retail, office, educational, and residential uses.

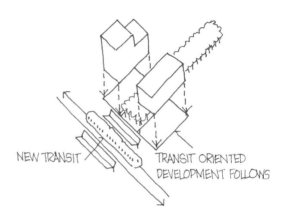

2. Public Facilities

New public buildings, such as airports, seaports, convention centers, ballparks, arenas, museums, performance halls, government offices, and cultural and educational facilities, create new jobs and bring in visitors. All can help improve a city's economy and desirability. Investment in public facilities also conveys a community's positive commitment to and faith in its future transformation. A new convention center, for example, attracts new hotels, whose guests attract new restaurants and entertainment venues and sometimes new cultural facilities. These amenities cannot be successful everywhere, but where they do succeed they bring new people to a city and begin that upward spiral of investment, hope, and confidence that is the diametric opposite of the "broken window syndrome."

6.1. Restoring a River (and Regenerating a City)

San Antonio River Corridor, Texas

The river corridor site in San Antonio

0	9.95(mile)
0	16(km)

Throughout the 1960s the inner city of San Antonio was a downtown on the way down. The city's economy was largely based on military spending from major army and air force installations. City officials, however, felt that it was important to diversify into other economic areas, such as tourism. An early first step was staging the San Antonio HemisFair in 1968, which enhanced tourism and focused attention on the historic San Antonio River. Prior to the HemisFair, the River Walk was considered isolated and so dangerous that it was off-limits to military personnel after dark.

At the time, things looked as unpromising for the San Antonio River as they did for the downtown itself. The U.S. Army Corps of Engineers had proposed flood-control construction that would channelize the river and destroy its natural, landscaped character. The prospects of a "river in a box" troubled local leaders, who rightfully viewed the San Antonio River as one of the city's key identifying features.

By the 1970s, a civic consensus had formed around preserving the river's natural charac-ter, enhancing water quality, improving public access and safety, and improving flood control. A subsequent study determined that these steps could transform the San Antonio River into a destination capable of attracting new commerce, housing, and tourism as well as the invest-ments to make those improvements possible. The phasing of river improvements over many years made the project economically feasible.

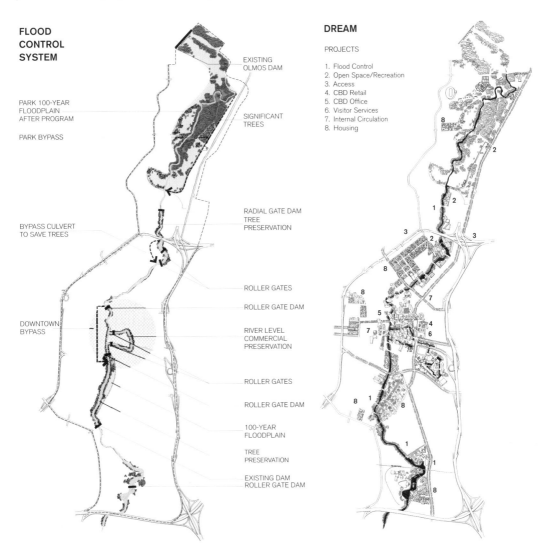

FLOOD CONTROL SYSTEM

EXISTING OLMOS DAM

PARK 100-YEAR FLOODPLAIN AFTER PROGRAM

PARK BYPASS

SIGNIFICANT TREES

RADIAL GATE DAM TREE PRESERVATION

BYPASS CULVERT TO SAVE TREES

ROLLER GATES

ROLLER GATE DAM

DOWNTOWN BYPASS

RIVER LEVEL COMMERCIAL PRESERVATION

ROLLER GATES

ROLLER GATE DAM

100-YEAR FLOODPLAIN

TREE PRESERVATION

EXISTING DAM ROLLER GATE DAM

DREAM

PROJECTS

1. Flood Control
2. Open Space/Recreation
3. Access
4. CBD Retail
5. CBD Office
6. Visitor Services
7. Internal Circulation
8. Housing

The San Antonio River Flood-Control System, designed to retain the landscape's character

A flood-protected and beautified river is planned to attract reinvestment to San Antonio's inner city.

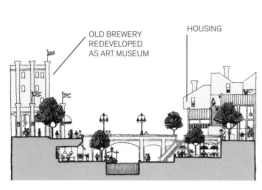

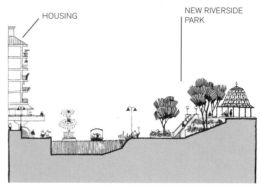

Section: Ninth to Thirteenth
River-level retail protected from flooding by a bypass channel

Section: Convent to Ninth
The river level widened and allowed to flood within its channel

The community rallied around river preservation and supported the new River Corridor Committee appointed to oversee the redevelopment. The committee was a model of public-private cooperation, with representatives from a remarkable range of private and public agencies and organizations.

The San Antonio River Plan challenged the belief that flood control was inimical to maintaining the natural character of a water feature. Equally to the point, it showed how a community could coalesce to create the incentives needed to conserve and beautify the river. The plan went beyond the Corps of Engineers' mandate and used beautification as an incentive to bring people, life, and investment back into a once-blighted area.

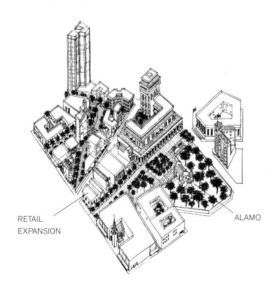

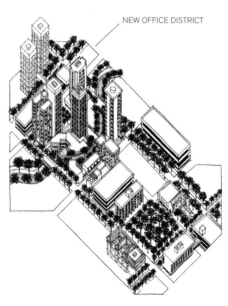

Reestablishing the downtown retail district with the river, the Alamo historic buildings, and an existing department store

Reestablishing the downtown office district with the river amenity and parking

The resulting amenity has attracted hundreds of new business, retail, entertainment, residential, and office uses in addition to its civic and cultural facilities, including museums and a new library. Today, the San Antonio River and its River Walk are widely recognized as the defining city landmarks and the heart of the city's cultural and civic life.

River Walk has a varied waterside landscape.

A tour boat serves hotels, restaurants, and the convention center.

A neighborhood park along River Walk

Each River Walk bridge is designed to look different from the others, which creates variety and a sense of place.

The historic flour mill, a preservation feature of River Walk

Rehabilitated work and living spaces along River Walk

A landscape area along River Walk that is allowed to flood without damage to buildings.

New office and residential buildings along the river

A new hotel and restaurant overlooking the river

San Antonio's new government and cultural facilities

A roller dam designed to hold the river's water at the proper level and to open during flooding

River Walk includes sidewalk cafes, small retail shops, and entertainment.

6.2. Rebuilding Downtowns in a Suburban Context: Good Intentions Get Snagged

San Jose, California, Master Plan

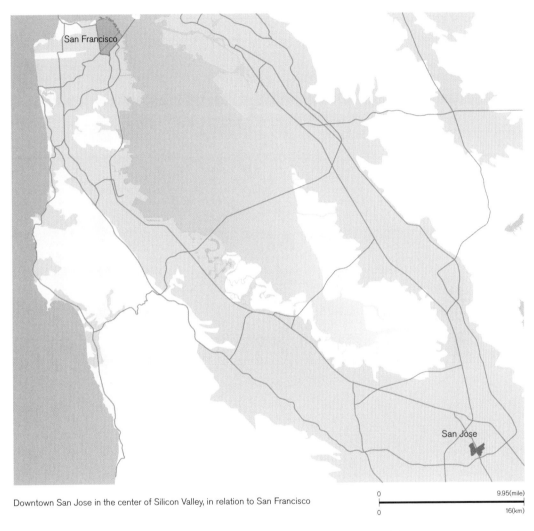

Downtown San Jose in the center of Silicon Valley, in relation to San Francisco

0   9.95(mile)

0   16(km)

In 1980 downtown San Jose sat depressed and blighted in the heart of the West Coast technology region that was fast becoming one of the world's celebrated economic engines. Various redevelopment plans had been proposed for a city that was about to surpass San Francisco as the most populous in Northern California. A few of the plans had been tried, but very little had been achieved. Large parts of the central area of downtown had, in fact, been cleared of existing buildings and then left to become vast parking lots.

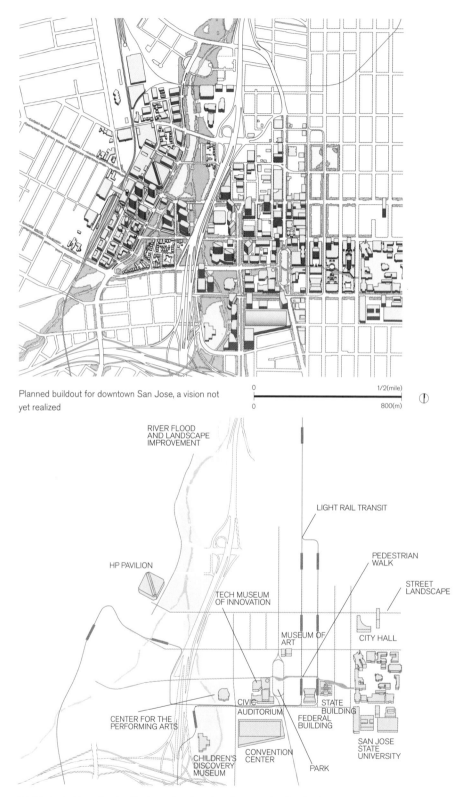

Planned buildout for downtown San Jose, a vision not yet realized

0	1/2(mile)
0	800(m)

RIVER FLOOD
AND LANDSCAPE
IMPROVEMENT

LIGHT RAIL TRANSIT

PEDESTRIAN
WALK

HP PAVILION

STREET
LANDSCAPE

TECH MUSEUM
OF INNOVATION

MUSEUM OF
ART

CITY HALL

CIVIC
AUDITORIUM

STATE
BUILDING

CENTER FOR THE
PERFORMING ARTS

FEDERAL
BUILDING

SAN JOSE
STATE
UNIVERSITY

CHILDREN'S
DISCOVERY
MUSEUM

CONVENTION
CENTER

PARK

Publicly funded incentives to attract new downtown investments and realize the vision

In 1983 a new San Jose mayor, Tom McEnery, proposed taking property taxes from increasingly successful Silicon Valley businesses and focusing that money downtown. He assembled a strong development team and endowed it with unprecedented political and financial clout. The team developed a plan for a classically compact, walkable downtown that balanced open space, residential development, retail, entertainment, cultural, civic, office, and other uses.

The Downtown San Jose Plan came together in phases, creating a dense, landscaped downtown center that mixed apartments and business towers with hotels, museums, a sports arena, the civic center, and a light-rail transit system. As the '80s progressed, San Jose's redevelopment garnered international publicity and was held up as a model for incentivizing downtown renewal.

Today, however, after nearly three decades of effort, intense public interest, and close-to-miraculous regional development, San Jose still struggles to find willing investors and companies eager to relocate downtown.

Why, with such intense cultivation, did San Jose's downtown fail to blossom?

The first answer is that San Jose has serious geographic challenges. While the plan strove for height and density, the nearby international airport limited building heights to twenty-five stories. Similarly chilling, a high water table limited the depth for excavating below ground level. The latter put a severe limit on underground parking, while the former demanded that buildings spread out instead of up.

The result was that nearly as much above-ground space had to be devoted to parking as to office space. Lacking the height, high-rise profile, and parking amenities to establish itself as a regional downtown in the minds of developers and potential tenants, San Jose was at a competitive disadvantage to the area's low-rise towns and commercial centers.

The city also found it hard to bring retail and entertainment uses into downtown. At first glance, this was difficult to understand, particularly because the working, residential, and student population was growing downtown. But urban "village" shopping was abundant in nearby cities and towns, and a plethora of shopping centers was already located within greater San Jose. These low-density, high-parking shopping streets and malls provided stiff competition to downtown San Jose with its higher costs and less-convenient parking.

Ultimately the difficulty in attracting and holding retail reduced the downtown's livability and the sense of community of its new population. With streets empty after dark, residents of award-winning housing developments were nevertheless made to feel like urban "pioneers," even after decades of investment and development. Today, after a banquet of incentives, a beautiful San Jose downtown remains a work in progress.

New art museum expansion and plaza

6.3. Incentivizing a Brownfield
The South Works Steel Plant/Lakeside Master Plan, Chicago, Illinois

Lakeside development site in Chicago

0   9.95(mile)

0   16(km)

The focus of a 1996 program called "From Steeltown to Hometown," the South Works development exemplifies Chicago's ability to muster the incentives to create a redevelopment program for a neglected "brownfield" site that had been the world's largest steel plant. The Lakeside Master Plan describes the creation of a sustainable new neighborhood destined to become one of twenty-first-century Chicago's most important rebirths and a catalyst for revitalizing the city's southeastern quadrant.

The former USX South Works Lakeside property was a shuttered 570-acre former U.S. Steel manufacturing plant and fabrication facility. It had lain fallow since its 1983 closure. Master plans developed by SOM and Sasaki called for transforming it into a new high-density, mixed-use South Side Chicago community of thirty thousand residents. While the value of of the site was never in question— it was universally considered the last piece in Chicago's lake-front development puzzle—the future of the slag- and rubble-strewn site had for more than a decade been the subject of debate and disagreement over how to incentivize development. The 1996 plan was a compromise that called for a mixed-use community with 5,500 homes, a school, a 500,000 square-foot retail/commercial/light industrial component, an entertainment complex, a marina, and a 75-acre waterfront park.

The plan proposed that Lakeside be built as a pedestrian-first, transit-friendly neighborhood, a prospect aided by the proximity of four Chicago METRA transit stations along the property's west side. To counter the argument that any development on the site would necessarily be a separate, gated neighborhood, the plan was explicit in integrating the new neighborhood into the adjacent South Side Chicago grid through incentives such as landscaped boulevards, bike paths, and a continuous lakefront park.

A new mixed-use community to replace a vacated steel plant on Lake Michigan

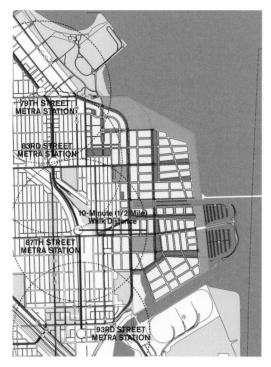

Create a transit-based community (METRA, bus, shuttle, bike paths).

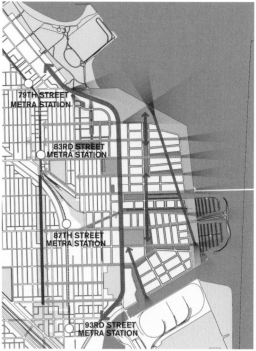

Connect the existing South Side community to the new public waterfront.

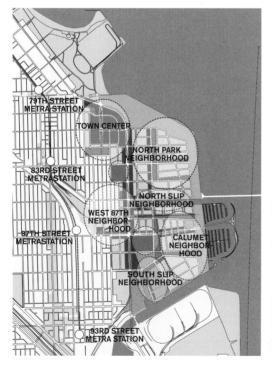

Emphasize a mixed land-use strategy with distinct, walkable neighborhoods.

Develop parks within a 3-minute walk of all neighborhoods.

The Lakeside Master Plan, a new community on Chicago's South Shore

The Lakeside park: A shoreline promenade and benches

Waterfront housing, wide sidewalks, and boat docks

Mixed-use commercial centers: Retail and office spaces

Restaurants and department stores

Nine Principles for Twenty-First-Century City Building   **167**

Principle Seven: Adaptability

Facilitating "Wholeness" and Positive Change

The Problem: Inflexibility to change a project's size or activity, rigidity, inability to compromise in terms of design.

Twenty-first-century city builders need to acknowledge that the final outcome of an urban design project can never be predicted with absolute precision. The time frame for these projects is generally long, and degrees of change inevitable, sometimes even before, but virtually always after, the project's official completion.

A roadway, for example, built to handle projected traffic levels, may in time be widened to accommodate even more traffic, or be converted into a pedestrian walkway or into a regional transit corridor. Because of the changing strength of the real estate market, a hypothetical planned commercial district might shift to serve a greater demand for residential uses; a housing project might be retooled as a research campus.

The principle of adaptability illustrates an important distinction between city building and pure architectural design. In designing projects, costly mistakes are often made by plans that reflect absolute architectural certainty. Such plans tend to be limited, too rigid, uncompromising, and impervious to change. Instead, good city design should anticipate that programmatic and other changes are inevitable over time. Ultimately, future-facing city building creates a compelling physical framework that can tolerate the ongoing change of physical elements and uses and still maintain a sense of wholeness over time.

Physical Change

City design can be thought of as creating a workable framework for urban life in terms of circulation, open space, and separate parcels that are ultimately filled in by buildings. At the beginning of the twenty-first century, many large cities, for various reasons, are without a framework and thus have limited opportunities to adapt. Changes then often require demolishing buildings and completely redeveloping sites.

Typically, projects without frameworks are large in scale, such as shopping malls and corporate office complexes—architectural islands surrounded by surface parking. Unlike a building within a street framework, these buildings do not exist independent of one another. Rather, they are completely subservient to the corporate or shopping center whole. If the entire complex fails economically or the developer wishes to sell off individual buildings, the parcels have limited adaptability, which makes attracting new tenants or buyers more difficult. To maintain adaptability, therefore, planners must consider three design elements: a rational framework, division of parcels, and street address identity.

1. A Rational Framework

Successful city frameworks typically involve simple organizations of movement corridors and open space that have multiple rationales to support them. An example is the circulation framework for the campus of the University of California, Merced. The circulation geometry and block orientation are based on the block size appropriate to the campus's largest proposed academic uses. The block grids are ori-

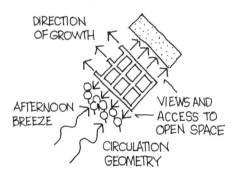

ented to capture the afternoon breeze, which is cooled by a heavily forested park on an adjoining lake. Grids are designed with view-corridors opening to the lake and athletic fields. The plan is also designed to connect the campus seamlessly with existing roadways and offers a geometric framework to guide university growth well into the future. A block's geometry, size, and orientation provide a framework adaptable to the inevitable changes that will take place over time.

2. Division of Parcels

Without the discipline of dividing large sites into parcels, human nature aims at placing new buildings in the center of whatever land is available. Doing so almost always destroys a number of additional potential building sites that would have been available if thoughtful parcelization had been accomplished at the

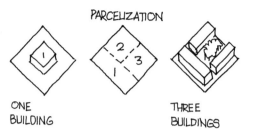

PARCELIZATION

ONE BUILDING

THREE BUILDINGS

outset. Design compactness and a unified campus feel can be lost as new buildings are positioned at the center of their individual sites, ignoring the context of a unified campus. Creating adaptable developments thus requires a system of defining parcels that can ensure efficient, compact use of the land. Parcelization also provides a way to easily remove and redesign buildings over time.

3. Street Address Identity

Buildings within a large campus or industrial park should never front on parking lots. Ideally, they should have a separate address and identity along publicly accessible streets. Separate addresses help maintain an individual building's value and ability to be repurposed as circumstances change, by giving it a separate identity and a clear public entrance.

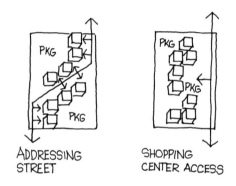

ADDRESSING STREET

SHOPPING CENTER ACCESS

Use Changes

During a building's lifetime, in the nature of things, old tenants give way to new, while changes in usage lead to new design requirements and sometimes a total renovation of a site. This mutability is organic to city life and must, therefore, be organic to city design. To enable adaptable use changes, three design elements should be considered: site adequacy, building adaptability, and open-space adaptability.

1. Site Adequacy

Initial parcel and block sizes should be established to accommodate a best-judgment range of possible building sizes. To anticipate very large buildings, such as campus medical laboratories, two blocks may need to be combined. In general, however, block sizes should be kept

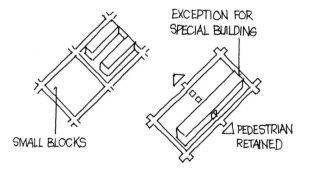

SMALL BLOCKS

EXCEPTION FOR SPECIAL BUILDING

PEDESTRIAN RETAINED

as small as possible, to support comfortable pedestrian access. In larger block sizes, accommodation should be made for pedestrian mid-block crossings.

2. Adaptability of Buildings

A building's initial design can be used to build in flexibility for different tenant needs and use changes over time. In creating the Chicago Civic Center Tower in the late 1960s, for example, designers engineered floors of a single-story layout for office space to be easily removable to accommodate double-height courtrooms. To enable maximum flexibility, a recently designed convention facility in central China similarly used easily removable floors to adapt to the needs of convention-goers and of displays of oversized goods or equipment.

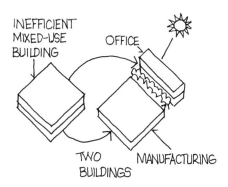

It is possible for buildings to be too adaptable. High-technology giant Hewlett-Packard required a building type with a very large floor area. Each building was two stories, and each floor had to be designed to accommodate research and development, office, administration, and manufacturing uses. The structural, electrical, and mechanical cost to achieve this flexibility was, of course, very high. Each use was to some degree compromised by the others, and ultimately the design offered very little resale value. The solution was to simplify, by separating manufacturing from research and office uses, and to create two different, more-efficient, and less-expensive building types.

3. Open-Space Adaptability

Designers need to think about adaptable open space in two ways. First, the space can be minimally programmed to provide flexible open areas for sports, community events, civic festivals, and the like. Second, open space can serve active and passive recreation needs and still be suitably classified as a future land reserve. Finally, naturally landscaped flood plains and other non-buildable land can be used for seasonal recreation use as long as no permanent structures are erected. An example of the first type of adaptability, Chicago's Millennium Park, also illustrates another kind of open-space flexibility. The park is designed with multiple outdoor "rooms," open space that is comfortable with a few people and vibrant with many.

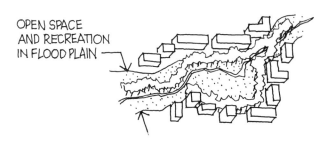

Millennium Park is often used as a place of citywide festivities and performances, yet it is easily transformed into numerous spaces for individual contemplation.

Minimal Disruption of Uses by Construction

Early phases of new developments need to be organized and sited so that they will be disrupted only minimally by subsequent phases of construction. Traffic, dust, and noise carried by prevailing winds can damage early-phase tenant and visitor mobility and comfort. These negative elements can be mitigated or avoided by careful contiguous phasing that is arranged to isolate completed parts of the project from new construction. Two design elements facilitate achieving that goal: traffic separation and downwind expansion.

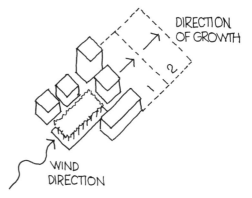

1. Traffic Separation

In an ideal situation, the first phase of a larger project can be located to keep construction traffic outside and away from the completed area. Subsequent phase construction should build outward from phase one so as not to affect the completed area.

2. Downwind Expansion

When possible, the phases of large projects should be programmed to take place downwind from a completed area. This can prevent most construction dust, debris, and noise from disrupting the completed environment. If later phases are not downwind, dust and noise management programs should be undertaken.

Project Location

New developments within what is seen as a hostile environment rarely succeed by themselves. To ensure overall success, a project's initial phase must be adaptable in a way that takes every possible advantage of the surrounding environment. Real value is gained by tying a project to existing amenities, such as parks, and natural features recognized as attractive and desirable. It is similarly important to locate a new development as close as possible to its strongest economically viable neighbor or to connect it physically with an already successful built environment. Three design elements are useful for locating new development: a healthy context, high visibility, and a sense of completion.

1. Healthy Context

A planned project should be located to take advantage of the most attractive amenities and the most economically healthy features of the area around its site.

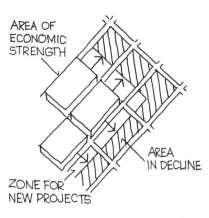

2. High Visibility

The planned project should have high visibility in both its neighborhood and the larger community. Visibility will help the project attract tenants, customers, and community acceptance and provide a positive signal of community renewal.

3. Sense of Completion

Almost always, portions of projects remain unbuilt until there is sufficient population. Supporting uses such as schools or shops may have to wait until they are feasible.

To eliminate the negative effects of vacant lots creating voids in the development pattern, future supportive uses are best located at the outside edge of completed areas. In this way the built environment can be made to feel complete, and disruption from new construction can be minimized.

When infilling development within an already built environment, it should be located nearest to the part that offers the greatest amenity to the project. Sometimes when building within areas of existing development, it is possible to lead with normally later-phase supporting uses. For a transit-based residential village north of Chicago, phase one involved the creation of a park, community center, and school. This communicated to future buyers and the existing community the design quality of the neighborhood to come.

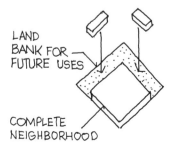

Use and Character

In the early stages of design development, it is crucial to find the right combination of uses that, even before project completion, can convey the look and feel of the finished product. On purely economic grounds, phase one of a project must include the mix and number of uses that can serve as the critical mass to attract the hearts, minds, and eyes necessary for success. This critical mass is achieved by leveraging economic strength and identity.

1. Economic Strength

A project must have sufficient size to create the necessary economic strength and "gravitational pull" to succeed in a particular market. Familiar examples include downtowns that struggle to revitalize retail districts previously undermined by suburban malls. Matching the size of the shopping center in a downtown is almost impossible. More success for downtown renewal comes from linking growth to new residential development in the downtown, helping to provide a "captive audience" for downtown commercial, retail, and entertainment uses.

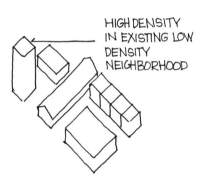

HIGH DENSITY IN EXISTING LOW DENSITY NEIGHBORHOOD

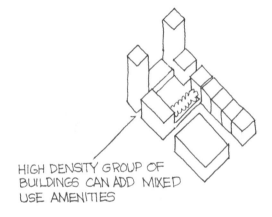

HIGH DENSITY GROUP OF BUILDINGS CAN ADD MIXED USE AMENITIES

2. Ultimate Identity

At a project's earliest phase, it is desirable to provide potential users with a sense of its ultimate mix of uses, design character, and overall quality. Through advertising, public and media relations, community gatherings, and word of mouth, communicating this sense of the ultimate character and use will help the project gain acceptance and success.

SENSE OF PLACE

VISIBLE LANDMARK

MIX OF USES

PHASE ONE

7.1. Planning for Continuous Change
Texas Medical Center, Houston

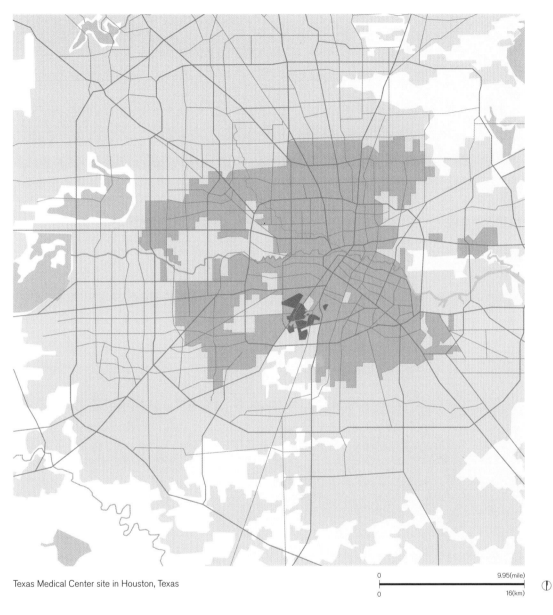

Texas Medical Center site in Houston, Texas

0	9.95(mile)
0	16(km)

The world's largest medical campus, the Texas Medical Center, is home to forty-three institutions with a daytime population of sixty to seventy thousand professionals, support staff, and patients. Physically, in the 50 years since its founding, the center has grown to 12 million square feet, with another 12 million planned for future growth. This makes TMC nearly the size of Houston's downtown. The center has, in fact, been prone to many of the problems of sprawl

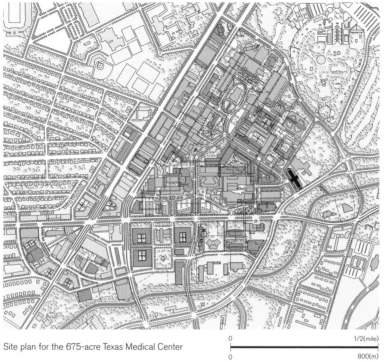

Site plan for the 675-acre Texas Medical Center

Dark color indicates new building sites

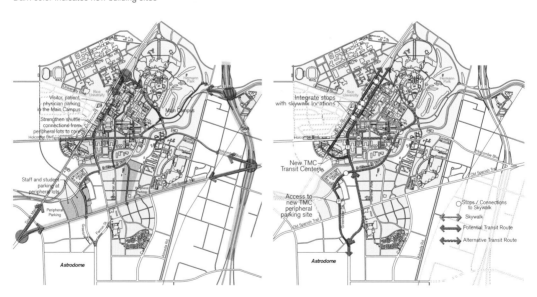

Establish a comprehensive parking strategy.

Link transit to ensure access to all campuses.

experienced by downtown areas. SOM urban designers were asked to create a plan for orderly development of an additional 9 million square feet over a 10-year period.

Until that point, TMC had grown in largely random fashion, with each of the dozens of medical institutions responsible for its own planning. Disparate programs, rarely shared, led to a chaos of competing and often clashing subcampuses. The new Master Plan for the Texas Medical Center, created in collaboration with nearby Rice University, focused on recognition of the medical campus as a "city," with a city's need for planned growth, and creation of a walkable campus with easily available public amenities and transit.

The goal was to create a unified, richly detailed, patient-friendly urban environment, rather than an oversized medical "business park" or "hospital mall" surrounded by parking lots. The plan ultimately provided a way for TMC to grow and adapt over time, with flexible plans for new streets, transit stops, pedestrian thoroughfares, commercial space, parking, and open space.

Aerial view of the center, with downtown Houston in the background

7.2. Guiding and Anticipating Growth with Principles

University of California, San Diego

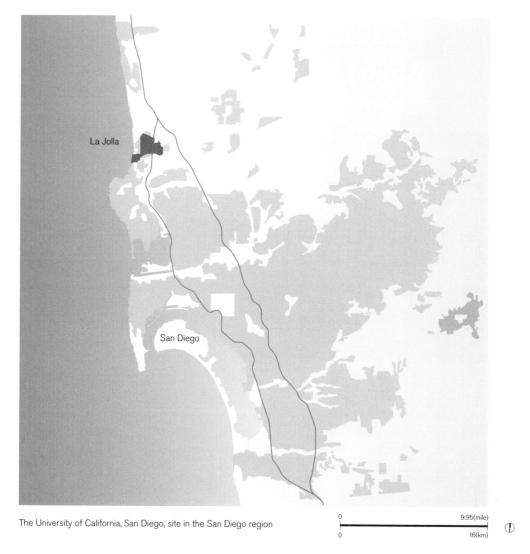

The University of California, San Diego, site in the San Diego region

0   9.95(mile)

0   16(km)

Sometimes, the simplest planning concepts can best anticipate the most profound changes. In the case of the University of California, San Diego, a master plan plus five simple tenets have, for two decades, guided more than $1.5 billion of campus development.

When master planning began for the nearly 1,000-acre University of California, San Diego, campus in 1989, there was simply no comprehensive framework for locating new campus buildings. What had begun as an idea to develop a series of separate colleges had degenerated into the academic version of urban sprawl. The ad hoc character of campus growth was fueled by the assumption that the eucalyptus grove running through the center of campus was a land bank for whatever new buildings the university desired.

The initial process for creating the campus master plan for future growth involved crafting easily understood rules to reestablish a coherent framework for five components: neighborhoods, academic corridors, the university center, the park, and connections.

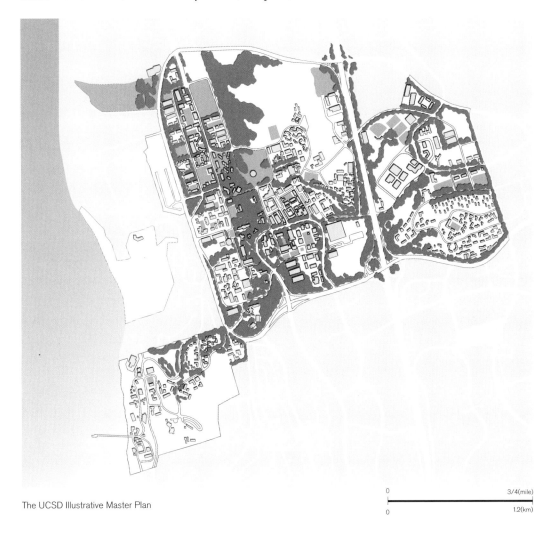

The UCSD Illustrative Master Plan

1. Neighborhoods

The first rule recognized that campus development should occur within established "neighborhoods." These were the building blocks of campus development and had to have clear boundaries and distinct characters. Campus neighborhoods provided an appropriate tool for siting individual colleges, clustering related disciplines, and providing housing.

Distinctive neighborhoods

Muir College is an example of a campus neighborhood.

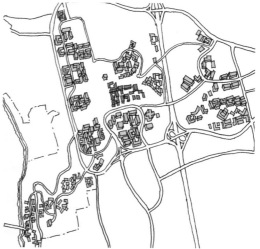

The campus is organized into neighborhoods.

2. Academic Corridors

The second rule established that most university departments and programs benefited from physical contiguity with related disciplines. The master plan, therefore, established "academic corridors" across neighborhood boundaries to bring related academic disciplines into proximity, locating academic facilities in those corridors. Initially five departmental corridors were identified: (1) marine science, (2) life sciences, (3) humanities, (4) social sciences, and (5) engineering, mathematics, and physics. The plan furthered and protected connections between campus parts by roads and pathways to facilitate access and ease of movement.

Road and path connections

The Social Sciences corridor will connect Muir College with a proposed sixth college.

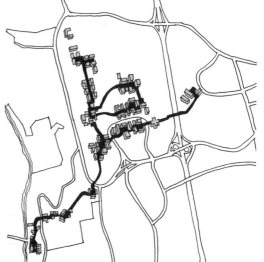

Related departments are linked.

3. The University Center

To provide a hub of student activities and a focus for undergraduate teaching programs, the campus clearly required a "university center." Similar in concept to a town center, this destination was to be easily accessible to visitors and campus neighborhoods and thus function as the social heart of the campus. UCSD was fortunate in already possessing a series of vintage wooden buildings from a former World War II army base. These had served as the first home of UCSD. Although they were old and had been designed to be temporary, the buildings were of a scale and design that made them an enduring—and endearing—part of campus life. The master plan suggested that some of these original buildings and their landscaped courtyards be maintained and serve, together with new infill buildings, as the center of the campus.

The UCSD centrally located social and academic heart

University Center will be the focus of campus activity.

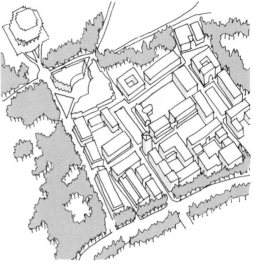

The Camp Matthews area will become University Center.

4. The Park

The Pacific Ocean shoreline and its mesas, canyons, and eucalyptus groves within the UCSD site constitute an ecologically sensitive natural setting. These environmental features

The eucalyptus forest, a unifying element

The park, a rich and varied natural setting, is at the heart of the campus.

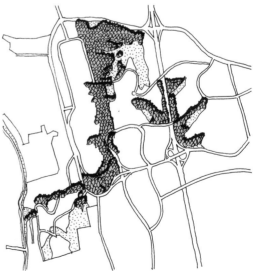

The park links the sensitive lands across the campus.

needed to be recognized and treated as parkland to be preserved and protected for future generations. An important rule, therefore, was that the university recognize its stewardship of and responsibility to conserve these natural resources and designate the eucalyptus grove as a permanent open space.

5. Connections

Enabling the university to function as a single "city" required connections between the various parts of campus. Connective "tissue" included roads, paths, public entries, landmarks, view-corridors, and landscape features. Establishing these links was necessary if the campus was to gain a coherent sense of place as well as functional access. It was also critical that the university build connections with adjacent towns and cities in the region in ways that the surrounding communities saw as beneficial.

New academic facilities will be located according to related disciplines and linked by academic corridors.

The Library Walk reinforces the connection of the parts to the center of the campus.

New roads and paths connect neighborhoods, open space, and the surrounding community.

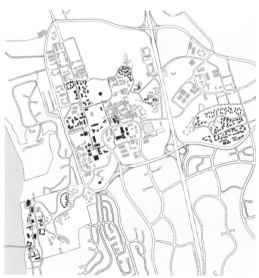

New Campus buildings (orange), as of 2005, completed according to the master plan

7.3. Recovering a Diamond in the Rust (Belt)

The Waukegan Lakefront Downtown, Illinois

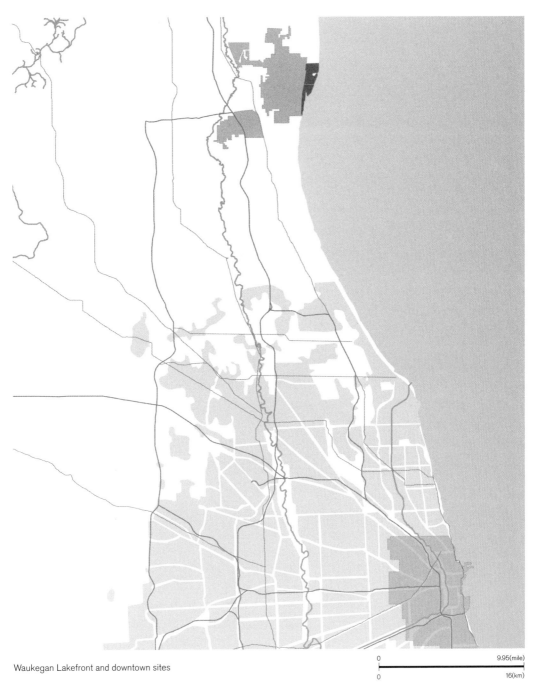

Waukegan Lakefront and downtown sites

0   9.95(mile)

0   16(km)

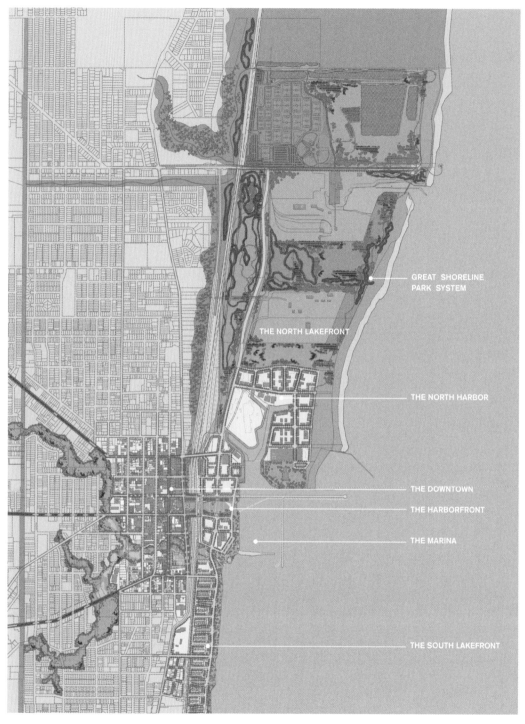

GREAT SHORELINE PARK SYSTEM

THE NORTH LAKEFRONT

THE NORTH HARBOR

THE DOWNTOWN

THE HARBORFRONT

THE MARINA

THE SOUTH LAKEFRONT

Waukegan Lakefront and Downtown Master Plan: reinventing an industrial waterfront city

Located on Lake Michigan halfway between Chicago, Illinois, and Milwaukee, Wisconsin, Waukegan is a classic midwestern town with a dried-up industrial base and thirty thousand lost jobs. In 2002 city officials asked SOM planners to develop possible scenarios for redeveloping Waukegan over 100 years as well as to produce a 20-year master plan.

The master plan focused on how, in the first phase of redevelopment, Waukegan's existing urban assets and amenities could be maximized and, more to the point, mobilized as incentives to advertise the town's enormous potential. Planners proposed first investing in assets that could have the most immediate benefit for the least initial cost. The first "bang for the buck" was renovating Waukegan's historic Genesee Theater and upgrading and infilling commercial and housing sites in the downtown that, together, could convey a sense of burgeoning activity and new life.

Two important factors differentiated Waukegan from typical "rust belt" cities, one hugely negative, the other positive. First, Waukegan had been home to the world's largest asbestos and gypsum processing plant, with its concomitant toxic legacy. Second, the defunct plant made available invaluable Lake Michigan waterfront adjacent to Waukegan's historic downtown with several miles of lake access. These factors gave the town of ninety thousand enormous potential as both a popular regional destination and an exurban home for commuters from both Chicago and Milwaukee.

The extensive open-space system along the waterfront areas

Reinvest in the downtown with new mixed-use development.

The SOM team's initial report, "The Waukegan Lakefront–Downtown Urban Design Plan," focused on this first-phase redevelopment and proposed to extend the city's road grid across the adjacent abandoned 1,200-acre industrial site. The effect would be to reconnect Waukegan's downtown directly to a lakefront that would be detoxified as the final element of the first phase. Along the newly energized waterfront, the proposal called for a maritime museum and environmental learning center. These would be the cultural base for a rich collection of uses, as the first phase of Waukegan's renewal became a springboard to subsequent transportation, commercial, residential, and recreational improvements.

Aerial view of downtown Waukegan and the redevelopment sites

7.4. Fitting Inside with Outside
Harvard North Precinct, Cambridge, Massachusetts

Harvard North Precinct, Cambridge, Massachusetts, and Boston Region

0	9.95(mile)
0	16(km)

In 2002 SOM began a study for the Harvard Faculty of Arts and Sciences to address the growing space requirements of departments constituting nearly half the university. What began as a short-term planning exercise grew into an ongoing relationship designed to help Harvard physically transform itself to maintain its place at the forefront of twenty-first-century academics and science.

The process began with a conversation with department chairs, administrators, faculty members, and others, after which the team identified several key principles. Subsequent proposals based on the principles related as much to evolving academic needs and priorities as to city design and architecture.

The first concern was the need for room for new offices, laboratories, classrooms, and other academic spaces. Harvard was simply running out of space north of the Charles River. This made it difficult to provide offices and labs for new faculty, a factor in the university's growth and financial well-being.

Another important issue was bringing individual departments closer together physically after decades of haphazard dispersion of classrooms and office spaces. This ran counter to the principle "Each tub sits on its own bottom," Harvard-ese for the historic responsibility of a department for its own financial stability and growth. Replacing the "tub" analogy was a consensus that research and academic problems would increasingly be solved through an interdisciplinary approach to the arts and sciences.

Thus individual departments needed space to coalesce and to be in proximity to related departments. These requirements were hampered by the fact that the only potential space available was within Harvard's North Precinct, an area thought of as "The Yard's backyard." It was a warren of storage and museum spaces, utility plants, and parking areas, surrounded by deeply rooted neighbors, including the Harvard law and divinity schools. It quickly became clear that the North Precinct was the last remaining piece of Cambridge into which the Faculty of Arts and Sciences could grow.

With these constraints in mind, the SOM team asked key questions about the possibilities for renovation and selected infill as well as new construction. In all cases, it turned out that the best solution would be creative uses of existing space.

A strategy to complete the Cambridge campus

0   3/8(mile)

0   600(m)

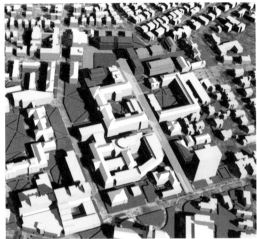

North Precinct Development Strategy

New buildings framing the revamped quad

light green: Divinity Avenue corridor

dark green: Harvard quads

dark orange: large footprint of science labs

light orange: small buildings transition to neighborhood

A third fundamental issue related to the activities that truly made sense on a modern college campus. Within the North Precinct, for example, sat a series of museum storage spaces. These housed Harvard's renowned glass flower collection and one of the world's most extensive herbaria. Could these be moved to outlying spaces to make room for more relevant uses?

Another important query was whether an academic "backwater" could be transformed to fit into the Harvard campus while remaining an "edge" where campus and local community could peacefully meet.

The answer was yes, particularly if Divinity Avenue could become the heart of an informal quad lined with small-scale buildings connected to the rest of the campus by a new passageway cut through an existing, and currently blocking, building. The ground level of this area would be designed to mirror the existing street scene and face outward. This orientation would allow the new space to welcome the community into the university while offering open spaces for multifaceted idea-generating, informal meeting places, which had been identified as an important model for the interdisciplinary future of academia.

The ultimate proposals followed this new multidisciplinary model by collecting departments such as chemistry, biology, and life sciences, no longer on their own architectural "bottoms," as it were, but rather in "condominiums" best able to exploit the multidisciplinary academic approach.

7.5. Working toward a Flexible Campus
Hewlett-Packard Worldwide

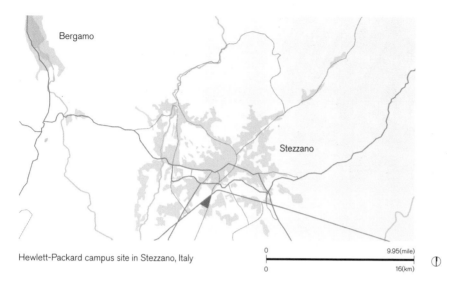

Hewlett-Packard campus site in Stezzano, Italy

Bergamo

Stezzano

```
0                          9.95(mile)
|———————————————————————————|
0                          16(km)
```

By the late 1980s Hewlett-Packard had grown into a giant company encompassing over 60 million square feet of property, which had been acquired without much consideration for even the most rudimentary principles of real estate. HP needed planning help to create new space to meet current manufacturing needs and business processes but that could be easily reconfigured for lease or sale to other companies.

Originally, HP had developed campuses around the world that integrated business, R&D, and manufacturing into single low-rise buildings. This space was flexible but usually had a large footprint and limited window exposure. The buildings were particularly unsuitable to office use and required extensive and expensive structural and mechanical changes to make them ready for manufacturing. The site plans for all HP campuses clustered these buildings together, generally surrounded by shopping-mall-style parking. The campuses were particularly difficult to reconfigure, and this lowered their potential resale or lease value.

The design team prepared new site plans for HP with a protocol that placed the business office functions in separate two- and three-story buildings. Manufacturing was moved to large single-floor buildings that were efficient and lower in cost.

The team modified existing site plans and created new ones to ensure HP's ability to expand or shrink on any site without loss of property value, employee comfort or work efficiency, or company identity. To meet these criteria, planners established guidelines to build the campuses along roads with street addresses. HP could then maintain its "brand" regardless of growth or downsizing but could also easily lease or sell a building that had its own "address identity."

Building heights and uses

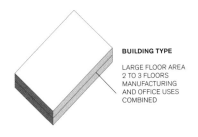

BUILDING TYPE

LARGE FLOOR AREA
2 TO 3 FLOORS
MANUFACTURING
AND OFFICE USES
COMBINED

Before

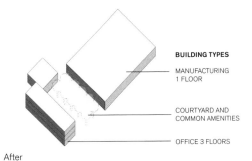

BUILDING TYPES

MANUFACTURING
1 FLOOR

COURTYARD AND
COMMON AMENITIES

OFFICE 3 FLOORS

After

Campus configuration

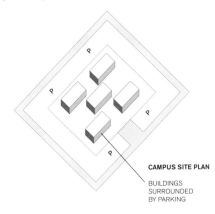

CAMPUS SITE PLAN

BUILDINGS
SURROUNDED
BY PARKING

Before

SERVICE

ADDRESSING ROAD

CAMPUS SITE PLAN

MANUFACTURING
LOCATED ACCROSS
COMMON AMENITY SPACE

OFFICE BUILDINGS FACE
ADDRESSING ROAD

PARKING DISPERSED

After

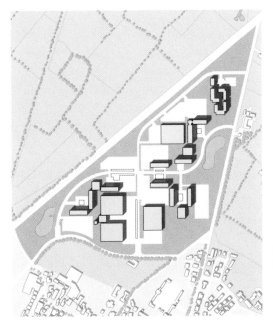

Hewlett-Packard campus in Stezzano with its addressing road
(the second road is for truck services)

0   3/8(mile)

0   600(m)

Nine Principles for Twenty-First-Century City Building

Principle Eight: Density

Designing Compact Cities with Appropriate Transit

The Problem: Sprawling development across valuable irreplaceable land, wasted energy and infrastructure, and millions of hours lost in commutes.

Density measures the number of people living or working on a unit of land. Density can be measured in different ways for housing and for work space. For residential use, density is the number of dwellings or people per acre or hectare. Worldwide, the density of cities varies greatly, because personal living space varies by cultural norms, what individuals and families can afford, and what they are willing to pay.

The average space per family can vary by a magnitude of more than ten. In the developing world, families may live in 10 square meters (100 square feet) while in developed societies 100 square meters (1,000 square feet) is considered an average unit size for two people. In developing cities, population growth and the need for density are products not only of the number of new arrivals but also of their economic situation and hopes for the future.

The second measure, work space density, is the ratio of a building's floor area to its lot or parcel size. For example, while a single-story manufacturing plant in an industrial park might have a floor-to-area ratio (FAR) of 1, the 110-story Sears Tower in Chicago has a FAR of 34.4.

The densities of both working and living spaces in cities vary widely. Asia today is experiencing unparalleled densities. Hong Kong, for example, has a population of approximately 8 million people, more or less equivalent to that in the San Francisco Bay Area. But the Bay Area is approximately 7,000 square miles, while Hong Kong is less than 50 square miles. This means that Hong Kong is 140 times denser than the Bay Area and 10 times as dense as the city of San Francisco. Other cities have equally varied densities.

The characteristic building block of Hong Kong is the forty-story residential tower. These towers and the many bridges connecting them make the city seem like a single science fiction "mega-structure." For the record, there are barely twenty single-family detached homes left in all of Hong Kong.

This is not to say that density doesn't have a number of important benefits. These include less need for infrastructure, lower costs for roads and utilities, conservation of valuable agricultural, scenic, habitat, and watershed lands, more choices of employment, wider cultural and educational choices, lower pollution, and less time loss in transit. Hong Kong's compactness, for example, supports a comprehensive rail system that can take riders from one edge of the city to the other in about 15 minutes.

While we view Hong Kong as a world wonder, its extreme density eliminates some of the qualities that define a livable city. The experience of dense cities like Hong Kong illustrates the need for new, attractive, desirable high-density neighborhoods that provide an alternative to both suburban living and tightly constrained tower-dwelling for at least some of the world's growing urban population. To create those neighborhoods, city builders need to discuss the benefits of compactness and proximity in terms of successful high-density design.

Compactness and Proximity

Sustainable, life-affirming cities need to offer many choices of both low- and high-density space for living and working. To support convenient and walkable services, suitable urban amenities, and public transportation, however, a threshold density of 15 to 50 dwelling units per acre is generally necessary. This density range is most often associated with the positive qualities of city living, compared with single-family suburban homes, which have a density of 5 dwellings per acre or lower and tend to be car- and mall-centric. The designer's tool kit contains three elements to achieve livable densities: transit-oriented development, development planning, and amenities.

1. Transit-Oriented Development

Today, in both the suburbs and the downtowns of North America, there is a serious effort to raise density to support efficient transit, encourage walking, and lessen dependence on private cars for everyday uses. Transit-oriented developments, such as those along Bay Area Rapid Transit and Hong Kong Rail Transit

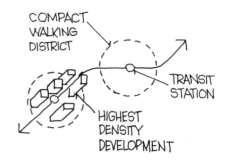

Airport routes, generally offer dense residential living in a setting that integrates transit with shopping, restaurants, and entertainment. Transit-oriented development offers a comfortable and safe walking environment from transit to home and a rich neighborhood life.

2. Development Planning

In dense transit-served North American cities, livable neighborhoods are being built at 300 dwellings per acre. This, however, is about the limit. Above 300, access to views, sunlight, and adequate open space is difficult to achieve. With most cities growing in population, raising density as much as possible is appropriate in order to limit mindless sprawl over increasingly valuable open land. But density must be done in compact, walkable districts in locations with transportation assets and access to the amenities of city life.

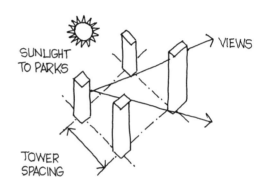

3. Amenities

To be successful, high-density living environments must offer their occupants amenities such as a short walk to work, exceptional views, close access to support services, cultural, recreational, and entertainment venues, and the generally exciting buzz of city life. These urban "assets of livability," are essential to tipping the balance in favor of living in denser neighborhoods in existing urban areas rather than the old preference, suburban living on previously undeveloped open land.

8.1. Using Brown, Saving Green: Urban Density for Regional Renewal

The Central Area Plan, Chicago, Illinois

The Central Area Plan site in Chicago

0   9.95(mile)

0   16(km)

Chicago offers a useful example of incorporating the principles of density into daily life and governmental decision making. The 2000 Chicago Central Area Plan and its 1983 predecessor were both commissioned to look ahead to the city in 2020 to determine how to accommodate employment, residential, commercial, and cultural growth within central city "brownfield" sites rather than through development in pristine outlying areas. The Central Area Plan identified sensitive, sustainable, and environmentally sound ways to increase density and expand the city's central core. The plan aimed to bring over $500 billion in new economic benefits to the Lake Michigan region. The plan's major theme was to create the equivalent of a sustainable new city of over fifty thousand people within Chicago's existing infrastructure, urban boundaries, and framework. Opting for this dense, urban infill approach had the potential to save over 500 square miles of precious undeveloped land in the region.

Various urban planning projects in downtown Chicago have provided examples of a best-practice approach to the problem of density and growth in the urban workplace. The Chicago Central Area Plan of 2000, like its 1983 predecessor, took a deep look into issues of creating affordable urban work space and into the potential for residential, commercial, and civic growth in the downtown.

One key issue addressed by the 2000 plan was identifying the basic requirements of livable and workable high-density neighborhood life. The goal was to enhance the city's

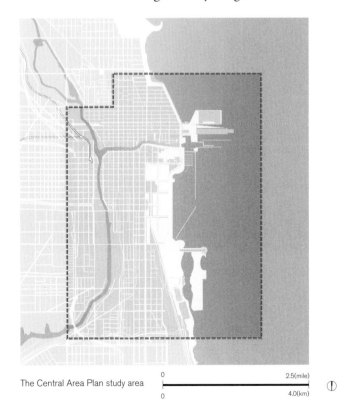

The Central Area Plan study area

0   2.5(mile)

0   4.0(km)

Principles of the Chicago Central Area Plan

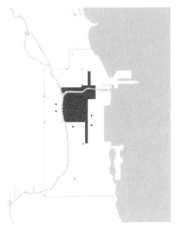

The Loop district, the existing core of the city

Introduce the expanded loop to embrace the rail stations.

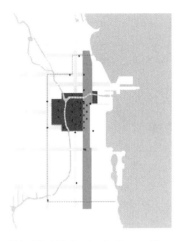

Extend the high-density, mixed-use corridors.

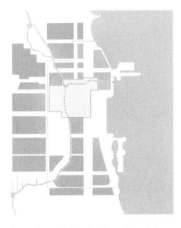

Strengthen neighborhoods and special places.

Protect landmarks and the special character of districts

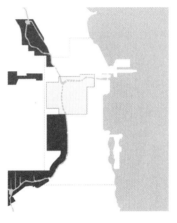

Reinforce industrial districts and corridors.

Strengthen education and learning.

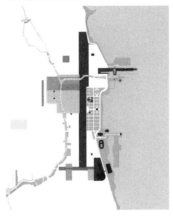

Connect cultural attractions and tourist destinations to the Central Area.

Extend the waterfronts, and create new open spaces.

gravitational pull and enlarge its status as the Midwest's hub for business, education, and style, providing a dense, livable alternative to creating new neighborhoods and cities in still-pristine areas of the region.

The plan aimed to create more than 180,000 new jobs, over 7 million square feet of retail space, 160,000 square feet of new museum and cultural facilities, 10,000 new hotel rooms, 3 million square feet of modern higher education facilities, and housing and services for over 140,000 pioneering urban residents who would be drawn into becoming residents of Chicago's Central Area.

To satisfy the best-practice principles of density, the 2000 plan established guidelines outlining a sensitive expansion of downtown Chicago beyond the city's famous and increasingly limiting Loop. The guidelines called for extensive use of infill development, most of all along existing transit corridors moving out from the city's core.

The 2000 Chicago Central Area Plan was one of the first programs designed to reduce both sprawl and car dependence on a regional scale. Three guiding best-practice themes emerged from it: the need for a sound developmental framework, provision of ample multi-mode transit, and commitment to expanding and enriching Chicago's parks, waterfront, and public spaces. At its finest grain, the plan recognized that infill, transportation, and open space must be developed in an integrated and mutually supportive way to successfully densify downtown Chicago.

View of the Central Area model, looking southeast
New infill development in blue

Extend the Loop to accommodate future growth.

Expand and connect the waterfronts and open spaces.

Strengthen and infill the diverse collection of livable neighborhoods.

Model of future growth within Chicago's Central Area
New infill development in blue

8.2. Accepting Density and Height
The Transbay Terminal Neighborhood Redevelopment Plan, San Francisco, California

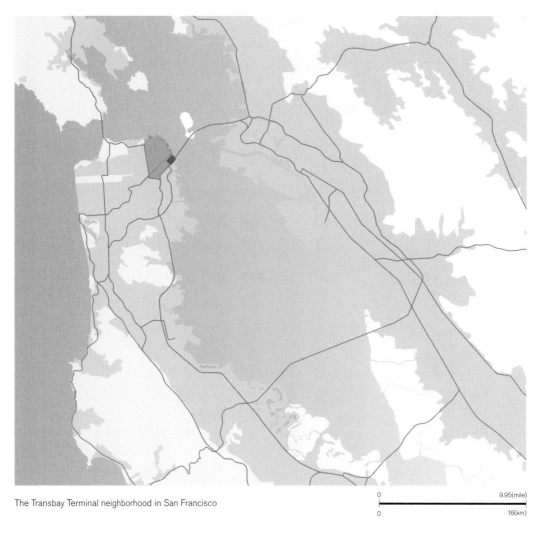

The Transbay Terminal neighborhood in San Francisco

| 0 | | 9.95(mile) |
| 0 | | 16(km) |

San Franciscans cherish their city as a place of unique individuals, institutions, and buildings in a singular natural setting. Not coincidentally, San Francisco is also famous for its contentious planning process and fierce resistance to altering the landscape, particularly by increasing the density of existing neighborhoods. Thus, when it came time to redevelop a decaying 40-acre downtown transit terminal and the adjoining property, conflict was virtually inevitable.

Surprising everyone, an amicable public consensus was reached that this area would be redeveloped as a new, high-density, transit-oriented neighborhood. The condition for public support turned out to be creation of a neighborhood that was comparable in livability and attractiveness to existing lower-density San Francisco districts. For San Franciscans, this translated into a development providing bay vistas without blocking existing views and providing parks, sunlit landscaped streets, and high-quality services in a walkable neighborhood with a recognizably local look and feel.

Plans for the new Transbay Terminal neighborhood relied on best-practice principles of fine-grained density, landscaped parks, and pedestrian alleys and lanes to make the surrounding area's large blocks friendlier and more walkable. The lanes were lined with four- to six-story residential buildings, with ground-floor units that opened directly onto the streets. One of the neighborhood's major streets was dedicated to the kind of ground-level retail, restaurant, and club uses that defined the social heart of many other San Francisco neighborhoods.

Designs were rendered of tall (up to fifty stories), slender, broadly spaced towers located so as to preserve existing views and avoid shading the new park. The streets were extensively landscaped to soften the area's otherwise harsh urban character, and the existing transit station redesigned to provide a variety of travel options, including bus and rail.

The cost for the transit improvements was to be borne by developers, partially supported by redevelopment of the adjacent, publicly owned land at a residential density of over 300 units per acre. The Transbay Terminal neighborhood's high-rise super-towers were necessary to create revenue to pay for rebuilding the decaying terminal.

SOM was then asked by the city planning staff to revisit the building sites closest to the terminal and study the feasibility of towers taller than previously recommended. The study suggested the allowable height be raised on three high-rise sites that would visually re-center the city's skyline around its area of highest transit access.

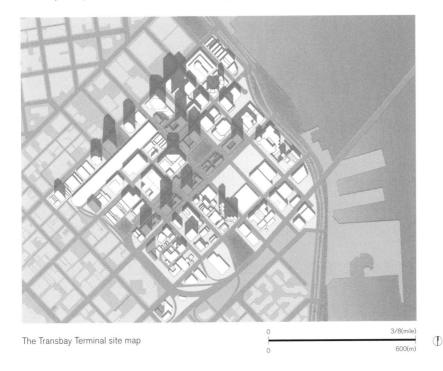

The Transbay Terminal site map

| 0 | | 3/8(mile) |
| 0 | | 600(m) |

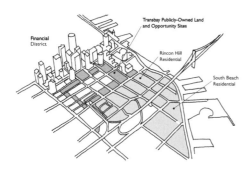

Context of the development near the financial district and residential neighborhoods

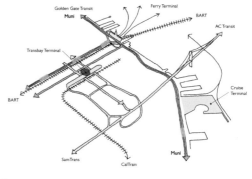

The highest transit access near the development

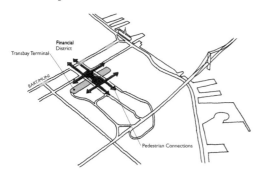

Pedestrian connections to the terminal

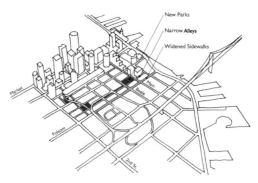

New open spaces in the neighborhood

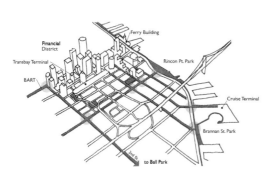

Open-space connections to surrounding areas

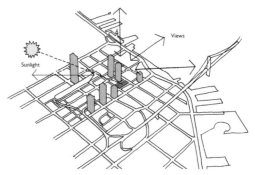

Preservation of sunlight and views by wide spacing of towers

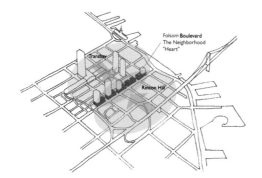

Connecting the neighborhood's social heart to the bay shoreline

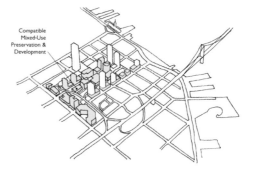

Existing low-rise context and compatible new infill

View of the San Francisco skyline from Treasure Island, before and after the development

View of the San Francisco skyline from the freeway approach to the city, before and after the development

Folsom Street, the social heart of the neighborhood

The new park and residential buildings with ground-level activity

Overview of the new high-density transit-oriented neighborhood

8.3. Taking Advantage of Existing Infrastructure

Lakeshore East, Chicago, Illinois

The Lakeshore East site in Chicago

0	9.95(mile)
0	16(km)

With a new, ornately landscaped 5-acre central park, the Lakeshore East Master Plan embraces a site that was the largest remaining undeveloped tract in downtown Chicago. The plan calls for seventeen buildings with a mix of uses, including retail, office, services, recreation, education, and, most critically, high-rise residential space for fifteen thousand people. Creating the new Lakeshore East neighborhood on a "brownfield"—a former Illinois Central switching

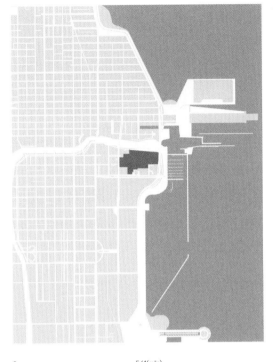

0   5/4(mile)

0   2(km)

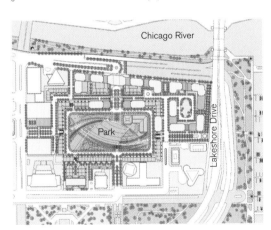

Master plan map for Lakeshore East

0   1/4(mile)

0   400(m)

yard—enabled planners to design a community that, rather than start from scratch, would keep hundreds of acres of pristine land on the urban periphery from development while saving tens of million of dollars by using extant transit, sewage, electrical, and other urban infrastructure.

The program for the 28-acre site addresses the portion of downtown Chicago where Lake Michigan meets the Chicago River, a site that was inherently difficult to develop. Essentially cut off on all sides from its surroundings, the Lakeshore East site was blocked by Columbus Drive to the west, Lakeshore Drive to the east, Wacker Drive to the north, and Randolph Street to the south. Rather than orient the development outward, the master plan instead focused the new mixed-use community inward toward the project's central park. This approach was able to break a 30-year stalemate and develop a brownfield site that had perplexed planners for decades.

The Lakeshore East Master Plan was also designed to gather the community support that had been largely missing from earlier efforts for the site. The team held a series of hearings and workshops and then made alterations based on the feedback: decreased density, increased open space, additional landscape setbacks, and interior gardens in residential areas. A public elementary school and a field house for the park district were added to the project in response to public support. The master plan also proposed ways to connect Lakeshore East with Lake Michigan and the Chicago River. Changes in grade across the site enabled the creation of terraces with panoramic views and a grand staircase along the central park's northern edge. The Chicago Planning Commission approved the Lakeshore East Master Plan in 2001.

A new elementary school will serve families moving downtown.

Townhomes can screen parking podiums from the street.

Access to the river provides great outdoor amenities.

Aerial view of the new Lakeshore East neighborhood

The new central park, focus of the neighborhood

Principle Nine: Identity

Creating/Preserving a Unique and Memorable Sense of Place

The Problem: Environmental sameness, repetition of elements, places hard to comprehend, a sense of being lost, a lack of natural features.

All cities aspire to success: economic, social, and, most recently, environmental. In a comparable vein, private investment aspires to minimize risk by replicating well-established and economically successful development. Not surprisingly, in the minds of many city builders, this translates into designing urban landscapes that mirror already successful places.

Similarly, all modern cities are built with much the same technology and many of the same materials. In the quest for easily developable sites, hills are flattened, waterways filled in, and forests cleared. Taken together, these factors favor fast-growing cities that look and feel alike and tend to degrade the environment. Good city building must therefore assert the public interest to protect and enhance the city's source of uniqueness over the private interests that threaten it.

At the beginning of the twenty-first century, city renewal projects are being built more quickly and at larger scales than ever before. This has made it increasingly difficult to build-in the variety and character that come from the finer scale and incremental evolution of older cities. Designing fast-growing yet livable new cities and neighborhoods has thus become the greatest challenge for modern city builders. They must take advantage of identifiable, unusual, and special features to help make each city unique and memorable. Ultimately, natural features, climate, culture, and design are the primary sources through which cities achieve individual identity.

Identity by Natural Feature

A significant source of civic identity can come from a city's relationship with its natural features. Consider, for example, the mountains and harbor of Hong Kong, the riverfront in Shanghai, the hills and bay of San Francisco, the harbor and rivers of New York, the lakefront of Chicago, the archipelago of Stockholm, and even the tiny, yet defining, rivers that run through San Antonio, Texas, and San Jose, California.

Water is the natural feature most closely associated with memorable cities. All cities seek freshwater to support their population needs, and many cities use their harbors for water-borne trade and distribution of goods. Most of the world's remarkable cities are built and celebrated in relation to their harbors, rivers, and lakes.

Hills or mountains also strongly identify certain cities. Some, like Rio de Janeiro, San Francisco, and Rome, are built on hills. Others gain their identity because of the steep hills or mountains at their edges. Tehran and Salt Lake City are notable for being backed up against tall, dramatic mountains. Hong Kong's urban image is framed by the interplay of water and peaks.

In cities lacking these natural identifiers, opportunities to create identity are often available through developing new water features such as lakes or lagoons, which have additional value because they can manage flooding, filter gray water, irrigate farms, and enhance the potable water supply. The lakes of Hanoi are exceptional examples. Originally excavated for soil to raise the surrounding land out of the floodplain of the Red River, they lace Hanoi with a jewel-like array of water features and small parks that define the city's identity.

In the name of flood control, scenic waterways have often been enclosed in concrete, as was the case with the Los Angeles River. Unfortunately, paved watercourses were once an engineering necessity. Today planners have a better understanding of how to maintain a river's scenic qualities while providing flood control. This was the positive lesson taught by the San Antonio River project of the 1960s and '70s.

Sometimes, in the name of making land "easier to build on," what might be considered "inefficient" topography is evened out, as large earth-moving equipment makes it relatively easy to do away with hills and harbors. Destruction of harbors has taken place in virtually all waterfront cities, eliminating natural features that designers now recognize as significant sources of identity and livability. City builders today use four tools to protect the natural features from which a city's identity can be derived: conservation, repair, visual and physical access, and view-corridors.

1. Conservation

Regulations are necessary to retain or specifically limit changes to existing natural features. Most often, regulations are applied to hillside topography, the boundaries and edges of water features, forests, species habitats, and watershed corridors.

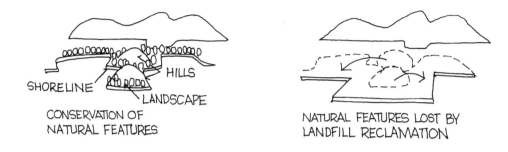

CONSERVATION OF NATURAL FEATURES

NATURAL FEATURES LOST BY LANDFILL RECLAMATION

2. Repair

Planning is required to repair or replace natural features that have been damaged or eliminated through thoughtless urbanization. Cities can restore creeks and streams that have been undergrounded, replant forests that have been overcut, remove landfill from water bodies, open up privatized waterfronts, and the like.

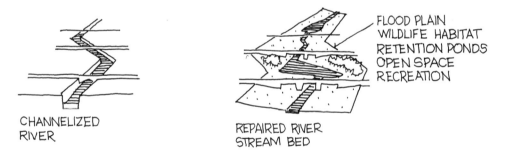

CHANNELIZED RIVER

REPAIRED RIVER STREAM BED

3. Visual and Physical Access

Regulations are needed to maintain and repair visual and physical access to prominent natural features. Rules can limit the scale of physical development, remove development that blocks views and access to natural features, and require public easements such as roads, trails, bicycle paths, and walkways to allow access to and enjoyment of natural features.

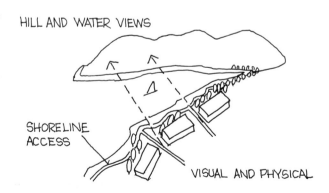

HILL AND WATER VIEWS

SHORELINE ACCESS

VISUAL AND PHYSICAL

4. View-Corridors

Gordon Cullen's Townscape movement, discussed earlier, showed designers new ways of viewing cities. Cullen illustrated the need for all cities to identify both new and existing view-corridors and cityscapes that expand personal space and promote the uniqueness and identity of a particular place. In cities like San Francisco, London, Washington, DC, and Chicago, view-corridors to central features such as San Francisco Bay, St. Paul's Cathedral, the U.S. Capitol Building, and Lake Michigan are protected by law.

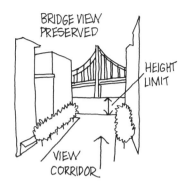

Identity by Climate

In hot climates, protection from the sun's heat is basic to human comfort. Successful hot-weather cities tend to shade their sidewalks with trees or arcaded walkways. Well-thought-out orientation and façade design prevent direct sunlight from entering buildings and raising indoor temperatures. Careful employment of water features can contribute to outdoor temperature comfort.

Conversely, in cool climates, direct sunlight is basic to outdoor comfort. Cool-weather cities promote sun on sidewalks and parks and limit building heights to reduce the shadows they cast. Cooler habitats tend to be more transparent, so that they can use the sunlight to help warm their interiors as well.

Wind is another natural feature that can influence city form. Projects such as the University of California, Merced, discussed later, illustrate how street grids are oriented to receive a cooling afternoon breeze. In other situations, buildings may be oriented to avoid the full force of recognized storm patterns. Rain or aridity should also be a factor in a city's approach to landscape creation.

City builders striving for a unique urban identity need to work within the context of climate-based elements: in warmer climates, sun protection and breeze and rain exposure; in colder climates, sun exposure and wind and rain protection.

1. Sun Protection in Warm Climates

In addition to regulations for thermal insulation, indoor comfort in warm climates can be aided by minimizing the outside surface area exposed to the sun in each building. For similar reasons window openings can be oriented to the north and south, to maximize lighting and minimize sun exposure during the day. Outdoor comfort in warm climates is achieved by creating places of shadow with landscaping and architecture.

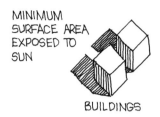

MINIMUM SURFACE AREA EXPOSED TO SUN

BUILDINGS

SHADED WALKWAYS

OPEN SPACE

Singapore is an example of a successful hot-climate city. Buildings there are mandated to be light-colored, so that they reflect the sun's heat. For similar reasons, the city is widely planted with trees that create both cooling shade and Singapore's unique green character.

2. Breeze and Water Exposure in Warm Climates

In warm climates, open spaces and buildings can be planned to receive the cooling effects of an afternoon breeze. This is accomplished by orienting streets, requiring operable windows, and channeling air movement. Channeling cools the air both by aspirating water from the leaves of trees and by exchanging heat when breezes pass over cooler water bodies, either natural or designed.

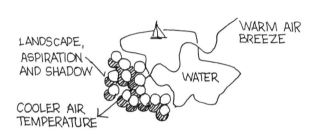

LANDSCAPE, ASPIRATION AND SHADOW

COOLER AIR TEMPERATURE

WARM AIR BREEZE

WATER

3. Sun Exposure in Cold Climates

In a cold climate, outdoor comfort can be achieved by maximizing sun exposure in parks and pedestrian areas that have heavy traffic. Guidelines need to limit building height to maximize sun on these outdoor places. Tree sizes and shadows may also be limited. Use of deciduous trees, which shed their leaves in winter, also helps maximize sun exposure. San Francisco, the cool "City of Fog," enhances outdoor comfort using all these approaches.

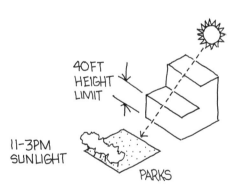

40FT HEIGHT LIMIT

11-3PM SUNLIGHT

PARKS

4. Wind and Rain Protection in Cold Climates

Outdoor comfort in cold climates also requires shelter from rain and the blocking, buffering, or deflection of wind. Building entrances should never be oriented to face typical oncoming storm patterns. Many large cities like Toronto have created climate-protected pedestrian networks below street level, or like Saint Paul, Minnesota, and Hong Kong, employ networks that bridge streets from above.

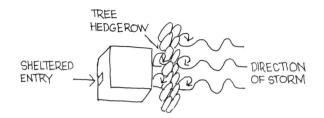

Identity by Culture

Cultural differences also provide strong sources of a city's unique form. Distinctions come from such cultural factors as the degree to which people seek privacy or community, the city's relative economic strength, its age, and its unique institutions of art, culture, and government.

1. Identity by Privacy versus Community

One of the key aspects of identity by culture is the cultural and historic preference for privacy or openness.

The best example of the cultural desire for privacy can be found in Islamic cities of the Middle East. Here buildings have historically been oriented inward. Windows facing the public tend to be translucent or shuttered. Perhaps not coincidentally, the Arabic proclivity for family privacy creates cities that are also well suited to hot climates.

A diametrically differing approach is taken in a place like Amsterdam. This quintessential northern European city features large, clear windows facing public streets, moderated only by virtually transparent lace curtains. Revealing private space to the public realm, together with nearly continuous commercial uses on the ground floors, suggests that Amsterdam uniquely expresses community, commerce, and openness.

To emphasize this kind of openness, buildings are often oriented to the public realm, and that realm itself is expansive with streets, pathways, parks, and plazas. Family life and the community's social life are played out in these public places.

To emphasize privacy, as in the Arab world, buildings are focused inward, for example, on a private courtyard. Family life and neighborhood life are then predominantly hidden from public view. Streets often dead-end, to discourage both motor and pedestrian through traffic.

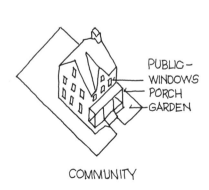

COMMUNITY

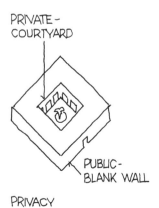

PRIVACY

2. Identity by Economic Resources

Economic resources can also be an important determinant of a city's sense of self as expressed in architecture and design. An economically weak city typically appears unfinished. Lower financial standing often equates with lower buildings and people living at higher densities with little personal space. The infrastructure of water, power, and waste management may also set limits in economically underdeveloped places.

Compensating mechanisms, however, enable the economically challenged city to enhance its individuality and livability by limiting or expanding its private or public realms. In a poorer city, public open spaces may, for example, be very large to provide social room and to compensate for limited personal space. While many cities seem frozen by their economic condition, others consciously compensate by transitioning to higher-quality public environments.

In places with fewer economic resources, an ironic saving grace for a unique city identity can be the tendency to hew more closely to traditional design. Conversely, with wealth often comes the will to modernize, conform, and tear down.

3. Identity by Age and Historic or Cultural Institutions

Regulations are often required to preserve a city's cultural identity. Certain institutions and places may need protection from the pressures of rapid growth and high-density construction. Other sites may require guidelines to ensure that new infill development does not overwhelm or compromise existing cultural institutions or the sense of place. City builders need to identify culturally important parts of cities so that they are not thoughtlessly lost to new development.

Older cities naturally tend to be richer in historic buildings and open spaces. They

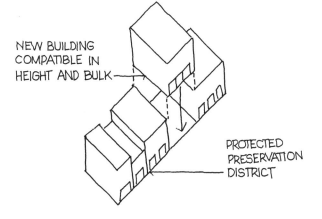

NEW BUILDING COMPATIBLE IN HEIGHT AND BULK

PROTECTED PRESERVATION DISTRICT

similarly have social and religious institutions, such as schools, museums, and churches, that influence behavior and social life. These older built elements, unique buildings, and historic parks often strongly define a city's physical character, as they do in Rome, London, Ho Chi Minh City, and Paris.

Identity by Design

City identity can be established by creating a group of buildings or even a single significant building or open space that stands apart from its context, such as Chicago's Sears and Hancock

Towers, Dubai's Burg Dubai, London's Canary Wharf, or New York's Rockefeller Center. Singular identities can also be created by a similarly scaled repetitive building type, such as the four-story residential units of San Francisco's Telegraph Hill or the forty-plus-story buildings of Hong Kong's residential districts.

City identity can be enhanced by many human-made features other than buildings. Famous streets, for example, provide a powerful sense of place. Chicago's Michigan Avenue, Tokyo's Ginza, London's Mayfair, and New York's Fifth Avenue are identified as premier shopping districts. Cities can be identified by designed open spaces. The National Mall in Washington, DC, and New York's Central Park are examples of elements as iconic and important as the buildings surrounding them. Large-scale public works like San Francisco's Golden Gate Bridge or the smaller-scale public art of Chicago's Picasso sculpture or the Band Shell and Plenum at Millennium Park also establish a world-renowned identity.

Finally, uniqueness can be created by a special sense of arrival or departure. Sometimes this kind of identity is dramatically revealed through a sequence of vistas and landmarks leading the viewer to a destination. The bridges that lead to San Francisco, Shanghai's tall bridges over the Huang Pu River marking the arrival to the city, or the peek-a-boo views of skyscrapers as one approaches Chicago's downtown all enhance this feeling of sequence and arrival.

Identity by Landmarks

Every city should identify the appropriate subjects and locations for landmark treatment. Typically, city landmarks have been places of worship, cultural facilities, civic buildings, tall downtown buildings, major open spaces, streets of citywide importance, and public works such as bridges and transportation terminals. City builders select locations for these icons often for their high visibility and general public accessibility. Key elements for suitable landmarks are the aesthetics of the landmark and the city fabric that forms the background.

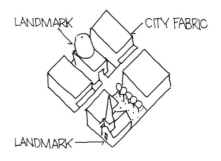

1. Landmark Aesthetics

Landmarks tend to have the largest human-made visual impact on a city. There is, however, a risk that the landmark will not fit in—will be too big, too different from its surroundings, or just plain ugly. Designers must reach a delicate balance to enable a landmark to stand out and at the same time be part of the larger city. Public and peer review have to be of the highest possible standard to reward subtleness and creativity and avoid the inappropriate scale or design.

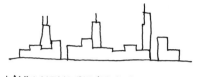

LANDMARKS RELATED TO CITY CONTEXT

LANDMARKS ALIEN TO CITY CONTEXT

2. City Fabric

Every city should identify areas that are suitable for compatible building treatment and note the architectural or natural fabric that gives such an area its uniqueness. The areas of that commonality will vary in building character, landscape, and streetscape, but within each area the compatible treatment should reinforce the area's unique character. Together, the separate and distinctive areas make up the sense of the whole. This overall urban fabric then becomes the background that allows landmarks to stand out. Compatibly developed districts often achieve a landmark status of their own.

LANDMARK CREATED BY COLLECTIVE CITY FABRIC

9.1. Developing Identity in Response to Climate

University of California, Merced

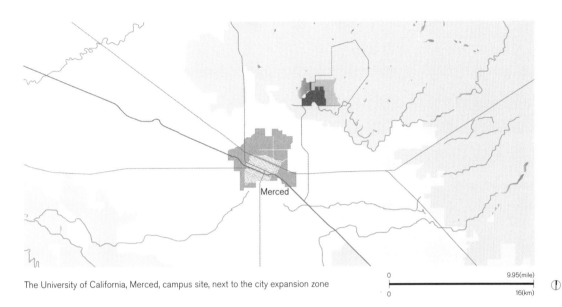

The University of California, Merced, campus site, next to the city expansion zone

Merced

| 0 | 9.95(mile) |
| 0 | 16(km) |

With enrollment beginning in 2005, UC Merced was the first new University of California campus to be built in over forty years. After much political maneuvering and debate, in 1988 the development team began looking for a site for a campus in California's Central Valley. More than eighty-five locations were evaluated. Ultimately, a 2,000-acre plot of former pastureland, donated by a private trust, was chosen.

The Initial Plan

The initial plan for UC Merced called for a campus serving twenty-five thousand students. Academic buildings, dorms, faculty housing, athletic facilities, and parking would be limited to 900 acres. An additional 340 acres were to be kept as a land bank for future development. The remaining 750 acres were permanently dedicated to natural habitat. A critical question posed by the planning of UC Merced was how to establish a meaningful framework to guide long-term campus development and create a sense of completion even in the earliest phases of development.

In previous experiences with campus projects, including UC San Diego, SOM planners had recognized that without a strong development framework these institutions often lapsed into unsustainable patterns of spread-out and disjointed development. For UC Merced, the remedy was to draw on the geometry of institutions like Stanford University, which was based on a simple grid that had worked as the school's organizing framework for nearly a century.

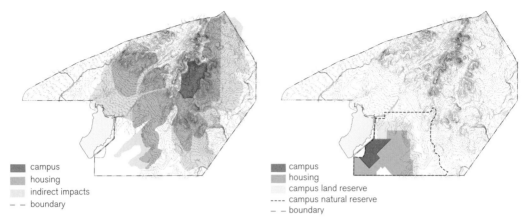

campus
housing
indirect impacts
— — boundary

campus
housing
campus land reserve
---- campus natural reserve
— — boundary

Hilltop campus location: The original campus location atop a hill was determined to contaminate a larger site area as well as extending travel impacts

Lakeside location: The new, compact site set closest to the city and the county park was deemed to have the least negative impact on the environment.

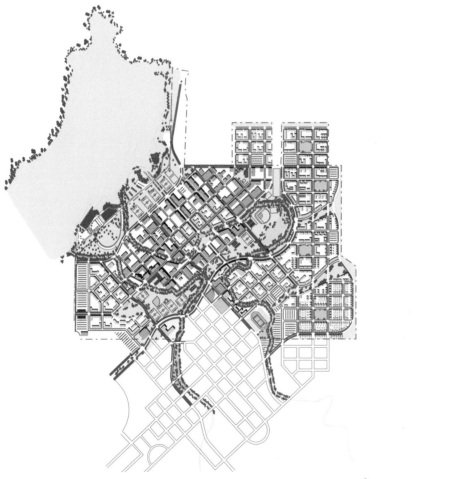

The overall campus plan beside Yosemite Lake, with student and faculty housing, on a mixed regular and irregular grid

0   3/4(mile)

0   1.2(km)

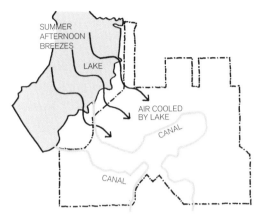

The lake sends cooling afternoon breezes onto the campus.

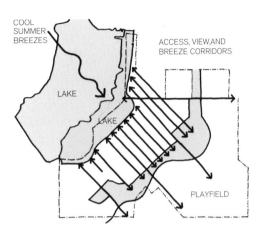

Campus corridors capture the lake breezes and connect the academic core to the park and playfields.

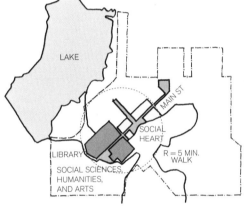

The main street is the campus's social heart and the major cross-campus link for academic neighborhoods.

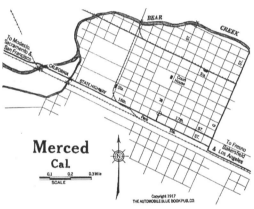

Early-twentieth-century Merced (circa 1917) had a grid similar to that planned for the campus in size and orientation.

Existing irrigation canals at the site were made a part of campus informal parks.

Similarly, in studying settlement patterns of the Merced region, the planning team noted the almost universal application of street grids to define compact urban settlements. As it developed, the plan focused on a simple, understandable grid shaped by the site's natural features. The lake, park, and canals were used as organizing ideas that could be connected to the campus's identity and daily life. The grid created movement corridors that were predictable and extendable. Establishing a grid helped ensure design continuity over what could be a number of decades and new school administrations. The grid concept also helped define the common size of development areas, which would strongly support compatibility among campus buildings over time.

Orientation

Located in the heart of the San Joaquin Valley heat belt, the new UC Merced campus critically needed an orientation that would offer physical comfort as well as institutional identity. Its final siting positioned the campus to exploit the cooling afternoon breeze that regularly blew across nearby Yosemite Lake. The campus grid was varied by landscaping existing irrigation canals that started at the lake and curved, following the topography, through the site. Juxtaposition of the grid with this curvilinear geometry created many varied open spaces and potential building sites.

With all of these ideas falling into place, a difficult and widely relevant question remained: Should the grid be oriented to emphasize access to the site's natural features? Or should it align north-south to minimize the sun's impact on the indoor temperature of the

Aerial view of the campus plan

buildings? A true north-south orientation is of indisputable value in virtually all arid climates. The north façade then receives no sun; the east façade is subject to the low-angle morning sun when the temperature is not yet high; and the south façade gets high-angle sun, which can be shaded by architectural features. The west façade presents the most difficult challenge, receiving low-angle sun during the hottest time of day.

Ultimately, at UC Merced, planners chose the lake orientation, to emphasize the connection of the natural features to the academic core. In deciding on this orientation, they considered the following arguments: The building orientation already provided maximum shadow while channeling the afternoon breezes to the pedestrian pathways between buildings. The planned landscape of large trees would further shade both buildings and pathways. The building façades would be protected by architectural treatments such as arcades, recessed windows, shading devices, and building materials; this result is visible in the three buildings of UC Merced's phase one. The lake orientation thus created a powerful and unifying architectural expression that was also climate responsive. The chosen orientation matched the experience of many of California's Central Valley cities, including Merced, which were not aligned truly north-south, yet functioned successfully, long before energy-consuming air conditioning was available.

Phase One

Phase one of the plans for the Merced campus would set the initial impression through which the campus would long be identified. To ensure that this "first take" was positive, early campus construction was designed to create an environment perceived as complete unto itself. Visual focus was achieved, to begin with, by designing an entry into the campus that gave a landmark view of the site along a main street, with student housing and services on one side and a view of the campus's lakes, canals, and sports fields on the other. The simple, yet majestic, view was designed to sweep down toward the city of Merced in the distance.

The Academic Core

The academic core of the campus was designed to be as compact as possible, to promote easy walks from class to class. Instead of locating student unions, faculty clubs, and administration buildings separately, the plan instead drew inspiration from the "main street" layout of nearby Central Valley towns. The plan thus established UC Merced's social heart as just such a main street, with student and faculty services at ground level and student housing above.

The First Quadrangle

The UC Merced entry road was designed to lead up to a five-story bluff on which the campus's first quad was set. The quad, heavily shaded by trees and closed off by buildings on three sides, had a commanding view on the fourth side. It was designed as both an informal place where students could sit and study, and a formal setting where official events such as graduations could be held.

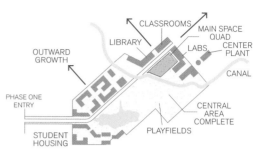

The first three buildings enclose the main quad. The open end of the quad provides distant views to the city of Merced.

Phase one buildings frame major open spaces.

The library building illustrates architectural guidelines to prevent solar heat gain by using recessed glass, glass louvers, roof overhangs, and shaded arcades.

The environmental guidelines for buildings unify the structures while allowing them separate identities.

View to academic main quad from student housing and athletic playfield area

9.2. Responding to Climate and Culture
Yanbu, Saudi Arabia

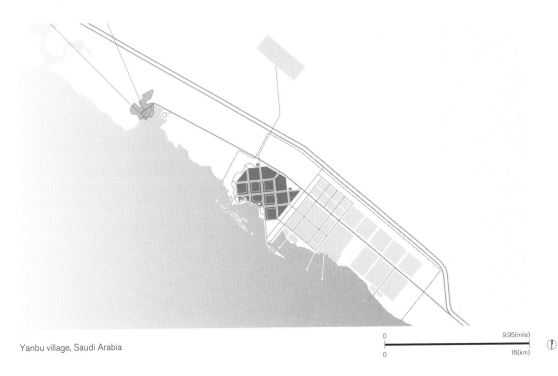

Yanbu village, Saudi Arabia

0		9.95(mile)
0		16(km)

Over the last half of the twentieth century, creating new cities became the option of choice in addressing urban growth, just as urban infill is likely to be the twenty-first century's growth mode of choice. While starting from scratch confronts city designers with entirely new sets of planning, phasing, and development issues, it also provides an opportunity to solve some of the most difficult issues of growth management.

In many parts of the world, particularly in the Far East, new cities have been established as part of a nation's economic growth policy, population growth management plan, or both. The impetus to build a new city typically evolves from such factors as new industrial development, increased tourism, or a growing need for affordable housing. In a number of related projects, particularly in the Middle East, new cities have been built to support development of the petrochemical industry and related port facilities. Such was the case of Yanbu, a new city on Saudi Arabia's west coast. In 1977 the Saudi government commissioned SOM to design Yanbu, a city of 150,000 to be built on the Red Sea coast. The central issue for Yanbu was to plan a midsized city that would be a good place to live and work despite a harsh desert climate, lack of amenities, and the disruptions of construction during early development phases.

From the start, to establish a strong sense of place, the plan located Yanbu's city center on the water, with new residential neighborhoods surrounding it. Yanbu's civic heart was designed

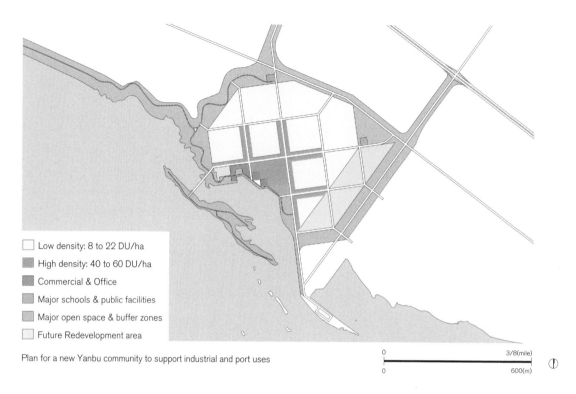

Low density: 8 to 22 DU/ha

High density: 40 to 60 DU/ha

Commercial & Office

Major schools & public facilities

Major open space & buffer zones

Future Redevelopment area

Plan for a new Yanbu community to support industrial and port uses

0   3/8(mile)

0   600(m)

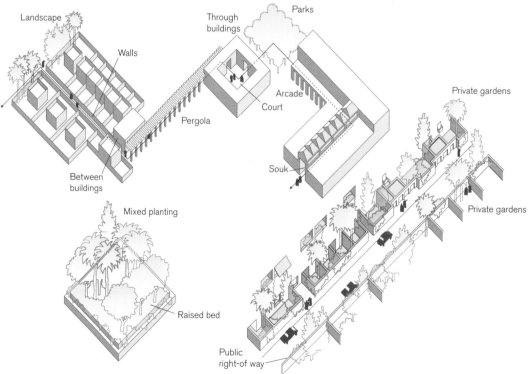

Landscape

Walls

Through buildings

Parks

Pergola

Court

Arcade

Souk

Private gardens

Between buildings

Private gardens

Mixed planting

Raised bed

Public right-of way

Places of shade created by architecture and landscape

to unite the main mosque, souk (marketplace), Royal Commission headquarters, and office buildings around a single open space connecting all civic, cultural, commercial, and work functions. The overall plan was organized on a 1,400-meter grid pattern defining individual neighborhoods that each included places of worship, educational facilities, which require separate schools for boys and girls, and a self-sustaining commercial infrastructure.

Like many large developments, Yanbu did not evolve entirely according to the master plan. The town's waterfront center, for example, developed more slowly than its residential neighborhoods. This partly reflected the fact that the city's early residents still preferred to drive south to the city of Jeddah, where they were in the habit of doing their major shopping. This drew much of the local commerce away from the new city center and instead to the highway leading to Jeddah.

The open spaces and landscaping for Yanbu were largely predicated on finding ways to mitigate a particularly harsh desert climate. The hot, dry environment led first to a street grid aligned with the coastline, an orientation selected to minimize exposure to the sun and maximize the cooling effect of the offshore breeze. This was followed by three other general techniques for promoting comfort in harsh climates: use of water elements, shadow, and breeze. Attached, rather than separate, buildings were favored, to limit surface exposure to the sun. Oriented to the water, Yanbu's streets also doubled as a storm drainage system without the need for underground drains.

Yanbu's dry climate and poor soil conditions made landscaping expensive and difficult to maintain. At the same time, the design team understood that vegetation was essential to relieve the harsh environment and temper the rawness of a new city. The landscape plan was thus designed to maximize the effectiveness and utility of its open space with a minimum of planting.

An extremely limited water supply demanded a new approach to landscaping. Three general principles applied.

Raised beds with dense plantings

Pergola-shaded walkways

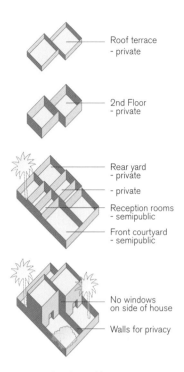

Roof terrace
- private

2nd Floor
- private

Rear yard
- private

- private

Reception rooms
- semipublic

Front courtyard
- semipublic

No windows
on side of house

Walls for privacy

Privacy planning for villas and for apartments

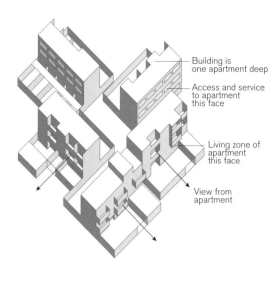

Building is
one apartment deep

Access and service
to apartment
this face

Living zone of
apartment
this face

View from
apartment

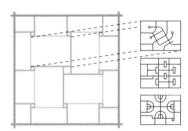

Neighborhood subdivisions are 1-mile square and are subdivided
by a secondary grid of streets. Inside the secondary grid, a variety
of residential neighborhood plans are encouraged.

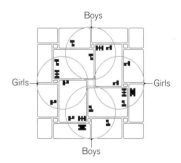

Boys

Girls

Girls

Boys

Schools are grouped in gender-separated K–12 clusters.

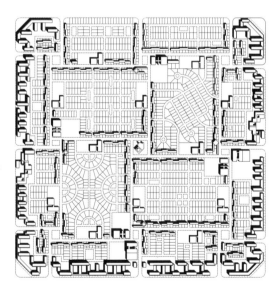

A synthesis residential module shows higher-density residential
buildings framing the primary and secondary street grids.

1. Shadow: Landscape elements such as trees, trellises, and walls were located to create maximum shade for walkways, courtyards, and buildings.

2. Shared Landscape: Trees were planted in private gardens fronting public streets, to help shade the public pathways.

3. Grouping: Trees in public parks were planted in clumps comparable to desert oases, to maximize visual shading effects as well as help protect the trees from wind and erosion.

In Saudi Arabia as well as in neighboring countries, there is a strong cultural requirement for family privacy. Typically, each home is zoned with private, family-only rooms as well as semiprivate rooms for meeting visitors. Views to and from a home are internally focused. Neighboring windows are never seen; residents look instead into their own walled gardens or courtyards.

Groups of these homes were similarly arranged into neighborhoods established inside a walkable primary transportation grid of 1.4 kilometers (1 mile). These neighborhoods were planned to divert through traffic around them. They were also designed to be populated densely enough to support services and K–12 schools that are physically separate for girls and boys.

In designing new cities, planners always encounter special problems, particularly when strong cultural requirements need to be met. In Yanbu, for example, building a city of 150,000 people over a short period of time also required addressing the needs of an initial population that was young, with few children and with a high number of expatriates or foreign nationals. The framework plan for the city was thus meant to avoid cultural clashes as well as to allow the city to easily evolve into the family size and population mix typical of other Saudi cities.

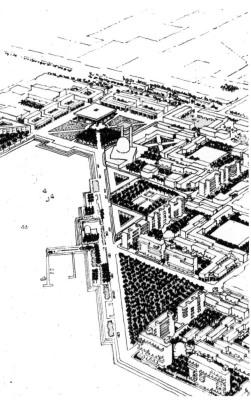

View of the community center, Royal Commission headquarters, main mosque, and souk, which are the community's civic and social heart.

9.3. Creating a New Downtown Identity
Beijing Financial Street, China

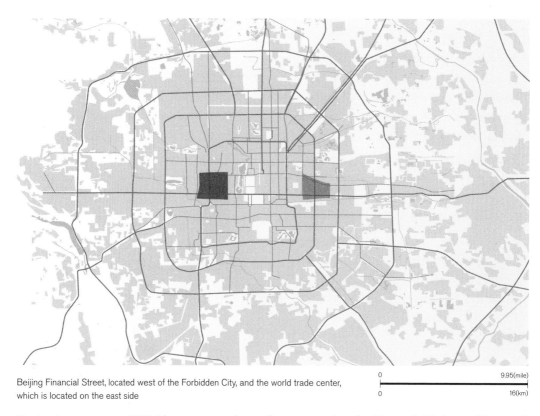

Beijing Financial Street, located west of the Forbidden City, and the world trade center, which is located on the east side

0   9.95(mile)

0   16(km)

Beginning in 2004, SOM began an update of a master plan for Beijing's Xicheng (Western) District, which had been created a decade earlier. The focus of the study was to develop a new set of principles for the area around what was being called the Beijing Financial Street. Spearheaded by the Bank of China, this project was designed to create a new downtown district in Beijing that could, in essence, become the city's financial center.

What had actually been created over a ten-year period, however, was a street without a real sense of place or point of arrival. A key task thus became to determine what would be necessary to create a vibrant, connected, and interconnected urban neighborhood rather than merely a new street with tall buildings.

The first question was whether the city of Beijing could actually support two downtowns. On the city's East Side was the Central Business District, where most of Beijing's commerce took place. Because of factors such as an underdeveloped transit system, however, the CBD was reaching the saturation point for new development.

For affirmation that cities could indeed support multiple business districts, planners had only to point to places like Manhattan, Tokyo, Los Angeles, and London, which, like Beijing, were all supporting populations above 10 million. Those examples made clear that each successful "alternate downtown" possessed its own identity and purpose. In London, for example, the Canary Wharf business district was defined as the European headquarters of many of the world's major international trading and brokerage firms. Typically, each of these downtowns was compact, walkable, and well-served by transit.

With this in mind, the SOM team analyzed how Beijing's West Side might differ in purpose from the East Side central district and then how that distinction could illuminate a new overall approach to development. Although the East Side had long been Beijing's commercial center, the West Side, near Tiananmen Square, had historically been the seat of government. This had encouraged the growth of services and businesses that focused on the needs of government throughout historical eras. Clearly this was a location where government and business uses could support each other, a powerful rationale for planning Beijing's alternative downtown.

With the theme of connectivity in mind, planners further considered why the West Side had not developed as planned in the 1990s, and what could be done now to facilitate growth. The obvious problem was the layout of Beijing's overall street grid. The city was divided into a series of giant blocks, each containing more or less haphazard filaments of fine-grained, almost villagelike, streets and alleyways.

Missing was a healthy grid of secondary streets to help take the pressure off increasingly crowded main roads while intelligently connecting them to the fine-grained environment. By breaking up the big blocks, these secondary streets would shorten routes, greatly ease traffic, and reduce pressure on the primary roads.

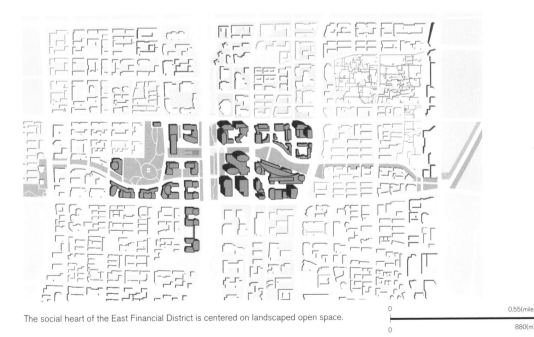

The social heart of the East Financial District is centered on landscaped open space.

0   0.55(mile)

0   880(m)

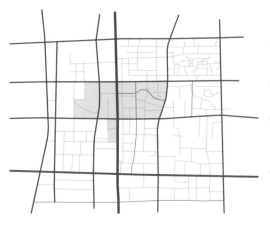

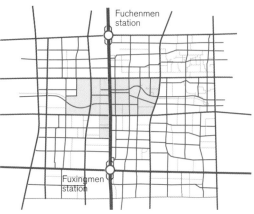

The existing large-scale grid of wide streets is subject to daily traffic gridlock.

The proposal adds narrower streets to better distribute traffic.

Hotel and retail uses are on the south edge of the central open space.

Landscaped steps connect lower levels to the central open space.

Diversity of open-space treatments at the district center

Another important missing element was a mix of uses. The offices that had originally been built on the Beijing Financial Street were highly repetitive in both look and use, and they lacked a 24-hour social and cultural hub. To mitigate the uniform office use, planners designed an open-space corridor at the district's center leading from a transit station to a park. The park was framed by recreational, commercial, cultural, and service functions and connected to the fine grain of streets of the surrounding neighborhood. The central park and its framing landmark towers created a social and economic heart and identity for the larger district, which now has the potential to grow organically into the world-class financial district envisioned a decade before.

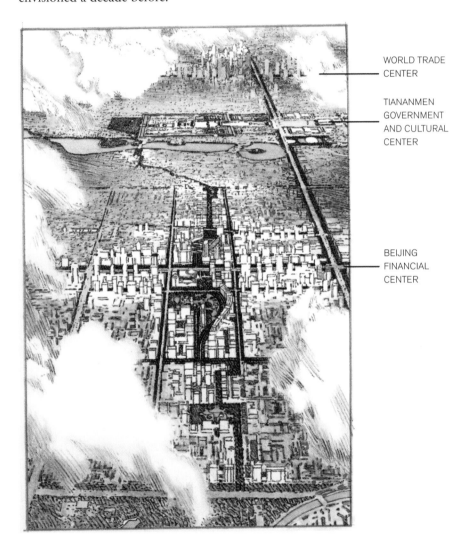

WORLD TRADE
CENTER

TIANANMEN
GOVERNMENT
AND CULTURAL
CENTER

BEIJING
FINANCIAL
CENTER

9.4. Harnessing the Potential of the Waterfront

Huang Pu River, Shanghai, China

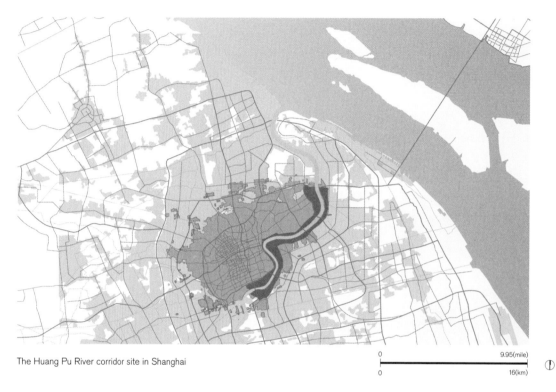

The Huang Pu River corridor site in Shanghai

0   9.95(mile)
0   16(km)

The Huang Pu River is to Shanghai what the Thames is to London and the Mississippi to St. Louis: the most prominent economic and natural feature and a unique source of both commerce and civic identity. The Huang Pu can also be thought of as an important open space providing visual relief from some of the world's densest development.

In the early 1990s SOM city builders crafted a proposal for the Shanghai Planning Institute that has become that city's basic document for waterfront redevelopment. The scope of the project was enormous, including 10 miles of the Huang Pu's waterfront, extending back into the city on both sides of the river for as much as 1,000 meters. The SOM Huang Pu River Waterfront Plan was selected in an international competition and is being incrementally realized. Its citywide public benefits are numerous, and it has enabled a number of new and creative urban redevelopment schemes along the riverfront.

Shanghai is bisected by the Huang Pu, China's most important trade artery, a river traversed yearly by thousands of large oceangoing ships. Shanghai's waterfront is China's largest port and grew, during a time of intensive industrialization, into a massive industrial area, largely walled off from the rest of the city. As containerization changed the nature of port activity, Shanghai city officials were given a unique opportunity to redevelop the port and maximize its benefit to the city as a whole. With a new and larger port facility being built north of downtown on the Yangtze, Shanghai was able to repurpose the old port.

The planning effort for Shanghai's historic waterfront was defined by two major principles. The first was to ensure maximum public access to the waterfront and visual access along its shoreline. The second was to extend to the shoreline major existing shopping streets that led to the river. These thoroughfares could then be transformed into neighborhood centers and gathering places. The plan called for them to be served by water taxi terminals, new services, and amenities. The plan also defined various types of open space to be developed on the waterfront, including park systems along the smaller waterways flowing into the Huang Pu.

Visually, the overall waterfront plan exploited the curving geometry of the Huang Pu, which presents outstanding views of river bridges, Pudong's soaring towers, the Bund, and other city landmarks. The neighborhood plans were also based on creating and maintaining views, best realized by varying building massings, setbacks, scales, and special uses. By promoting different building characteristics for these purposes, the plan established a unique identity for each new, view-rich shoreline neighborhood.

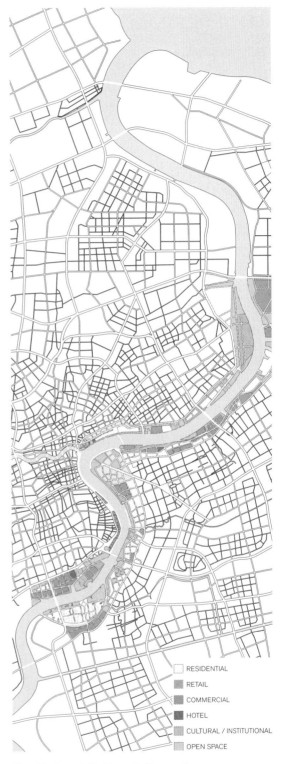

RESIDENTIAL
RETAIL
COMMERCIAL
HOTEL
CULTURAL / INSTITUTIONAL
OPEN SPACE

Plan of land uses in the Huang Pu River corridor

0   15/4(mile)

0   6(km)

Public access to the waterfront

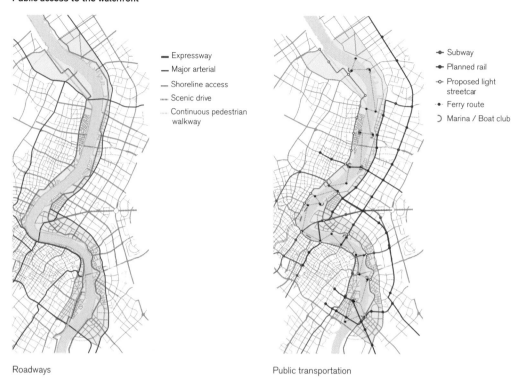

Expressway
Major arterial
Shoreline access
Scenic drive
Continuous pedestrian walkway

Subway
Planned rail
Proposed light streetcar
Ferry route
Marina / Boat club

Roadways

Public transportation

Shoreline open space
Regional open space

Open space

Commercial node
Commercial district
Commercial corridor

Gathering places

The Huang Pu River as Shanghai's central public open space

A grade change separates the public shoreline from hotels' semi-public open space.

The river's curving geometry allows views downriver to city landmarks.

Gathering spaces connect the city to the waterfront.

Open space extends views of the waterfront deep into shoreline neighborhoods.

Part III:
The City of the Future/ The Future of the City

The City Is the Solution (Not the Problem)

This book began with Lewis Mumford's powerful observation, "With language itself, the city remains man's greatest work of art." It ends with it as well, because, from first to last, city builders are lovers of the aesthetic, the design, the life, the physical, cultural, and social texture that is the essence of the city. Urban life may not be a panacea, but contrary to the twentieth-century critics—who viewed the city as the medium of plagues, poverty, heretical thinking, crime, and gridlock—I believe that enlightened city planning can be an important way to solve many of the problems that confront society in these still-foundational years of the twenty-first century.

The city, in fact, is a font of saving solutions for humankind because the way that urban settlement takes place links virtually all other environmental and social concerns. How humans come together in cities is nothing less than a key to the long-term stewardship of the land, air, water, and energy use, as well as to habitat preservation, health, security, and positive social interaction. Particularly in the face of the current—and long overdue—response to climate change, planners need to think ever more forcefully in terms of the city's ability to provide sustainable solutions.

A New Urban Model

Even if the earth's population was not increasing so rapidly, and its resources not being burned through at such a rate, people would still need a handbook for twenty-first-century city building. Possibly the urgency would be less, and designers might have been content tinkering at the margins of the low-density, monocultural, auto-dependent lifestyle that is not only the suburban reality in North America but also the ideal in much of the rest of the world. This model might have worked if population growth had remained at its mid-twentieth-century levels. It has not: 1 billion became 3 billion and then 6 billion. It seems likely that by 2050, 6 billion will become 10 billion. There are some hopeful trends, including the decline in birthrate in the developing world, a surprising consequence of the increasingly popular microloan programs, which enable women to start small businesses and, critically, take control of both their finances and their biology.

Like it or not, however, life in the future will be lived at urban densities. As noted at the beginning of this book, the first decade of the twenty-first century was the milestone at which a majority of the human race began living in cities.

With urban life inevitable, it makes sense to identify and then implement ways to make its structure as livable as possible. This means creating urban settings that are healthy, clean, energy-efficient, exciting, and minimal in their carbon footprint; it demands a daily life at work and home that strives to stay in balance with natural and human ecology. Designing and building sound, motivating, life-affirming cities requires that the architecture and planning not be fragmented or project-based. Instead, design needs to exist, and be measurable, at scales ranging from the personal to the planetary. As planners, designers, and architects, we cannot limit our vision to isolated, single-use projects: we need to focus our energies on how these works can lead to healthy and sustainable settlement on the land. We also need to take into account the changes to our cities—inevitable now—from global climate change and the consequent rise in sea level.

A Developmental Moore's Law

One of the great ironies of the last half-century is that, armed with what seemed like limitless energy, ideas, and materials, we wound up building sprawling, auto-centric cities that, we now see, were tenable only if hydrocarbons remained inexpensive and without environmental impacts. Perhaps that irony can be made to stretch another way: that, in a climate of energy shortage and economic limitations, we find ways to build better cities based on those very limitations. Perhaps we will discover a city-building equivalent of Moore's Law: that just as the power of microprocessors is exponentially increasing, so our ability to design more livable cities will increase in relation to their growing density and urban richness.

Learning from Asia

To see how density and urbanity can complement each other, it makes sense to examine city building at its most intensive and extensive, which is to say in Asia during the last decade. Whereas in North America the requirement to urbanize has been buffered by a plentiful supply of land and superhighway-induced suburban growth, in Asia, and particularly China, urbanization has been and continues to be in crisis mode. Development in North America has appeared to be almost static, while in Asia the rate of change is rapid and enormous. We can see, virtually in real time, how the Chinese government is grappling, for example, with the need to provide infrastructure for the most people at the lowest possible expense and greatest possible speed. In the pressurized realm of Chinese development, not only are the positive aspects of compact urbanization on display, but also the mistakes are magnified and sped up.

Chongming Island is a Chinese project that exemplifies the need for thoughtful development in a context that Americans and others should study and understand. The key to Chongming, why it is so important, is the imperative to keep the land largely agricultural in the face of seemingly inevitable massive Shanghai urbanization. Recognizing a limited supply of prime agricultural land, a history of famine, and the increasing cost of transportation,

Chinese officials understood the importance of maintaining agricultural uses close to its cities. Even as the United States enjoys the bounty of fruits and vegetables flown by jet from Chile, wisdom suggests that imitating China's protection of agricultural lands close to cities for social survival insurance would be prudent, to say the least.

Other developmental lessons from China are more problematic. In Shanghai, for example, development has tended toward strip high-rises fronting major roads and avenues. The problem is that signature high-rises now string far out into the suburbs, defeating critical principles of compact, walkable, transit-served neighborhood development. The antidote lies in projects such as Xintiandi, which give a recognizable and desirable identity to transit-rich neighborhoods that concentrate development and celebrate density.

Similarly, projects like Saigon South show how development can be used both to take pressure off historic neighborhoods and to build adequate infrastructure and amenities, like power stations, transportation corridors, environmentally sound waterways, and walkable neighborhoods. Taken together, these elements offer a positive model for developing Vietnam's urban future.

The Need for a Framework for Settlement

At the beginning of the twenty-first century, we are overwhelmed with environmental challenges. A highly simplified list might include the following:

1. Environmental exploitation and overconsumption, energy waste, degradation of land, pollution and misuse of air and water resources.

2. Traffic congestion, gridlock, time lost in travel, gated and walled-off neighborhoods, auto dependence, lack of pedestrian safety and comfort.

3. Degraded support services, lack of visual interest, unsatisfying environments, lack of affordability.

4. Loss of natural habitat, inadequate recreational space, overbearing buildings and hardscapes.

5. Out-of-place, discordant, and confusing neighborhoods and buildings.

6. Cities and neighborhoods in economic decline, with underused infrastructure and empty buildings.

7. An environment that is resistant to change in size or use, rigid, or unnecessarily costly to fix.

8. Sprawling urban development over valuable, irreplaceable land, long-distance commutes that waste time and energy.

9. Environmental sameness, repetition of elements, lack of identity that gives a sense of being lost, illogical and hard-to-comprehend places.

This list is long and by no means comprehensive. To attack the problems separately seems daunting and open to unforeseen consequences. The question arises: by solving one problem, do we make the others worse?

So, where to start?

The answer I have pursued in my city-building practice and in this book is to strive to create and implement a sustainable and livable framework for settlement. City builders must intelligently guide where and how people settle on the land as they renew and rebuild cities in the twenty-first century.

In our work on building cities, my colleagues and I have established the nine principles for making livable and sustainable cities that I describe and illustrate in this book. Each deals with a different subject area. In the end, however, all are interrelated and mutually reinforcing. By now, I hope, readers will recognize them as familiar and desirable, if not necessary, goals.

I hope that these principles help readers as they have helped me to focus, organize, and simplify the tangled, often incomprehensible mess we identify as the current global environment and development crises. As the nine principles reinforce one another, they also provide multiple arguments for making cities sustainable and livable. It is the inter-connectedness of the principles that gives them their power both in attracting public support and in the ultimate development process. They are foundational to the work of building cities, prerequisite building blocks of the city builder's craft.

One: Sustainability

Sustainability can be defined in terms of a commitment to an environmental ethic. As a separate principle, sustainability means taking responsibility for stewardship of the land by providing a way to eliminate or reduce damaging patterns of consumption of nonrenewable resources. More specific ways to achieve sustainability are addressed and reinforced by each of the other principles.

Two: Accessibility

Accessibility is defined as facilitating the movement of goods and people. As a separate principle, it argues for a new emphasis on safe and comfortable foot traffic. The automobile's domination of travel in many world regions has compromised walking, bicycling, and transit travel. Accessible movement is ultimately aided by remaking streets to better serve these missing modes of travel.

The principle of accessibility supports sustainable behavior by keeping cities compact as opposed to sprawling and by concentrating work destinations to make transit feasible for home-to-work travel. Accessibility serves the goals of preserving open land, reducing energy waste, improving air quality, and shortening commute times.

Three: Diversity

Diversity is defined as maximum variety and choice in an urban environment. It is axiomatic that the best cities offer their citizens the most diverse choices that can be practically supported. The principle of diversity supports sustainability by promoting the widest variety of choices for employment and education and by maintaining affordable choices for living and working. By contributing to city livability and attractiveness as a place to live, diversity is inherently sustainable. Diversity supports accessibility by arguing for the benefits of multiple travel modes. Diversity supports the principle of identity by promoting a city's visual variety in a mix of buildings old and new, large and small, and everywhere promoting separately identifiable places and buildings.

Four: Open Space

Open space is a principle defined as regenerating natural and human-made systems to make cities verdant. All open-space systems reinforce sustainability goals. Making cities and their surrounding regions as green as possible provides wildlife habitats, protects agricultural land, and improves air quality. In hot climates, open space can reduce outdoor temperature; in cold climates, it can buffer and moderate wind chill and allow more sun to reach public spaces. Open space supports diversity by creating a variety of green softening effects within urban hardscapes. It also supports the principle of identity by protecting natural features such as shorelines, hills, and important views that help create a city's unique sense of place.

Five: Compatibility

Compatibility relates to the ability to maintain visual harmony and balance among a city's built elements. This principle is important as a guide for designing new buildings to fit in with existing neighborhoods and districts. Tools for compatibility include standards for height, bulk, setbacks, materials, and building character. These help avoid the visually destructive juxtaposition of buildings of widely varying dimensions and styles. Compatibility supports the principle of sustainability by keeping neighborhoods attractive and desirable places to live and work. Neighborhoods of compatible buildings and landscape also support the principle of identity by maintaining their distinctive sense of place.

Six: Incentives

Incentives are defined as ways to renew declining cities and rebuild underused industrial brownfields. Incentives can support sustainability by promoting reuse of empty buildings, unused infrastructure, and land made toxic by industrial pollution. Incentives also relate to accessibility, open space, and density, and all of those may be used as incentives to attract new investment for sustainable renewal.

Seven: Adaptability

Adaptability can be defined as facilitating wholeness and positive change. As a principle, its purpose is to anticipate change by making buildings, streets, and blocks adaptable to new uses and even eventual replacement. Adaptability ensures that change can take place at minimum cost and disruption to nearby uses. Adaptability recognizes the often-overlooked factor that cities are in constant change. It supports sustainability by facilitating renewal of cities to achieve greater density and higher environmental standards.

Eight: Density

Density is defined as compact, highly accessible concentrations of people at home and at work. A primary reason for density is to make transit service feasible, neighborhoods walkable, and convenient neighborhood services supportable. Density supports sustainability by reducing the land needed for population growth in expanding suburbs. Density relates to incentives because it is often used to attract new investments. Density also relates to the principle of compatibility in that high-density, tall building districts have to taper down to fit within the scale of their surroundings.

Nine: Identity

Identity is defined as a unique and memorable sense of place. The purpose of identity is to make every city distinct from other cities and to create and preserve the special character of neighborhoods and districts. A unique sense of place can be established by protecting natural features such as rivers, harbors, forests, and hills, which, as part of the ecology, support sustainability. Cities in hot climates may gain identity by planting drought-resistant landscape and designing shading devices for buildings, which reduce energy and water consumption, promoting sustainability. Unique urban identity can also be saved by conserving local culture—preserving and reusing historic buildings and identifiable places. These techniques also contribute to the diversity of buildings and their neighborhoods.

Taken together, these broad and interrelated principles establish a sustainable and livable framework for settlement. Though the examples above are not exhaustive in their detail, they do communicate their interrelatedness. The nine principles promote a comprehensive approach to the long list of challenges facing humanity in the twenty-first century.

Refocusing Planning Theory and Practice

For some planners, the emphasis here on principles of city building may seem "pie in the sky." How can we realistically achieve the goals of intelligent city building, given the almost universal appeal of the single-family suburban home with private lawn, garden, and adjacent open spaces?

The answer is that while there will always be people who choose low-density living, the solution is primarily a matter of emphasis. Over many years, the best urban design talent in North America has focused on designing new suburban neighborhoods. By now, this movement has spread worldwide and has unfortunately increased the taking of rural land to accomodate population growth. Increasingly neglected are new approaches to making cities, large and small, better. The world needs a new vision and increasing choices to create highly desirable, higher-density city neighborhoods that can compete with the appeal of suburbs.

Rethinking Single-Purpose Design Education and Problem Solving

One reason for the lack of overall, comprehensive plans to create dense, transit-endowed neighborhoods is the fact that architecture education tends to focus on "the building," landscape education on "the open space," planning education on "the regulatory framework."

By remaining largely disconnected, the design disciplines are unable—and often unwilling—to consider the overall idea and ideal that is crucial to all of them: the design of sustainable human settlements. In this respect things have changed little since the days of the California Tomorrow Plan, which argued that planning needed to focus not on the symptoms but on the underlying causes of environmental dysfunction.

Future answers are not likely to be found within individual disciplines but, as Nathaniel Owings suggested, in "the spaces in between" and the connections between them. Design and planning require not so much a new aesthetic as a recognition of the unique relationships that define sustainability, livability, and perhaps even survivability. Academics today speak of the power of interdisciplinary thinking, but in the "real world" the professional design focus remains within the "silo" of individual disciplines, where the rewards of career advancement are still stubbornly centered. Creating an educational system that connects the various design disciplines will help close the gap in a profession that largely fails to understand the importance of city design issues at the highest, most wide-ranging, and interrelated scales.

A Call for National Plans

In my mind, there is no question about the link between successful city design and environmental sustainability. The number of people who occupy space on this earth continues to grow. Much of what is being built today will likely need to double in size and square footage over the next 20 years. At the same time, some cities will experience serious population decline because of the loss of jobs, and reclaimed land along urban waterfronts will likely be subject to rising sea levels and more intense storms.

This slow march toward ecological imbalance cannot be remedied without a comprehensive plan for the use of land, air, and water in cities, regions, and nations. The need for national land-use planning is absolute. It requires leadership in nations around the world to undertake a planetary inventory, the first step in creating a sustainable world with a base of knowledge about population and resources.

To implement planning at this scale will require altering some governmental structures and mechanisms. It almost certainly will change current approaches to public and private spending, alter lifestyles, and demand new ways of thinking. It will be no easy task.

Conclusion

Finally, to get personal, I hope that the ideas contained in this work provide some new insights and tools, and encourage people, especially architects, landscape architects, and planners, to step up and view their discipline in the context of city building. Ultimately, sustainable, livable city design does not come from complex statistics, functional problem solving, or particular decision-making processes. Successful cities instead come from advocating easily understood human values about the sensory qualities of the environment and then designing to transform those qualities into sustainable realities. The nine principles can be applied globally, recognizing that they will vary by local climate, culture, and geography. I hope that the projects chosen to illustrate the principles provide a "way of work," showing how cities can be designed, built, and rebuilt to create human habitation that is sustainable, humane, and a gift to future generations. Now, that is an effort worth undertaking.

Project Credits

Many people have contributed to the career experiences that have led to this book. Of them, I want to note eight up front—Jerry Goldberg, Marc Goldstein, Craig Hartman, Alan Jacobs, Ellen Lou, Kathrin Moore, and Carolina Woo. They and a host of others who participated in specific projects are noted in the credits that follow. I must also acknowledge Keiko Nakagawa for helping prepare the project images and Peter Bosselmann for the use of his city mapping research.

1.1 The Federal Service Systems for National Land Use
Client: U.S. Bureau of Land Management

Plan prepared by:
Skidmore, Owings & Merrill, San Francisco
Nathaniel Owings, Management
Jerry Goldberg, Planning
John Kriken, Urban Design

1.2 The California Tomorrow Plan
Client: California Tomorrow, Alfred Heller, President

Plan prepared by:
Skidmore, Owings & Merrill, San Francisco
Marc Goldstein, Director
John Kriken, Urban Design and Sketches
Jerry Goldberg, Planning and Management
Christopher Adams, Planning

Consultants:
Samuel E. Woods
John W. Abbot

Members of Plan Task Force:
Alfred Heller, William Bronson, Willie Brown, Sumar Elshar, Theodore Foin, Nathaniel Owings, Victor Palmieri, Harvey Perloff, William Roth, Frank Stead, Kenneth Watt, Samuel Woods

Photo: Marin Headlands, Larry Orman

1.3 The Chongming Island Master Plan
Client: Shanghai International Tendering Co., Ltd.

Plan prepared by:
Skidmore, Owings & Merrill, Chicago
Philip Enquist, Urban Design and Planning
Peter Kindel, Urban Design and Planning
Jeannine Colaco, Graphic Design
Robert Forest, Management
Thomas Kerwin, Management

Consultant: Norman Kondy, Illustrator

1.4 The Bahrain National Plan
Client: Kingdom of Bahrain, Economic Development Board

Plan prepared by:
Skidmore, Owings & Merrill, Chicago
Philip Enquist, Urban Design and Planning
George J. Efstathiou, Director
Alexander Barker, Management
Daniel R. Ringelstein, Planning
Peter Kindel, Planning
Graham J. Wiseman, Management

Consultants:
Atkins Environmental Engineering
Battle McCarthy
DTZ Pieda Consulting
HR Wallingford
JMP Consultants
MSCEB Architects & Engineers

2.1 The Baltimore Expressway Plan
Client: State Road Commission of Maryland in cooperation with the U.S. Department of Transportation

Plan prepared by:
Skidmore, Owings & Merrill, Washington, DC
J. E. Greiner Company, Inc.
Parsons Brinkerhoff Quade & Douglas
Wilbur Smith Associates

2.2 Canary Wharf, London
Client: Canary Wharf Contractors, Canary Wharf Group, PLC

Plan prepared by:
Skidmore, Owings & Merrill, Chicago
Philip Enquist, Urban Design and Planning
Adrian Smith, Architectural Design
William F. Baker, Structural
Drohmer Korista, Structural
Edward Thompson, Management
Todd Halamka, Architectural Design
Jason Stanley, Technical Coordinator
Anwar Hakim, Technical Coordinator
Jeffrey J. McCarthy, Project Management

2.3 The Treasure Island Master Plan, San Francisco, California
Client:
Kenwood Investments, LLC
Lennar Corporation
Mayor's Office of Business and Economic Development
Treasure Island Community Development, LLC
Treasure Island Development Authority
Wilson Meany Sullivan

Plan prepared by:
Skidmore, Owings & Merrill, San Francisco
Craig W. Hartman, Architectural and Urban Design
John Kriken, Urban Design and Planning
Mark Tiscornia, Management
Bill Paluch, Design Architect
Carrie Byles, Management

Consultants:
Aidan Hughes, Arup
Hans Baldauf, Baldauf Catton Von Eckartsberg Architects
Chris Von Eckartsberg, Baldauf Catton Von Eckartsberg

Architects:
Kevin Conger, CMG
Christopher Guillard, CMG
Concept Marin Associates
ENGEO, Inc.
Mark Hornberger, Hornberger + Worstell
Korve Engineering
SMWM
Tom Leader Studio Landscape
Treadwell & Rollo

2.4 State Street, Chicago, Illinois
Client:
City of Chicago

Plan prepared by:
Skidmore, Owings & Merrill, Chicago
Philip Enquist, Urban Design and Planning
Adrian Smith, Architectural Design
Paul DeCelles, Management
Peter Van Vecten, Architectural Design
Kevin Pierce, Architectural Design
John Zils, Structural Engineer
Robert Wesley, Management

Consultants:
Baker Heavy & Highway, Inc.
Rust Environmental & Infrastructure
Avila & Associates, Inc.
Consoer Townsend Envirodyne Engineers, Inc.
Culture Walk
DuSable, Inc.
McLean Design Corporation
O'Brien & Associates, Inc.
Schuler Shook, Inc.
Wolff Clements & Associates

2.5 Far East Side, Detroit, Michigan
Client: Kimball Hill Homes

Plan prepared by:
Skidmore, Owings & Merrill, Chicago
Philip Enquist, Urban Design and Planning
Christopher Hall, Management
Andre Brumfield, Planning
Etka Naik, Urban Design
Matthew Stegmaier, Urban Design
Richard F. Tomlinson II, Management

Consultant: Madison International

2.6 ProCentro, São Paulo, Brazil
Client: ProCentro

Plan prepared by:
Skidmore, Owings & Merrill, San Francisco
John Kriken, Urban Design and Planning
Kathrin Moore, Project Planner and Manager

Participant: Braconsult, São Paulo

3.1 The Pennsylvania Avenue Renewal, Washington, DC
Client:
President's Council on Pennsylvania Avenue
National Capitol Planning Commission
District of Columbia Government and Department of Highways

Plan prepared by:
Skidmore, Owings & Merrill, Washington, DC
John M. Woodbridge, Design
John F. Kirkpatrick, Planning

Consultants:
William Turnbul
Rolf Ohlhouson
Arnold Savrann
Robert Becker
Peter Walker
Larry Smith and Company

3.2 Saigon South, Ho Chi Minh City, Vietnam
Client: Phu My Hung Corporation, Ho Chi Minh City, Vietnam

Plan prepared by:
Skidmore, Owings & Merrill, San Francisco
John Kriken, Urban Design and Planning
Kathrin Moore, Management, Planning
Ellen Lou, Urban Design
David Nieh, Urban Design
Terezia Nemeth, Urban Design
Carolina Woo, Management

Associated Planners:
Koetter, Kim & Associates
Kenzo Tange Associates
Yu Wong Design Co., Ltd.

Consultants:
Woodward-Clyde, Hydrology, Water Quality, Flood Control
Barton-Aschman Associates, Traffic Engineering, Road Design
Moh and Associates International, Highway Engineering
Ebasco-CTCI, Electrical Engineering
Christopher Grubbs, Illustrator

Project Architects:
Design International, Janet Morell-Bernier
KORN Architects, Axel Korn
KYTA, Kudo Norihiko & Tan Gek Meng
NQH Architects, Ngo Quan Hien
RTA Associates, Ryoji Terajima

Landscape Architect: Primeclass, Lim Hse Jinh

Project Coordination: Sino-Pacific Construction & Consultancy
Company

3.3 Tianjin Economic Development Agency Residential Neighborhood, China
Client: Tianjin City Planning & Land Management Authority

Plan prepared by:
Skidmore, Owings & Merrill, San Francisco
John Kriken, Urban Design and Planning
Ellen Lou, Urban Designer and Planning
Brian Lee, Architectural Design
Eric Keune, Design Architect
Andrea Wong, Management
Silas Chiow, Management

Consultant: Christopher Grubbs, Illustrator

3.4 Knowledge and Innovation City, Shanghai, China
Client: Shui On Group

Plan prepared by:
Skidmore, Owings & Merrill, San Francisco
John Kriken, Urban Design and Planning
Ellen Lou, Urban Design
Kathrin Moore, Management
Carolina Woo, Management

Consultant: Christopher Grubbs, Illustrator

3.5 Park Boulevard, Chicago, Illinois
Client: Mesa Development Company and Stateway Associates

Plan prepared by:
Skidmore, Owings & Merrill, Chicago
Philip Enquist, Urban Design and Planning
Daniel R. Ringelstein, Urban Design
Andre Brumfield, Urban Design
Peter Ellis, Design
Joseph Reibel, Architectural Design
Michael Fink, Structural Engineering
Mark Andersen, Civil Engineering
Richard F. Tomlinson II, Management
Christopher Hall, Management

4.1 Hong Kong Central Waterfront, China
Sponsored by: Swire Properties Ltd.

Plan prepared by:
Skidmore, Owings & Merrill, International, Ltd.
John Kriken, Urban Design and Planning
Steve Townsend, Urban Design

Consultants:
MVA Hong Kong, Ltd., Transportation
Master Plan, Ltd., Development Advisors
Architech, Computer Simulations
Christopher Grubbs, Illustrator

4.2 Los Angeles River Program, California
Client: Los Angeles Department of Public Works

Plan prepared by:
Skidmore, Owings & Merrill, Chicago
Philip Enquist, Urban Design and Planning
Peter Kindel, Planning
Teresa Fourcher, Management
Jack Swenson, Management
Elena Stevanato, Urban Design
Thomas Kerwin, Management

Consultants:
Bruce Mau Design, Inc.
Gehry Partners, LLP

4.3 The Millennium Park Master Plan, Chicago, Illinois
Client:
Chicago Department of Transportation
Chicago Public Building Commission
Chicago Office of the Mayor

Plan prepared by:
Skidmore, Owings & Merrill, Chicago
Philip Enquist, Urban Design and Planning
Leigh Breslau, Design
Adrian Smith, Design
Raymond J. Clark, MEP Engineering
Jason Stanley, Technical Coordinator
Thomas Kerwin, Management
Robert Wesley, Management

Participants:
Frank O. Gehry
Hammond Beeby Rupert and Ainge
Harley Deveroux
Kathryn Gustafson
McDonough Associates, Inc.
O'Donnell Wicklund Pigozzi & Peterson
Renzo Piano
Schuler Shook, Inc.
Talaske Group, Inc.
Teng & Associates
Terry Guen Design Associates
Thornton-Thomasetti
Wolff Clements & Associates

4.4 Greenbelt Alliance/Bay Conservation and Development Commission Programs, San Francisco Bay Area, California
Client:
People for Open Space/Greenbelt Alliance
Executive Director, Larry Orman

Future of the Metropolis Report Committee:
Paul DeFalco, Chair, Nancy Alexander, Don Dickenson, Chuck Forester, Jerry Goldberg (SOM), Marc Goldstein (SOM), Allan Jacobs, T. J. Kent Jr., John Kriken (SOM), Bob Mang, Michelle Monsten, Roberta Mundie, Martin Paley

Research and plan prepared by:
Skidmore, Owings & Merrill, San Francisco
John Kriken, Urban Design and Planning
Phil Enquist, Urban Design
Jerry Goldberg, Planning and Management

Consultant: Larry Orman, Risk Map

4.4 Bay Conservation and Development Commission, California
Client: BCDC, Will Travis, Executive Director

Staff Coordinator: Brad McCrea, Design Analyst

Design Review Board:
John Kriken, Chair, Karen Alschuler, Cheryl Barton, Ephraim Hirsch, Roger Leventhal, Michael Smiley, Steve Thompson

Consultants: BCDC Public Access Map, Brad McCrea

5.1 Taipingqiao, Shanghai, China
Client:
Fuxing Yimin, Ltd.
Shui On Properties, Ltd

Plan prepared by:
Skidmore, Owings & Merrill, San Francisco
John Kriken, Urban Design and Planning
Peter Ellis, Architecture
Silas Chiow, Management
Ellen Lou, Urban Design and Planning
Carolina Y. C. Woo, Management

Consultants:
J. Harlan Glen & Associates
Shanghai Urban Planning & Design Research Institute
Tim Griffith, Photographer
Christopher Grubbs, Illustrator

Xintiandi (Historic District):

Architecture:
Wood + Zapata
Nikkan Sekkei International
Tangji Design Institute

Landscape: Pete Walker and Partners

5.2 Foshan, China
Client: Shui On Properties, Ltd.

Plan prepared by:
Skidmore, Owings & Merrill, San Francisco
John Kriken, Urban Design and Planning
Ellen Lou, Urban Design and Planning
Andrea Wong, Management
Gene Schnair, Management

Consultants: Christopher Grubbs, Illustrator

5.3 Opérations d'Intérêt National, Paris
Client: Mission de Préfiguration, Opération d'Intérêt National

Plan prepared by:
Skidmore, Owings & Merrill, London
Daniel Ringelstein, Urban Design and Planning
Ilaria Di Carlo, Urban Design
Emmanuel Ramirez-Ruiz, Urban Design
Bernhard Rettig, Urban Design
Anna Gasco, Urban Design

5.4 Elephant & Castle District, London
Client: St. Modwen Properties, PLC

Plan prepared by:
Skidmore, Owings & Merrill, London
Daniel Ringelstein, Urban Design
Ilaria Di Carlo, Urban Design
Emmanuel Ramirez-Ruiz, Urban Design
Bernhard Rettig, Urban Design
Anna Gasco, Urban Design

6.1 San Antonio River Corridor, Texas
Client:
River Corridor Committee
City of San Antonio
Bexar County
San Antonio Development Authority
San Antonio River Authority
with participation of
Alamo Area Council of Governments
San Antonio Independent School District

Study conducted by:
Skidmore, Owings & Merrill (SOM) and Marshall Kaplan Gans and Kahn (MKGK), a joint venture
SOM, San Francisco:
Marc Goldstein, Management
Jerry Goldberg, Management and Planning
John Kriken, Urban Design
Kathrin Moore, Urban Design

MKGK, San Francisco:
Sheldon Gans, Partner in Charge
George Williams, Manager

Consultants:
Robert Conradt, Transportation
Cyris Wagner, Architecture, Illustrations
Sherry Wagner, Urban Design
Paul Sharkey, Hydrology
Robert Copeland, Ecology
Groves, Fernandez, Ludwig, Barry, Telford & Associates, Inc.,
Hydraulic Engineering

6.2 San Jose, California, Master Plan
Client: Kimbel, Small

Plan prepared by:
Skidmore, Owings & Merrill, San Francisco
Larry Doane, Architectural Design
John Kriken, Urban Design and Planning
Burton Miller, Urban Design

6.3 The South Works Steel Plant/Lakeside Master Plan, Chicago, Illinois
Client: McCaffery Interests/U.S. Steel Corp.

Plan prepared by:
Skidmore, Owings & Merrill, Chicago
Philip Enquist, Urban Design and Planning
Douglas Voigt, Urban Design and Planning
Andre Brumfield, Urban Design and Planning
Ekta Naik, Planning
Richard F. Tomlinson II, Management
Sasaki, Associated Master Planners

Consultant: Norman Kondy, Illustrator

7.1 Texas Medical Center, Houston
Client: Texas Medical Center

Plan prepared by:
Skidmore, Owings & Merrill, Chicago
Philip Enquist, Urban Design and Planning
Leigh Breslau, Design
Raymond J. Clark, MEP Engineering
Brian Jack, Management
Teresa Fourcher, Management
George Tingwald, M.D., Planning
Daniel R. Ringelstein, Planning
Peter Kindel, Planning
Douglas Voigt, Urban Design
Richard F. Tomlinson II, Management

Consultants:
Barton Aschman Associates, Inc.
CH2M Hill
FKP Architects, Inc.
Harza Engineering Company
McGowan Brothers Engineers, Inc.
Morris Architects
Rowan Williams Davies & Irwin, Inc.

Walter P. Moore
Zimmer Gunsel Frasca Partnership

7.2 University of California, San Diego
Client:
Chancellor's Council
Campus/Community Planning Committee
Marine Sciences Physical Planning Committee
Undergraduate Affairs Master Plan Committee
Campus Planning Office

Plan prepared by:
Skidmore, Owings & Merrill, San Francisco
John Kriken, Co-Director for Urban Design and Planning
Jerry Goldberg, Management and Planning
Phil Enquist, Urban Design
Kathrin Moore, Design and Management (Scripps Institution of Oceanography)

Consultants:
Richard Bender, Co-Director with John Kriken
Alan Jacobs
Emment Wemple & Associates, Landscape
Basmaciyan-Darnell, Traffic
Economic Research Associates
Robert Pervy, Native Plants
Norman Kondy, Illustrator

7.3 The Waukegan Lakefront Downtown, Illinois
Client: Waukegan Department of Planning and Zoning

Plan prepared by:
Skidmore, Owings & Merrill, Chicago
Philip Enquist, Project Urban Design and Planning
Christopher Hall, Manager
Peter Kindel, Manager
Lucas Tryggestad, Urban Design
Jeannine Colaco, Graphic Designer
Thomas Kerwin, Project Management

Consultants:
Development Consulting Services, Inc.
Land Strategies, Inc.
Mary Ellen Tamasy
Norman Kondy, Illustrator

7.4 Harvard North Precinct, Cambridge, Massachusetts
Client: Harvard University

Plan prepared by:
Skidmore, Owings & Merrill, Chicago
Philip Enquist, Urban Design and Planning
Adam Thies, Management
Douglas Voigt, Planning
Richard Tomlinson II, Management

Architectural Design:
Skidmore, Owings & Merrill, San Francisco
Craig Hartman, Project Architectural Design
Carrie Byles, Project Management

7.5 Hewlett-Packard Worldwide
Client: Dennis Raney, Director of Facilities, Palo Alto, California

Plan prepared by:
Skidmore, Owings & Merrill, San Francisco
John Kriken, Urban Design and Planning
Craig Hartman, Architectural Design
Kathrin Moore, Management and Planning

8.1 The Central Area Plan, Chicago, Illinois
Client: Chicago Department of Planning and Development

Plan prepared by:
Skidmore, Owings & Merrill, Chicago
Philip Enquist, Urban Design and Planning
Christopher Hall, Management
Douglas Voigt, Planning
Jeannine Colaco, Graphic Design
Richard F. Tomlinson II, Management

8.2 The Transbay Terminal Neighborhood Redevelopment Plan, San Francisco, California
Client:
San Francisco Redevelopment Agency
San Francisco Planning Department, Transbay Citizen Advisory Committee

Plan prepared by:
Skidmore, Owings & Merrill, San Francisco
John Kriken, Project Urban Design and Planning
Ellen Lou, Senior Urban Design and Planning
Steven Sobel, Management
Gene Schnair, Management
Rosie Dudley, Planning

Consultants:
Alfred Williams Consultancy, LLC
BMS Design Group
Peter Bosselman
Dowling Associates
Jacobs Macdonald City Works
Seadway Group/CB Richard Ellis Consulting
Urban Explorer
Wilbur Smith
Michael Reardon Illustration

8.3 Lakeshore East, Chicago, Illinois
Client: Magellan Development Group, Ltd.

Plan prepared by:
Skidmore, Owings & Merrill, Chicago
Philip Enquist, Urban Design and Planning
Adrian Smith, Design
Christopher Hall, Management

Daniel R. Ringelstein, Planning
Richard F. Tomlinson II, Management

Consultant:
Office of James Burnett
Michael McCann. Illustrator

9.1 University of California, Merced
Client:
Carol Tomlinson-Keasy, Chancellor
Christopher Adams, Campus Planning

Plan prepared by:
Skidmore, Owings & Merrill, San Francisco
John Kriken, Urban Design and Planning
Ellen Lou, Senior Urban Designer
Gail Collins, Manager
Gene Schnair, Project Management

BMS Design Group
Barbara Maloney, Planning
Michael Smiley, Planning

Peter Walker and Partners Landscape
Peter Walker
Douglas Findlay

Consultants:
Kenedy/Jenks Consultants
Fernau & Hartman Architects
EHDD Architects
Fehr & Peers Associates
Sandis Humber Jones
Simon & Associates
Rocky Mountain Institute
Richard Bender Architects
JCM/PB, Rod Rose
Arup, Alisdair McGregor, Principal
David Langdon Adamson
Christopher Grubbs, Illustrator

9.2 Yanbu, Saudi Arabia
Client: Royal Commission for Jubail and Yanbu

Community plan prepared by:
Skidmore, Owings & Merrill, San Francisco, as consultant to Saudi Arabian Parsons Limited
John Kriken, Urban Design and Planning
Howard McKee, In-Country Project Management
Kathrin Moore, Management and Planning
John Merrill, Management

Consultants:
Arthur D. Little, Inc., Program, Policy
Deleuw Cather International, Transportation
Dames and More, Civil Engineering
TetraTech, Soils
Tom Aidala, Urban Design

Roger Boyer, Illustrator
Steve Wanat, Photos

9.3 Beijing Financial Street, China

Plan prepared by:
Skidmore, Owings & Merrill, Hong Kong and San Francisco
John Kriken, Urban Design and Planning
Craig Hartman, Architecture Design
Michael Duncan, Architecture Design
Steve Townsend, Urban Design (HK)
Ellen Lou, Planning
Toby Bath, Management (HK)
Andrea Wong, Management
Patricia Yeh, Architectural Management
Gene Schnair, Management

Consultant: Christopher Grubbs, Illustrator

9.4 Huang Pu River, Shanghai, China

Client: Shanghai City Planning Administration Bureau

Plan prepared by:
Skidmore, Owings & Merrill, San Francisco
John Kriken, Urban Design and Planning
Ellen Lou, Urban Design
Craig Hartman, Architecture
Brian Lee, Architecture
Mark Sarkisian, Structural Engineering
Carolina Woo, Management

Consultant: Christopher Grubbs, Illustrator

Index